INTRODUCTION TO PSYCHOPATHOLOGY

Alessandra Lemma

SAGE Publications
London • Thousand Oaks • New Delhi

SAGE Publications Ltd
6 Bonhill Street
London EC2A 4PU

SAGE Publications Inc
2455 Teller Road
Thousand Oaks, California 91320

SAGE Publications India Pvt Ltd
32, M-Block Market
Greater Kailash – I
New Delhi 110 048

British Library Cataloguing in Publication data

A catalogue record for this book is
available from the British Library

ISBN 0 8039 7470 1
ISBN 0 8039 7471 X (pbk)

Library of Congress catalog record available

Typeset by Mayhew Typesetting, Rhayader, Powys
Printed in Great Britain by The Cromwell Press Ltd,
Broughton Gifford, Melksham, Wiltshire

For my students who asked me the questions
and my clients who shared their answers with me

Contents

Acknowledgements

There are always so many people whom I feel it is important to acknowledge when I have completed a piece of writing. They have all contributed in their own unique way through their support, encouragement, friendship and teaching. I will not have enough space to mention them all here but I trust they know how much I have appreciated them.

I would especially like to thank the School of Psychotherapy and Counselling at Regent's College for offering me an opportunity to work there as it is through my experience of teaching that the idea for this book was first conceived. I would also like to thank my clients whose experiences have taught me so much about the nature of emotional distress. I am indebted to Dr Anthony Roth and Professor Peter Fonagy for having kindly allowed me to read, prior to its publication, their authoritative review of the psychotherapy outcome research literature to which I have repeatedly referred in this book. I would also like to thank Central Book Publishing for their permission to reproduce parts of my book *Starving to Live: the Paradox of Anorexia Nervosa* in Chapter 8. Finally, I would like to extend my warmest appreciation to Gill Cruisey, Dr Peter Shoenberg and Stephen Wright who worked closely with me in the production of this book – the nature of their contributions was quite different but they were all equally invaluable.

Preface

Increasingly, counsellors and psychotherapists are being employed in GP practices or working within hospitals. The clients that are being referred to them are more likely to present with identifiable psychiatric problems. This means inevitably that they will see a different range of clients from the one normally seen in private practice. This shift calls for a more thorough understanding and knowledge of psychopathology. This book aims to bring together research and clinical practice to enhance the practitioner's understanding of the various manifestations of psychopathology. Although the book is written primarily for counsellors and psychotherapists, it does not concern itself with specific assessment of the suitability of such approaches in any of the problems considered in this book.

An important proposition underlying this book is that it is essential to good practice to consider what research has shown in the field of psychopathology with as few preconceptions as possible so as to examine the available data, critically assess their relevance to clinical practice and ultimately to the struggles facing those individuals who seek our help. This book therefore aims to provide a concise review of the literature as an essential springboard for subsequently questioning it. The process of questioning the research findings is an individual enterprise and is not the primary focus of this book.

Having just stated my aims in writing this book, I would now like to invite you to pause and reflect on why you feel you need to read a book on psychopathology. What is it that you are hoping to learn and in what way will this knowledge enhance your work with people in emotional distress? It may be, for instance, that you simply want to turn to the relevant chapters to read up on particular psychiatric problems or perhaps to the section on assessment, hoping to find the guidelines that will make your task as therapist that little bit easier when confronted with the sometimes complex stories and series of symptoms that your clients present with. If this is so, you may be tempted to skip this preface and perhaps also the introductory chapter on the nature of psychopathology. I hope, however, that in this instance you will make an exception and give some consideration to the issues raised here and in the next chapter.

The aim of Chapter 1 is to highlight some of the long-standing problems that have surrounded the issue of psychiatric diagnosis and classification and our attempts to define mental health and illness, paying particular attention to the challenges posed by the questions of gender and culture when considering any type of psychopathology. The focus on psychopathology and the distress which clients present with has detracted important attention away from the equally significant concept of resilience, namely why individuals who face the same degree of adversity or difficulty in life do not all develop psychiatric problems. Chapter 2 will therefore consider psychopathological manifestations across the lifespan, focusing on the question of the continuities and discontinuities between problems in childhood and adulthood.

When we consider the question of psychopathology and how it may manifest itself it is also important to consider the question of assessment. Chapter 3 will outline a framework for assessing clients which takes into account psychological, social and physical factors. The assessment of specific psychiatric problems is dealt with separately in the later chapters. One of the important purposes of assessment is to determine whether we, as practitioners, feel that there is something that we can offer our client or whether it is either not our role or not within the limits of our expertise to offer help to a particular individual. The aim of Chapter 4 will be to examine the question of referring on to, and of working alongside, other professionals, as well as bringing to the fore the legal and ethical aspects of therapeutic work with people with psychiatric problems.

Chapters 5–10 deal with some of the most common psychiatric problems, including (Chapter 6) the question of suicide and self-harm. It is beyond the scope of this book to review exhaustively all current psychiatric problems. The choice is therefore to some extent arbitrary, but not entirely so as it reflects some of the most frequently encountered clinical problems. I have chosen this structure because it is important to have some way of breaking up the material into manageable sections, preferably on the basis of a system which is readily comprehensible to the reader. However, there are undoubted disadvantages to dividing the material in terms of clinical categories. One of the most significant problems in using a classificatory system based on clinical categories is that labels like 'depression' or 'anorexia nervosa' are not actually analogous to familiar diagnostic concepts from general medicine which in many instances carry specific implications for aetiology, treatment and prognosis. However, to say that a person is depressed carries a much weaker set of implications. In particular it says little, if anything, about the aetiology of the problem.

I hope that the division of material in this way will not be construed as confirmation that such categories and labels refer to immutable entities but merely reflect one way of grouping together research findings which correlate with particular manifestations of emotional distress. Such categories and labels are among the current tools we have available to think about such distress. They can, of course, be refined, rejected or replaced by more appropriate ones, but we always need a framework within which to organise our experience and thoughts about particular issues. Scientific work could not proceed without guiding hypotheses and theoretical frameworks. However, models of psychopathology are never definitive – 'their truth', as Benedetti put it, 'lies in what we do with them' (1987: 2). All approaches to psychiatric classification can only provide more or less arbitrarily constructed guides to further investigation, but they must undergo change and adaptation to serve better the purpose of any given enquiry. They are inevitably subjective and selective – that is, they all depict selected features of reality and consequently ignore other features of the same reality. At present all approaches to classification must contend with certain intractable and unavoidable limitations.[1]

One of the unfortunate consequences of the process of reification – that is, of talking about psychopathology as if it referred to real entities or categories in the world – is that it can mislead us into seeing the diagnostic categories used, for example, in DSM-IV (*Diagnostic and Statistical Manual*, APA, 1994) as concrete diseases rather than useful abstractions, thereby resulting in the false sense that if we know the diagnosis we also know the person.

Terminology

The language we employ to describe what interests us is not without consequences. All terminologies are value laden. In view of this, it seems important to clarify how some more controversial terms will be used in this book.

In referring to those individuals who seek professional help for their emotional distress, I use the term 'client'. I do so with some misgivings, however. Although the term 'patient' in the context of a therapeutic relationship can give the mistaken impression that there is, on the one hand, a therapist who is strong and healthy and, on the other hand, a 'patient' who is sick and weak, we must not lose sight of the person's own reality and how they perceive themselves and the nature of their distress. Many people who present with mental health problems see themselves as being in some way 'ill'. Others do not experience themselves as 'clients' in the sense of having entered a voluntary, consensual relationship when they may have been, for instance, admitted to a psychiatric institution against their will. In such instances, the word 'patient' is a more accurate reflection of the reality of the person's situation. Changing the label will not change this reality. When referring to particular studies where the individuals concerned were labelled 'patients', or when referring to hospital-based treatment, I shall retain the term as it is in keeping with the views of the authors and the label given to the recipients of hospital-based care.

Another controversial area is the overlap between counselling[2] and psychotherapy. This book is aimed at practitioners, from varied backgrounds, who engage in contracted, boundaried, psychotherapeutic relationships with people with mental health problems with the aim of helping to alleviate their emotional distress. Their theoretical allegiances will also be varied. Only some of these practitioners will have undergone additional training in counselling or psychotherapy. Others may none the less have acquired general psychotherapeutic skills as part of their core training in other mental health professions, such as nursing and psychology. These skills are applied in the course of their exchanges with clients in a structured and formal manner. It is difficult to know how one refers to this endeavour. If the client is being seen on a weekly basis over several years, is this counselling or is this psychotherapy? The distinctions between the two are not as clear cut as we might wish them to be. In the interests of clarity, in this book the term 'therapy' will be used to refer to both counselling and psychotherapy offered on a once-weekly basis, unless otherwise specified. The more generic term 'therapist' will be adopted to refer to the practitioners who offer counselling and/or psychotherapy, irrespective of their core professional backgrounds.

The term 'psychopathology' is also, of course, somewhat controversial given its medical connotations. This will be explored more fully in the next chapter.

Note

1. It is important to remember that in clinical settings clients often present with a number of difficulties (for example, low mood, anxiety and difficulties around eating) rather than fitting neatly into any one of the diagnostic categories.

2. Generic counselling *per se* as an intervention has not been widely evaluated in the treatment of the various clinical problems reviewed in this book. This has most certainly been complicated by the fact that counselling as an intervention means different things to different people. Broadly speaking, however, the available evidence points to the appropriateness of counselling with those clients who are less severely impaired and chronic. This underscores the importance for counsellors to be sufficiently knowledgeable about the various manifestations of psychopathology so as to make appropriate referrals to other professionals and/or agencies.

1
What is Psychopathology?

Any attempt to define what psychopathology is presupposes that we really know what normality is. In view of this, any consideration of psychopathology requires an examination of the notions of mental health and illness and their inherent assumptions and biases. This will be the aim of the first part of this chapter. It will be followed by an exploration of some of the functions served by the notion of mental illness.

Throughout history, people's understanding of psychopathology has constantly shifted; different cultures and historical periods have labelled 'mad' those whom other times and societies have regarded as 'sane'. Indeed, it has been argued that madness is nothing but a label pinned by the respectable on those they cannot tolerate or that society is in actuality so demanding or alienating that it drives the most vulnerable souls to distraction. Psychopathology or madness can even be seen as being merely sophisticated euphemisms for human anguish. Since the ancient Greeks, psychopathological manifestations have been treated by a variety of social organisations including the Church, the law and medicine. In modern Western society medicine is the main source of identification and care for psychopathology. In spite of the attempts of the medical profession to use scientifically loaded terms reified within systems of psychiatric classification, the question of psychopathology has nevertheless remained shrouded in mystery.

The term 'psychopathology' generally refers to patterns of mal-adaptive behaviour and states of distress which interfere with some aspect of adaptation. Implicit in the American Psychiatric Association's (1994) *Diagnostic and Statistical Manual* (DSM-IV) definition of 'mental disorder' is that the mental condition causes significant distress or disability (impairment in one or more important areas of func-tioning) and that it is not merely an expected and culturally sanctioned response to a particular event. The effectiveness of the person's adaptation is thus implicit in the definition.

When people seek professional help this is generally because they are distressed by some aspect of their experience. The overt signs of distress, which may manifest themselves as psychological or physical symptoms, or even both, indicate a sense of 'dis-ease' (Ashurst and Hall, 1989) within the person's internal and external worlds. Language can only give us a poor approximation of another's experience of their states of 'dis-ease', yet it is through the use of labels that we categorise such differing and unique experiences in an attempt to make sense of them.

Notions of health and illness

Within the realm of physical medicine there is little dispute as to the precise nature of health. The physician is not required to make a moral or philosophical decision when declaring someone to be physically ill or healthy. Physical health can be stated in anatomical and physical terms. In medicine, statistical abnormality of physical structure and function is synonymous with pathology. Ideal and statistical norms are roughly equivalent so that no subjective values are involved in determining whether someone is physically ill or not. Equally, medical treatment is generally tailored to the correction of some deviation which is more or less the same for everybody and generally desired.

The notion of mental illness is the cornerstone of a working hypothesis which was set up in order to determine to what extent the medical model could explain and provide remedies for psychological disturbances. What often gets lost when we talk about mental illness or psychopathology is that all models are nothing more than 'abstractions. They are our inventions created to place facts, events and theories in an orderly manner and are therefore not necessarily either true or false' (Siegler and Osmond, 1974: 71). Although the application of the medical model to the understanding and treatment of psychological disturbances is still widely subscribed to, it has also been severely criticised.

Definitions of health and illness in psychiatry are highly problematic. Normality in the context of mental health has been variously defined, for example: as the absence of disease; as an ideal state of mind; as the average level of functioning of an individual within the context of a total group; as a capacity to function autonomously and competently; as a subjective sense of contentment and satisfaction; and as an ability to adjust to one's social environment effectively. As will be immediately apparent, all such definitions, besides their vagueness, presuppose that other factors are clear; for instance, that we know what constitutes mental illness or an ideal state of mind. Such definitions can therefore only be subjective. Mental health is not the converse of mental illness, and is generally conceptualised as something wider than the absence of mental illness. For example, Maslow (1968) equated mental health with a process of self-actualisation and defined it as the person's use and exploration of, their talents and potentials. This comprised ten components including, for example, acceptance of self and others and autonomy. While few would dispute that these are laudable qualities which some might choose to strive towards, the problem in adopting them as criteria for mental health is that, on the basis of such a definition, the majority of the population could be considered to be maladjusted.

As Kakar (1982) has suggested, mental health is a label which covers different perspectives and concerns, such as the absence of incapacitating symptoms, integration of psychological functioning and feelings of ethical and spiritual well-being. It is clear, however, that culture will play an important part in determining both the perception and level of concern in the case of each of these qualities. For example, Fernando (1991) has pointed out that in the cultures of Asia, Africa and pre-Columbian America, in contrast to Western culture, there may be less concern about varieties of inner experience or altered states of consciousness, whereas in the West these would be seen as abnormal experiences and in some cases as evidence of illness.

Mental health or normality has proved challenging to define and some authors suggest that normality may in fact not even be something to which we should aspire. Indeed, Donald Winnicott (1945: 150) wrote that 'we are poor indeed if we are only sane', which suggests that the need for normality is perhaps exaggerated. This is echoed by another psychoanalyst, Joyce McDougall (1990), in the evocative title of her book *Plea for a Measure of Abnormality*, where she argues that 'to be caught in the grip of an overly powerful social ego, over reasonable and over adapted is no more desirable than the dominance of unleashed instinctual forces. The point at which [the norm] becomes the straightjacket of the soul and the cemetery of the imagination is a delicate one to define' (1990: 484). McDougall thus suggests that, faced with the inherent difficulty of the human enterprise, we may well respond by an over-adaptation to the world of external reality by becoming what she calls 'supernormal'. It is not that such authors glorify madness, but rather that they point to the equally undesirable aspect of what we might otherwise call normality and, of course, remind us of the corresponding difficulty in defining normality.

Defining mental illness has proved as difficult a project as defining mental health. In Hamlet, Polonius hints at the problem when he concludes that to try 'to define true madness, what is't but to be nothing else but mad'. Despite the attendant problems, attempts at defining mental illness have none the less persisted. In Britain, in the Mental Health Act 1983, section 1, mental disorder is defined as 'mental illness, arrested or incomplete development of mind, psychopathic disorder and any other disorder or disability of mind'. Four categories of mental disorder are specified as follows:

- *mental illness*: not defined
- *severe mental impairment*: 'a state of arrested or incomplete development of mind which includes severe impairment of intelligence and social functioning and is associated with abnormally aggressive or seriously irresponsible conduct on the part of the person concerned.'
- *mental impairment*: defined in the same way as severe mental impairment except that the phrase 'severe impairment' is replaced by 'significant impairment'.
- *psychopathic disorder*: 'a persistent disorder or disability of mind (whether or not including significant impairment of intelligence) which results in abnormally aggressive or seriously irresponsible conduct.'

Such definitions are clearly problematic as one might well ask what constitutes 'abnormally aggressive behaviour' or 'seriously irresponsible conduct'. Unlike general medicine, where statistical abnormality is synonymous with pathology, in psychiatry an individual may well exhibit very unusual behaviour and yet not be diagnosed as mentally ill. Whether a person is thus labelled may therefore be under the influence of other factors. Sarbin and Juhasz (1967, 1978) for example, have suggested that psychiatrists are more likely to judge reported hallucinations as pathological, that is, as symptoms of schizophrenia, when the hallucinating individual has already been devalued in some way, as for example when he or she is of low social status and poor education. It was convincingly argued by Scheff (1966) that everyone performs actions that do not correspond with our definitions of normal behaviour but that only in certain circumstances do they receive a stigmatising label. Along with Szasz (1961) and Goffman (1961), he argued that diagnostic labelling occurs *after* the person has violated social norms. While this is a very important and interesting hypothesis, there is unfortunately no conclusive evidence to support it.

Littlewood and Lipsedge (1989), discussing a wide range of behaviour, have suggested that it is not necessarily the performance of certain behaviours *per se* which invite pathological labels but their performance outside a prescribed social context. While reporting hallucinatory experiences as being real is negatively valued in modern Western society, there are some exceptions to this, for instance when such experiences occur in a religious context. Such factors point to a fundamental problem in defining mental illness, namely that statistical data in psychiatry may be misleading in that they can be based on assumptions which include unacknowledged value judgements.

The contamination of the raw facts of someone's behaviour by the psychiatrist's or other mental health practitioner's own subjective judgement leads to a number of worrying situations whereby one person may be labelled mentally ill in one institution or even country and not in another; political dissenters who were labelled as mentally ill in the former Soviet Union are a prime but sinister example of this possibility (Fulford et al., 1993). It was with such factors in mind that critics of the medical model and the political use of psychiatric diagnosis in the 1960s and 1970s, such as David Cooper, Ronald Laing and Thomas Szasz, argued the importance of clearly distinguishing between organic and mental illness and suggested that the latter is no more than a mere label to stigmatise non-conforming individuals. Szasz argued that madness was erroneously termed mental illness. Rather, he said, it was more appropriate to refer to it as 'problems in living' but that the label of illness was awarded by the medical profession in order to legitimise its own authority. The essential message was that mental illness could not be considered in a value-free scientific framework but rather needed to be understood in its sociopolitical context.

The above position is hard to refute and several lines of evidence converge to support it. The way we define mental illness changes with time and depends on the rules by which a given society lives which include the behavioural norms that determine within that society what a person can or cannot do: where, when and with whom. A historical perspective on the concept of deviance, in the sense of deviating from given societal and cultural norms, soon highlights that the norm has always had a sociotemporal dimension. How a particular society defines deviance, which may be couched in terms of mental illness, depends on how wide a range of behaviour that society allows to be acceptable. How a society explains deviance from the so-called norm will, in turn, depend on its own prevailing beliefs. Historically, such deviance has been variously explained by possession by evil spirits, as a loss of divine grace, as a result of early or severe toilet training, as a function of biochemical imbalance, to name but a few of the accounts put forward. Accordingly, the same behaviour has received different labels at different times in history. Raimbault and Eliacheff (1989), in their study of anorexia, have shown how changing cultural environments have determined whether the individual who self-starves is seen as saintly, hysterical, sick or mad.

Finally, how a society manages deviance will, once again, be according to the nature of that society. A more traditional society will handle deviance quite differently from a large industrialised society, which may make it harder for the person who has deviated to become reintegrated into that particular society. Warner (1994), in a very thorough study and critique of our ways of dealing with schizophrenia in the West, has argued that the outcome of schizophrenia is better in the non-industrial world, despite the low priority given to psychiatric care in such countries. Warner explains such results in terms of the opportunities offered to the individual in the non-Western world to find a valued social role, particularly through work, and therefore to be reintegrated within the community. In industrial societies, on the contrary, little leeway is given to adapting the job to the abilities of the worker. It is therefore more difficult for individuals to regain a valued social role within their communities from which they may have become estranged during the period of their psychotic episode (see Chapter 9).

Such studies point to the importance of understanding behaviour in its cultural context and highlight the ways in which the overall worldview within a culture, appertaining to health, religion, psychology and spiritual concerns, determine the meaning within that culture of mental health and illness. Fernando (1991) has argued that the current medical model of psychiatric illness in the West is one that is relatively, if not completely, free from religious, ethical and spiritual aspects of the culture in which it is based. However, in the medical traditions of Asian culture, for instance, medicine, religion and ethics are integrated together. Jean Pouillon (1972), the French anthropologist, argues that there are many different approaches throughout different cultures to the concept of sickness that depend to some extent on a three-way relationship between the sick individual, the healer and the conception of sickness itself. Crucial to this argument is the idea of another anthropologist, Levi-Strauss (1955), that in some cultures termed 'exorcistic' all pathology is regarded as alien to the self and so to be removed by the healer on behalf of society. In other cultures termed 'endorcistic' pathology is regarded as potentially helpful to the self and so to be integrated into the self. Western medicine and hence psychiatry can thus be seen as a product of an 'exorcistic' culture where the primary aim of treatment is to 'get rid' of a person's experiences of mental anguish or suffering rather than helping the person to integrate them into the self.

Notions of health and illness can only really be considered in the context of particular cultural worldviews. In the West, Fernando (1991: 16) argues, 'health is felt as something that is attained by control and domination', in keeping with a worldview that emphasises control of emotions by reason, and of nature by people. By contrast, the Western concept of health is a matter of overcoming illness. The worldviews of Africa and Asia, however, promote 'a sense of health arising from acceptance' (Fernando, 1991: 16). Together with this there is a striving for harmony both within the person and between people and their environment, in nature and the spirit – a way of thinking that is often dismissed in the West as superstitious. A cross-cultural perspective thus emphasises the importance, when discussing the concepts of mental health and illness, of remaining aware that a true picture of cross-cultural difference is often distorted by the imposition of value judgements of the constituent cultural system. The application of the Western medical model to people from other cultures is therefore problematic.

The problem of classification and diagnosis

Classification

Classification refers to the dividing of a given set of abstract entities into sub-classes and is the fundamental activity of any science. Our current systems of psychiatric classification are derived from medical classificatory models described in France and Germany in the second half of the nineteenth century and the early twentieth century when leading clinicians defined some of the major syndromes of psychiatry. These included, most notably, Kraeplin in Germany who assumed that there were groups of symptoms and signs occurring together with sufficient regularity to merit the term disease.

The aims of classification are twofold: by permitting adequate description, it is argued that classification enables communication, and by grouping together entities assumed to share common characteristics it allows the possibility of general laws and theories to be inferred. Kraeplin's classificatory system forms the basis of the descriptions of syndromes and diagnostic categories still used today. The existing categories are now established within 'the bibles of psychiatry' (Ussher, 1991), namely the American Psychiatric Association's *Diagnostic and Statistical Manual of Mental Disorders* (DSM-IV, APA, 1994) and the *International Classification of Diseases* (ICD 10). In this book we shall refer to the DSM-IV classificatory system.

DSM-IV is a manual of 'mental disorders', but as Frances points out 'it is by no means clear just what is mental disorder or whether one can develop a set of definitional criteria to guide inclusionary and exclusionary decisions from the manual' (1994: VII). Furthermore, 'mental' implies a mind–body dichotomy that is becoming increasingly outmoded and untenable – any division between purely mental and purely physical disorders ignores that these conditions often result from an interaction that belies the distinction. Unlike earlier classificatory systems, DSM-IV provides specific diagnostic criteria to enhance reliability, even though it is admitted that most diagnostic criteria are based on clinical judgement and have not been validated through empirical research (APA, 1994).[1]

Classificatory systems hold the appeal of clarity but they also present difficulties. First, 'the correlation of a particular word with a particular meaning derives not from any natural divisions in reality but from convention, and any vocabulary reflects established, though possibly arbitrary, distinctions' (Mullen, 1979: 26). In order to classify the variant presentations of emotional distress we invariably divide our observations into manageable units and assign a label to each, but this process is, of necessity, an arbitrary one which cannot capture the subtlety of experience. Though the separations, it can be argued, facilitate comprehension and communication, they may also place limitations on what can be observed.

Secondly, an examination of psychiatric classificatory systems also requires some consideration to be given to the question of the challenges posed by any attempt to study the human mind. The mind as an object of study is problematic. In any science, whatever is to be studied and spoken of must become in effect an 'object' for the scientist. However, unlike other sciences, those seeking to study the minds of others cannot directly contemplate their object, 'for the mind of the other is never an object for us and can only be apprehended in its productions such as speech, actions and writing' (Mullen, 1979: 27). The problems inherent in such an enterprise are great for, as Merleau-Ponty (1962) observed, the existence of other people creates difficulties in our pursuit of objective thought. If the mind of the other is to be the object of any study, we have to acknowledge that the consciousness that we are trying to study also has us as an object of its consciousness, thereby placing us as an object within our object. This immediately imposes restrictions on any attempt to study the mind of another objectively. This, in turn, raises an important issue because psychiatry does not restrict itself to observing behaviour, if the observable is taken to mean 'overt behaviour' exclusively. On the contrary, psychiatry regularly refers to 'mental events'. A quick glance through DSM-IV confirms this: hallucinations, delusions, low self-esteem, feelings of hopelessness, to name but a few. Such mental occurrences are frequently expressed through speech or overt behaviour. But one individual's mental processes are never directly observable by another person and the observer therefore always has to interpret the meaning of the overt behaviour to decide which mental events are correlated with it (Wiggins and Schwartz, 1994).

Thirdly, while the DSM-IV claims to be atheoretical with regard to aetiology, there are good reasons to be sceptical about such a claim. It can be argued that classification cannot be atheoretical because observations are invariably influenced by theoretical allegiances. Observations are made by people whose personal histories and sociocultural backgrounds influence them to perceive things in a particular way. This carries implications for the aetiology of psychopathology because if the observer accepts only a particular worldview, then only certain predetermined options are considered when that person contemplates possible causal factors. Philosophers of science (for example, Popper, 1968; Harré, 1972) have held that any classificatory system in any field of the basic natural sciences cannot claim to be atheoretical as these are influenced by the purposes and aims of the classifiers.

The view that disease concepts are inevitably bound up with theoretical assumptions is a corollary of the widely embraced view of science, namely that observations are inevitably based on theory. As a result, there cannot logically be any neutral concepts of disease.

Although classifications are predominantly descriptive, they also contain value judgements. Distributed throughout DSM-IV are value terms expressing judgements of 'good' or desirable and 'bad' or undesirable; for example, disturbance, failure and distortion. Moreover, Fulford et al. (1993) point out that the criteria we use to evaluate symptoms of psychopathology, such as anxiety, are different from those we use to evaluate symptoms of physical illness such as pain. They argue that

> people disagree about what is good or bad, welcome or unwelcome, in respect of anxiety to a greater extent than in respect of pain. For most people anything but the wildest pain is at best a necessary evil. On the other hand, while some people avoid anxiety, others actively seek it out . . . where pain is a narrow-band experience, evaluatively speaking, with little scope for individual variation in the way in which it is evaluated, anxiety is a broad-band experience. (1993: 807)

To recognise an evaluative element is merely to acknowledge it for what it is and to clarify its contribution to the conceptual framework of classificatory systems. Indeed, it is not really possible to make neutral descriptions. Values, not cognition, determine what we select as important or in some way related. In other words, values lend structure to our field of attention. It would therefore be nonsensical to argue that any scientific endeavour in the field of psychopathology should set aside all values and create a value-free science, but it remains essential to good practice in this field that values, as one of the major determinants in psychology and psychiatry, are openly and critically debated and not simply taken for granted or ignored.

One final but important criticism that may be levelled at DSM-IV is its focus on the individual person as the basic unit of concern. In DSM-IV the focus is on individuals with psychopathology, not social systems or communities or families which might be regarded as dysfunctional (Sadler and Hulgus, 1994). Notions of context-dependent psychopathology or interactive psychopathology of social groups do not appear. However, the problem will be obvious to any practitioner, namely that all forms of psychopathology are inevitably embedded in a social or family network and this has important implications for practice. To ignore this is to disregard the vast literature of preventive psychiatry and family psychiatry which attests to the aetiological as well as the practical relevance of social systems to understanding and alleviating the distress associated with individual manifestations of psychopathology.

Diagnosis

A number of serious criticisms have been levelled at the current psychiatric classificatory and diagnostic systems. 'Diagnosis' means 'to distinguish' and as such refers to the process of applying a given classificatory system. Boyle (1990: 223) sums up some of the difficulties in this process:

> Classification systems in the natural and biological sciences are based on groupings in terms of stable attributes and from which concepts such as mammal and fruit are inferred. It is not difficult to see how problematic it would be for researchers working within those systems if, say, the same cow sometimes reproduced by giving birth and suckling and sometimes by laying eggs ... but it can be argued that this is exactly the situation faced by psychologists and psychiatrists with respect to behaviour and one which has been widely ignored; rather than confronting the fact that the same person may behave in very different and quite opposing ways, and attempting to account for this variability, a search has been made for underlying stable attributes, whether they be 'mental illnesses' or 'personality traits', in terms of which, it is supposed, people may be grouped.

For a diagnostic system to be of either scientific or clinical utility, it has to be both reliable and valid. The *reliability* of a diagnostic system refers to the consistency with which clients are diagnosed; that is, if the same person presents with the same symptoms in two different places, they should receive the same diagnosis. The *validity* of a system refers to the meaningfulness or usefulness of the diagnostic categories as judged by other criteria. For instance, on the basis of diagnosis, the therapist should be able to predict the course and outcome of the disorder and which treatments are likely to be the most effective. This is, in fact, largely the case in physical medicine. There should also be some relationship between diagnosis and aetiology. It is important to remember that, while reliability is a necessary condition for validity, it is not sufficient. This is because any combination of symptoms can be made reliable simply by specifying them clearly enough so as not to leave too much room for interpretation.

Early studies addressing the question of reliability found that psychiatrists were often inconsistent in assigning individuals to diagnostic categories. Beck et al. (1962), for example, using the first *Diagnostic and Statistical Manual* of the American Psychiatric Association, assessed the rate of agreement between four experienced psychiatrists trained in the use of this particular system. Each of the 153 psychiatric patients was interviewed by two of the psychiatrists. Beck found a very poor agreement rate among the psychiatrists, a rate of only 54 per cent. Other studies found similar results. In response to the criticisms following such worrying findings, psychiatrists developed more precisely defined criteria for the different diagnoses as well as interview schedules which were meant to ensure that people were questioned about their symptoms in a standardised fashion and not at the whim of a particular psychiatrist. This led to the development of the research diagnostic criteria of Spitzer et al. (1978) and to the *Diagnostic and Statistical Manual* (which is now in its fourth edition), using more clearly defined criteria and a more structured, seemingly objective, approach to eliciting information from clients. The expectation was that these new developments should produce a far higher degree of agreement in diagnosis. However, the results do not unequivocally support the expectation. If we take as an example the diagnosis of schizophrenia, which is one frequently in dispute, a high degree of agreement should be observed when different criteria are compared. In a study by Brockington et al. (1978) ten sets of criteria were applied to 322 patients in a large psychiatric hospital. The concordance between the different diagnostic systems was, however, very low.

The now famous study by Rosenhan (1973) highlighted the ease with which the 'sane' may be labelled as 'insane'. Psychiatric and nursing staff in twelve institutions diagnosed as schizophrenic colleagues of the experimenter who had been instructed to report auditory hallucinations. Once admitted, they behaved in a perfectly sane way but their insistence on their sanity was interpreted as symptomatic of the illness. Their true clinical status was never suspected – all were discharged with a diagnosis of schizophrenia in remission.

It is clear that psychiatrists have made great efforts to improve their methods of diagnosis and, on the whole, now no longer use their own idiosyncratic approaches to diagnosis, which we are not surprised to discover originally gave rise to considerable disagreement between them. Nowadays, there exists at least an equivalent degree of disagreement about the different diagnostic systems available to psychiatrists. But if the entities described in these different systems were valid scientific concepts, then it would not be unreasonable to expect to know which set of criteria is the right one. However, social constructionist approaches to particular psychiatric categories, using discourse analysis, highlight how these categories are social artefacts, products of historically situated exchanges among people (Harper, 1994).

The problem of validity has on the whole been ignored by psychiatrists and the results, as in the case of reliability, are not encouraging (Bentall, 1990). One statistical technique which has been applied to test the validity of diagnostic systems is 'cluster analysis' which looks at the similarities between people and attempts to assign individuals to groups according to simple rules. As an example, a cluster analysis programme might search through a database of hospital patients and begin by placing together (that is, in clusters) those patients with the most similar symptoms. If patients fall into natural groups which, in turn, correspond to traditional psychiatric diagnosis, this would suggest that such diagnoses reflect true divisions in nature and would be powerful evidence of validity. However, several studies using this method have not yielded encouraging results. Everitt et al. (1971), for instance, claimed to have identified clusters corresponding to the depressive and manic phases of manic depression and to the diagnosis of paranoid schizophrenia. However, over 60 per cent of their patients fell into two or three 'dustbin' clusters containing patients with various diagnoses.

It will be apparent by now that the process of diagnosis is not always reliable and may not even be valid. On the whole, mental health professionals outside the medical system have been less concerned with classification and diagnosis because the symptoms of various syndromes are often indistinguishable and syndromes are not immutable. It is indeed mainly the psychiatrists who, in order to retain respectability within the medical fraternity, adhere to those approaches deemed closest to the positivistic scientific method underpinning physical medicine. Interestingly, Berg (1992) has highlighted how the process of diagnosing physical illness is also far from straightforward, noting how the formal medical criteria for diagnosis and other supposedly fixed givens are but one factor in a complex web of influence. This serves as an important reminder that even within the realm of physical medicine, where one would expect diagnosis to be more reliable, data obtained do not necessarily count for or against a diagnosis because diagnostic criteria are in fact but one element in the whole diagnostic decision-making process. Other factors, such as institutional culture, range of disposal options, extent of resources, time and the personal agenda of the diagnostician, all play a role.

Gender, culture and psychopathology

As we have seen so far, psychiatry's claim to be a scientific enterprise has been criticised from a number of angles. Some of the most important challenges have come from feminist and cross-cultural critiques of the concept of mental illness, and we shall briefly review some of their main arguments here.

Feminist critiques

Both feminist and cross-cultural practitioners have postulated that psychiatry, in its theory and practice, inevitably carries with it the ideologies of Western culture which value certain types of behaviour and not others. Undesirable behaviour, it is argued, can then be controlled through being labelled deviant. In this manner women, for instance, can be labelled mentally ill for not conforming to prevailing stereotypes of femininity (Penfold and Walker, 1984; Ussher, 1991). Chessler (1972) strongly argued that sex-role stereotypes are at the heart of much of what we call mental illness. According to her, women are frowned upon and often punished by men for independent or self-assertive behaviour. In the mental health field, she contends that such behaviour is pathologised and hence controlled.

Numerous psychological studies have pointed out that in the West what is generally regarded as the woman's role coincides with what is typically considered to be mentally unhealthy. In a study carried out by Broverman and colleagues (1972) a group of 71 clinicians (including psychologists, psychiatrists and social workers) found that they strongly agreed on the behaviours and attitudes that characterised a mentally healthy man, a mentally healthy woman or a mentally healthy adult independent of gender. The description of the latter matched closely the description of a healthy man but not that of a healthy woman. This confirmed the notion that a double standard of health is applied, depending on the person's gender. Healthy women are perceived as less significantly healthy by adult standards. These differences parallel the sex-role stereotypes in the West and also relate to what is socially valued. According to the Broverman study, healthy women differ from healthy men by being more submissive, less independent and adventurous, more cooperative, more excitable in minor crises, more concerned about their appearance, to name but a few familiar stereotypical female attributes which are usually devalued in our society.

The relevance of such a study to the question of psychopathology will be readily apparent: if a woman breaks out of the female role Western society has cast her in she may be more readily regarded as mentally unhealthy. The general findings of Broverman have been supported by later studies (for example, Penfold and Walker, 1984) and serve to underscore the important point that to talk about psychopathology all too often conceals the fact that the notion itself embodies a moral dimension that may well work against certain groups in Western society, including women.

Such views cannot be separated from the discourse, well established since the nineteenth century, that positions women as biologically inferior and thus vulnerable to both physical and psychological disorders. Such a notion was very clearly evident in the early choice of the term 'hysteria', meaning 'wandering womb', to describe a problem which in the main was said to affect women, along with the category of 'menstrual insanity'. Today, women are still seen as biologically labile whereby puberty marks 'the beginning of a process which links female reproduction to weakness and debilitation, defining women through [their] position in the reproductive life-cycle (Ussher, 1989: 13).

From a feminist perspective, the female body is seen as a scapegoat which allows internal, individualised and medicalised attributions to be made for women's psychological distress. Research and theoretical analysis examining the influence of the reproductive cycle on mental health is largely equivocal, challenging both the validity and the reliability of such constructs as, for instance, premenstrual syndrome and postnatal depression, which are presently in vogue. On the contrary, research has suggested that menstrual and premenstrual disorders are related to undesirable life events and that increases in life stress are associated with increases in menstrual cycle complaints (McFarland et al., 1987; Ussher and Wilding, 1991). While the validity of the reproductive syndromes may be questioned, they none the less appear to act as a salient source of attribution for many women. If a woman is feeling depressed but may be unsure why, the premenstrual syndrome affords a ready-made, culturally sanctioned explanation for the distress. This particular type of attribution may well be a consequence of the discourse which has linked women's psychological distress to biological factors – an idea which has now been taken on board uncritically by many women who are often among some of the most fervent supporters of the reproductive syndromes.

Cross-cultural critiques

Cross-cultural critiques have focused in the main on the seemingly implicit assumption that psychiatry is devoid of cultural and racial bias. Ideas and observations from the basic sciences have influenced psychiatry and an attempt has been made to apply a scientific method to the investigation of the concepts so derived. The process is none the less essentially one that has grown in a particular social, cultural and political climate. The predominant paradigm in psychiatry is one which has been developed in Europe and North America.

In considering the question of diagnosis, it has been strongly argued that we have to remember the essentially ethnocentric nature of psychiatry as well as the fact that its ways of diagnosing are influenced by the social ethos and the political systems in which such diagnostic systems evolved. These aspects of diagnosis need to be borne in mind when considering, for instance, such facts as the higher incidence of compulsory admission into psychiatric hospitals among people from ethnic minorities (Khan, 1983; Ineischen, 1984; Thomas et al., 1993). Furthermore, members of ethnic minorities who become involved with psychiatric services are more often diagnosed within psychotic categories than their indigenous counterparts. One study of psychiatric admissions in Leicestershire in Britain (Shaikh, 1985) compared two matched groups of Asian and white patients. While the study did not reveal any significant differences between the two groups in the number of compulsory admissions, nor in the length of stay in hospital, it highlighted the fact that the diagnoses applied to the Asian patients were significantly different from those applied to the white patients. The Asian patients were more likely to be diagnosed as psychotic.

Moreover, the treatment administered to the two groups differed. ECT (electroconvulsive treatment) was given to those Asian patients diagnosed as schizophrenic more frequently than to the white patients with the same diagnosis. The latter finding has been supported by other research which shows that people from ethnic minorities are more likely on the whole to receive medication than to be referred for psychotherapy (Campling, 1989). Variations in the incidence of diagnosed illness may then be understood as partly arising from social influences on the construction of the illness.

Human experience, individual and collective, and concepts of normative personhood have varied greatly across time and place. Moreover, pathological manifestations are themselves shaped to a degree by the culture's prevailing schemata and categories of abnormal experience or behaviour. For example Simon (1978, quoted in Wallace, 1994) pointed to certain fixed cultural patterns of madness in ancient Greece, such as the hearing of animal sounds and the music of flutes and cymbals – patterns which would not have applied in other cultural milieux. Similarly, while the structure of delusions appears to be similar across cultures, their content is strongly influenced by culture: content that might be considered delusional in one culture may be regarded as normal elsewhere. Even when we consider psychiatric problems such as depression or schizophrenia, so-called 'local knowledge and understanding' of their origin, course and outcome highlights the considerable variation across cultures so that it becomes apparent that it is nonsensical to discuss such presumed universal, biologically determined problems in any universal manner. Such considerations have led some authors to argue that all illness is culture bound and therefore needs to be understood in culturally specific terms (Harkness and Super, 1990). Such a position does not deny the possibility that there is a biological dimension to psychopathology but it stresses the importance of addressing the 'cultural organisation of psychopathology' which purely medical models evolved in the West fail to consider.

Research into the different conceptualisations of abnormal behaviour suggests that what is normal and what is pathological is shaped by cultural definitions of personhood, social identities and role expectations. In a study of the Asian community in London, Beliappa (1991) showed that while emotional difficulties were recognised by those included in the sample, they were not classified as pathological. Those individuals who were facing emotional difficulties were less able to compartmentalise their experiences as affecting the individual psyche but were more likely to use a holistic model where the whole person was felt to be affected and to line their experiences within a normative structure of roles and expectations. Rather than viewing emotional distress as a sign of illness, it was understood as a condition that signalled a need to restore lost meaning with reference to expected roles. Such different conceptualisations of psychological distress may help to account for the low uptake of statutory services by ethnic minorities who consider a medical approach as inappropriate to deal with their distress (Cullen and Fernando, 1989).

In summary, both the feminist and cross-cultural critiques remind us that abnormality is always recognised against a background of particular beliefs about normality which are themselves partly culturally determined and therefore reflect the prevailing norms of a given society at a given historical period. The investigations in the fields of social science, history and cross-cultural studies foster our humility as well as encourage more phenomenologically orientated approaches to the question of psychopathology along with greater appreciation of culture-specific conceptualisations of 'mental illness' and how to help people who are distressed (Patel and Winston, 1994). By alerting us to the external determinants on our perceptions and interpretations, they also broaden our understanding of the therapeutic relationship by reminding us of the interactional, mutually determining nature of psychological investigations taking place in any given sociocultural context.

Mental illness: a barrier to understanding?

The various criticisms that have been levelled at the notion of mental illness, as we have seen so far, are not simply part of a convincing rhetoric. On the contrary, they are well documented and backed by research which brings into question the validity and reliability of the various diagnostic systems, as well as highlighting the inevitable cultural and gender bias inherent in such an enterprise. Notwithstanding such serious challenges, the notion of mental illness has, in the main, been retained. We do well to ask ourselves 'why?' The answer to this question lies, at least in part, in an understanding of the functions it serves in Western society, that is, the reasons why we apparently *need* to believe there exist diseases of the mind. Three of these functions are particularly relevant to our discussion and to the spirit in which this book is written.

Legitimising psychiatry

First, many of the critics of psychiatry have argued that psychiatry as a profession could not justify itself without a notion of mental illness. As noted earlier, psychiatry is, unlike other branches of medicine, the poor relation in the eyes of the medical fraternity. This is attributable to its dubious scientific status which, in turn, can be understood as a consequence of the difficulties of studying the human mind. In spite of the attendant problems in any attempt to study the human mind scientifically, the idea of particular behaviours as 'illnesses' has maintained at least the impression of some similarity between psychiatry and the rest of medicine.

While it is important to recognise the limitations of applying the medical model to the study and treatment of psychopathology, medicine none the less may have a potentially useful contribution to make to our understanding of abnormal behaviour, or indeed any kind of behaviour, as nothing takes place in a neurophysiological vacuum. That a neurological substrate is what makes the life of the mind possible cannot be in doubt; mental activity can reasonably be regarded as a natural function of neurological complexity. Changes in brain chemistry do correlate with particular moods or behaviours. However, it is this activity as experienced by the individual that is the province of the therapist. If interventions at the level of neurochemistry relieve the emotional distress reported by some people, then that is reasonably one of the ways we can approach treatment. It would, however, be a mistake to infer from this either that the most useful statements that can be made about an individual's so-called psychopathology must be expressed in the language of neurochemistry and treated accordingly through medication, or that brain chemistry is the cause of particular behaviours or moods. Although some psychiatrists still uphold a narrow and heavily medical approach to treatment, it is important to appreciate that modern approaches to psychiatry are by no means restricted to a biochemical or neuropsychological point of view. They include social and other varied psychological approaches that reflect the developments in the understanding of psychopathology that have taken place over the past century.

Relieving our anxiety and guilt

In considering the second important function served by the notion of mental illness, we need to look to ourselves for the answer. It may be easier to think of the pain and confusion some people present with as resulting from an illness. Such a conceptualisation may reassure us. If the distressing behaviour we encounter can be firmly located in the 'other' and the cause of the behaviour can in turn be located in brain chemistry or genes, then we have temporarily created the illusion that this kind of thing only happens to 'them' and not 'us'.

In an essay entitled 'What is schizophrenia?', Manfred Bleuler commented that 'we conceive of ourselves, our personalities and our own egos as being steady and firm. The fact that we could disintegrate mentally . . . is a monstrous, uncanny concept' (1984: 8). The fear of

collapse and the sense of dissolution which Bleuler refers to con-
taminate the Western image of all diseases. Disease of any kind evokes
the most profound sense of the self's fragility. Sinason (1992) has
suggested that as biological organisms we seem to carry within us a
sense of the whole. The intactness of our bodies and our minds
confirms this sense of wholeness. Any threat to this wholeness evokes
deep-seated anxieties against which we need to defend. In line with
such thinking, Gilman (1988) makes the point that at the root of all
bipolar images of difference, for instance disease versus health, which
underpin our construction of stereotypes, lies the fantasy of wholeness.
He argues that our internalised sense of difference is the product of the
primal moment in our experience when we first become aware that we
are separate and different from our care-giver, most typically our
mothers, and no longer able to live in the illusion of omnipotent
control of our environment. The anxiety inherent in this realisation is
reawakened when we are confronted by the possibility of mental or
physical disintegration.

We find it very hard to own and hold on to such a fear of our own
collapse; we find it easier to project it outwards into the world in order
to localise it in the 'other', thereby creating an illusion of being in
control. That which is projected is ultimately our sense of what some
have called 'ontological insecurity'. In some cases the fearful is made
harmless through being rendered comic – after all do we not sometimes
laugh at the person who believes he is Jesus Christ? In other cases, the
fearful looms as a threat controlled only by being made visible. To
illustrate the latter we can turn to the construction of the image of the
mentally ill as violent. The mentally ill person, especially in the
incarnation of the violent schizophrenic, is one of the most common
focuses for the general anxiety felt by most of us. If we are afraid that
we might be attacked, we do not want this fear to be universal. Rather,
as Gilman (1988) suggests we want to know and be able to identify
who is going to attack us. In order to increase our sense of being in
control, each society selects a certain number of categories into which it
projects such anxieties and at different times and different places some
have been, and still are, afraid of black people, homosexuals, Jews,
mad people and any 'other' a particular society chooses to designate as
different (Gilman, 1988).

Our anxieties are not unjustified as not only do violent individuals
exist but it is also very difficult to predict a person's dangerousness.
Our efforts to render dangerousness visible, by identifying particular
groups as the ones most likely to aggress against us so that we can
avoid them, match the clinician's and the researcher's efforts to
diagnose dangerousness. Yet dangerousness is often the result of a
complex interaction of personal and situational factors. It is not merely
the presence or absence of any particular factor but their combination

that gives some indication of the volatility of the individual and her violent potential (Clarke, 1990). The label schizophrenic may well be associated for some of us with violence, largely because of the emphasis placed by the media on those incidents of violence involving individuals labelled schizophrenic, but the label itself is in no way a reliable predictor of violence. Most of the people with such a diagnosis never attack anyone but they are often sadly imprisoned in a world in which they feel themselves to be persecuted and attacked by internal aggressors. As Monahan (1992: 510) put it: 'Compared with the magnitude of risk associated with alcoholism and other drug abuse, the risk associated with major mental disorders such as schizophrenia and affective disorder is modest indeed. Clearly, mental health-status makes at best a trivial contribution to the overall level of violence in society.'

The move towards de-institutionalisation of the 'mentally ill' means that it is now very common to encounter on the street someone who behaves oddly. When we do so we often cross the street if we feel that such a person is actually heading for us or we smile politely if they sit next to us on a bus, but we seldom engage with them. They are the terrifying 'other', keepers of our worst fears of chaos and disintegration. But what happens when it is not the identifiable mad person who turns out to be aggressive or odd but rather someone close to us? We are shocked if this happens and the moment when we recognise that the 'other' is, in fact, just like us is terrifying as we then no longer know where the line lies that divides our so-called normal, reliable world from the chaotic world we fear. We thus need the mad to be different. However, the reality is that most people who are labelled as mentally ill do not correspond to prevailing stereotypes. It is the perception of a small number of such individuals as the embodiment of our image of the mad which leads us to place all people who are labelled mentally ill into the category of the dangerous person who needs to be avoided and feared.

How we see the so-called mad is determined in part by our need for psychological coherency and consistency. Ross (1977) has suggested that there is a strong tendency to explain other people's behaviour in terms of internal, stable dispositions, particularly when the behaviour in question is in some way distinctive and is perceived as uncommon. The desire to demarcate clearly what is normal from what is abnormal in matters of mental health was the basis of the most popular forensic psychiatric system in nineteenth-century Europe. Cesare Lombroso, in his studies of criminal men and women, saw the criminal as a sub-type who possessed specific physical characteristics (particularly physiognomic) which identified his or her madness. Gilman (1988) makes the important point that the tradition of visually represented madness in the form of various icons, whether body type, gesture or dress, points towards our need to identify the mad in absolute and incontrovertible terms. This underscores Western society's need to localise and confine the mad. While there may well be specific physical abnormalities which precipitate, or at the very least correlate with, particular manifestations of psychopathology, it is none the less important not to lose sight of our *need* to see such clear, identifiable, concrete patterns behind all such manifestations for the reasons outlined above. Even though we may fear the person labelled mad, we need to recognise that we are often endlessly fascinated by him. Echoing a point made originally by Foucault, Ussher (1991: 141) writes: 'the outsiders are not merely functional in defining ourselves or our social groups. They have an intrinsic fascination – possibly because they represent that part of ourselves which we most fear.'

The conceptualisation of certain behaviours as illnesses may also serve to absolve society of any responsibility for having caused the behaviour – if it's an illness it's not our business, as it were. An exclusive focus on organic processes may then detract important attention away from the societal and/or familial contributions to the development of particular behaviours. This is not to advocate a 'I blame the parents/society' position, but merely to acknowledge that all behaviour occurs in a context and that this context plays its part in giving shape and content to the behaviour and how it is managed. As we will see in Chapter 9 on psychosis, studies have shown that particular types of family interaction and the structure of society itself, while not necessarily causing psychotic symptoms, certainly play a very important part in the course and outcome of a psychotic episode.

The promise of 'cure'

The third function served by the medical model of distress meets the needs of at least a proportion of those people who are labelled as having a psychiatric illness. The notion of mental illness is seductive, for if the distress can be shown to result from organic dysfunction we then only have to wait for cure by the physician. This is an important point to consider when working with clients whose own beliefs about the cause of their distress may become the focus of therapeutic work. I can vividly recall in my early days of clinical work seeking to challenge my clients' beliefs about the organic nature of their distress. In my *naïveté* I hoped to free them, as I saw it then, from an understanding of their predicament which I believed to be erroneous and which I thought further disempowered them. I also remember quickly realising that some of my clients found a measure of relief in the labels that they had been given as they were seen to contain the hope of cure. Moreover, several felt that the drugs that they had been prescribed helped them to manage a life which would otherwise have been unmanageable.

Although such realisations did not necessarily lead me to change all of my assumptions about the nature of the distress I was observing, I none the less had to accept that, given our very limited knowledge in this area, I had no right to force them to accept my own view of the world. It also encouraged me to adopt a more open attitude to the potentially helpful role of medication for some people. When considering the notion of mental illness and the disadvantages of labelling generally, we should not lose sight of the client's perspective and the function that such labels, and the notion of mental illness itself, may serve for them. The rhetoric of antipsychiatry can leave us, as practitioners, stranded and speechless when confronted with someone in the grips of a terrifying psychotic episode. Labels at that point may help the client to make sense of such internal chaos by attributing it to a process which has a name and, which suggests that it may be treated.

Implications for practice

This chapter has reviewed the notion of mental illness from a number of different perspectives, highlighting the problems such a notion poses as well as the functions it serves. While the criticisms that have been levelled at this notion cannot be easily discarded, neither can the reality of the psychic pain our clients present us with. This reality needs to be acknowledged and responded to. It can be all too easy to argue that psychiatry and psychotherapy are abusive and oppressive practices and that there is no such thing as mental illness (Szasz, 1961; Masson, 1990). While some psychiatrists and some therapists may well be abusive, to argue that all are such is not only quite clearly untrue but it is also of very limited use to those whose emotional well-being is at stake.

It is indeed sobering to ask ourselves what those critics of psychiatry and psychotherapy have to say to those in real distress. The deconstructive approaches to the notion of mental illness that have underpinned the antipsychiatry movement highlighted how labels might be masking the far from laudable motives of the labellers. However, this was only a first step and not an end in itself, as removing the label does not, unfortunately, also remove the distress and misery which afflict some of us. Moreover, changing the label may be seen itself as symptomatic of the difficulty we experience in facing differences because of the guilt this triggers in us for being different from the one who is labelled (Sinason, 1992). Sinason (1992) also points out that mental illness is one of the areas around which euphemisms have proliferated. She argues that this phenomenon reflects those areas of human experience where 'wishes cannot change or put right differences; they are differences that thwart omnipotent wishes to be able to change and control' (1992: 42). But she also soberly reminds us that 'word changes are symptomatic, they do not solve problems' (1992: 43). Even though the acknowledgement of difference may be difficult for us, for the reasons outlined by Sinason, acknowledging similarity is equally threatening as it challenges us with the possibility, as pointed out earlier, that our world may become chaotic and that we may lose our grip.

Ussher has aptly noted that the critics of psychiatry 'can become captivated by their own mesmerising arguments, moved or thrilled by the shocking horror of the extremes they portray, forgetting the essential reality and unglamorous actuality of madness as it is for the majority' (1991: 221). Once we deconstruct the notion of mental illness, 'something' needs to take its place as there is 'something' that needs to be understood. It is this 'something', however we choose to label it, that prompts people to seek psychological help. Their problems are real and their message is often painful to bear and to contain. The client's palpable signs of pain and suffering cannot be dismissed purely as a social construction.

The task of those in the therapeutic professions is a most difficult one. While focusing much of the time on the client's internal reality and her perception of the world, we also need to remain attentive to the social and cultural context within which such personal realities develop and acquire meaning, including the reality of the therapist–client relationship. No therapeutic endeavour can be completely divorced from a sociopolitical discourse even though each one of us will conceive of our role differently in relation to such a discourse. How active or otherwise we choose to be at the sociopolitical level, beyond the boundaries of our consulting room, does not, however, relieve any of us of the burdensome responsibility of continually challenging our assumptions about the nature of our clients' distress and the ways in which we feel it appropriate to intervene therapeutically when presented with such distress.

While there can be no simple answer to 'what is psychopathology', one thing seems clear, namely that normality and abnormality are relative concepts representing arbitrary points on a continuum. The most formidable barrier to understanding psychopathology lies in the often implicit premise that the professional's account of the client's behaviour constitutes an explanation but that the client's account of his behaviour, on the whole, does not. The reluctance to grant explanatory status to the client's own theories about his distress is an integral part of the modern deification of science as the only key to correct explanations. This does not mean that we should reject the findings of scientific approaches. Rather, it means that the stories clients construct about their difficulties are at least as relevant, if not more so, to our understanding of psychopathology as any of the stories we, the 'experts', might like to entertain on the basis of our preferred theoretical models.

The practitioner looking for universal features or factors in the otherwise highly individual fabric of emotional distress is undoubtedly laying essential foundations for a more scientific approach to understanding psychopathology. But those who by virtue of particular theoretical commitments to the presumed 'disorder' never really see the client as a person with his or her own stories and theories are neither good therapists nor good scientists. In clinical practice, our primary task is to maintain a constant and conscious effort to free our observations from the distortions of pre-judgement and to challenge continually our assumptions about notions of mental health and illness. This way we may come closer to offering our clients a 'good-enough' therapeutic space, within which to explore the meaning of their experiences. In the end, all our observations of psychopathology can only inform us about a part of a person and, even if accurate, they should never be divorced from the sociocultural context in which the person lives.

Note

1. The DSM-IV divides psychopathology into five different axes. A multi-axial assessment requires that every case be assessed on several axes. Each axis refers to different classes of information. The first three axes constitute the official diagnostic assessment and refer respectively to: Axis I: clinical syndromes; Axis II: developmental disorders and personality disorders; Axis III: physical disorders and conditions. Axes IV and V refer respectively to the severity of psychosocial stressors and the global assessment of functioning and are generally used in research settings where they provide additional information to the official diagnoses; for instance, information about the stressors in an individual's life.

2
Developmental Psychopathology

Developmental psychopathology contributes a developmental perspective to the study of abnormal behaviour. It is also concerned with the study of the prediction of the development of maladaptive behaviour processes (Lewis, 1990). The scope of this investigation bridges the fields of child and adult psychopathology, allowing us to examine the continuities and discontinuities between mental health problems and risk factors in childhood and later difficulties in adulthood, as well as understanding the internal and external sources of competence and vulnerability. A developmental approach strives to conceptualise how the processes underlying an individual's adaptation in her development lead to a particular outcome in a given developmental period. This requires an examination of a person's current functioning in the context of how this level of functioning was achieved over the course of her development.

A developmental approach to psychopathology emphasises not only how knowledge of normal development can inform our understanding of psychopathology, but also how the study of risk and pathology can enhance our comprehension of normal development. Rather than conceptualising psychopathology in a fixed and stereotyped manner, the emphasis is on the heterogeneity of behavioural outcomes as well as on the developmental process. This chapter will explore some of the challenges facing the study of developmental psychopathology as well as distilling the broad conclusions that may be drawn from the research regarding change and stability in psychopathology across the lifespan. Such issues are relevant for the practising therapist as they help us to appreciate the complexity of individual problems and the aetiological factors which need to be considered in any formulation of problems at the assessment stage (see Chapter 3).

The legacy of childhood

When we are faced with a client with mental health problems, a common question to consider is 'why and how did they arise?': why did one person become depressed; why did another develop an eating problem and yet another develop obsessive-compulsive symptoms? This question raises a related question, namely that of specificity. By this we mean whether there are particular patterns of adversity or risk factors which predict specific manifestations of psychopathology.

The study of psychopathology has traditionally been dominated by a deterministic approach. Whether it be the genes we inherit, the environment we grow up in or both, such factors are seen to shape the adults we become and to be somehow causally related to the psychological difficulties we may experience in adult life. Many therapists would argue strongly against the biological reductions of some aetiological models of psychopathology, while endorsing either explicitly or implicitly the notion that early childhood experiences are aetiologically significant in the development of mental health problems. This is reflected in the focus of a lot of the work in psychotherapies of differing theoretical orientations on a revisiting of the past, inevitably from the perspective of the present, so as to make sense of the psychic pain which clients present with. On one level, therapists are professional advocates of personal responsibility; on another level, many are, in their own belief systems, environmental determinists (Yalom, 1980).

The belief in the importance of the uncovering of the past, and particularly of early childhood experiences, dates back to Freud who held that the exploration of the past was essential to understanding our development and any deviations from so-called normal development. In his clinical work, Freud painstakingly traced meaningful and seemingly causal connections between childhood experiences and current psychopathological manifestations, lending support to his contention that psychological events were not haphazard. This belief was at the core of his principle of psychic determinism. However, such a notion does not imply a simple relationship of cause and effect in our mental life. Indeed, Freud was well aware of the complexity involved in the development of maladaptive as well as normal behaviour. He was in fact quite sceptical about the possibility of predicting outcome, a scepticism which, as we shall see, has been borne out by research.

The limits of prediction

The study of developmental psychopathology is integral to our attempts not only to understand why some people experience mental health problems but also to prevent such problems from arising in the first place. If it is possible to identify 'at risk' groups in childhood and make available the necessary resources to support them, we can, it is hoped, pre-empt the development of difficulties in childhood and subsequently in adulthood. This presupposes that it is possible for us to predict who is more likely to develop mental health problems on the basis of their early histories.

When faced with a young child, for example, who comes from a broken family where he witnessed violence between the parents, who now lives with his mother, who is depressed, and several siblings, in a socially deprived area, and who presents with behavioural problems, we are unlikely to be surprised that such a child is experiencing problems given his history and circumstances. Indeed, we might have predicted, given these facts, that this child would experience some difficulties. If this same child, as an adolescent, uses drugs, is involved in petty theft and truants from school, once again, we would not be surprised by this turn of events and we could predict a likely continuation of behavioural difficulties into adulthood. Such speculation constitutes prospective prediction. Conversely, if we are faced with a female client who is anorexic we would be likely to speculate, if we are psychoanalytically inclined, that the history of her early experiences will reveal complex interactional dynamics in the family of origin and more specifically in her relationship with her mother. This represents a retrospective prediction.

Prediction – both prospective and retrospective – is a very complex matter. The study of developmental psychopathology has largely relied on retrospective analyses which are vulnerable to what are referred to as 'base rate errors'. For example, the common assumption that children who have been abused are more likely as adults to abuse their own children has arisen from studies which rely, in the main, on retrospective analyses. Typically, in such studies, the mothers of children who are being abused are asked if they were themselves once abused. When the question is thus researched, it is reported that the vast majority of mothers reveal a personal history of abuse. This has typically led researchers to conclude that if the parent was abused as a child, he or she is more likely to behave similarly towards his or her own children. These findings do tend to confirm clinical experience but when considering such data we need to remember that in order for it to be meaningful we also need data on those children who are *not* abused and on whether their parents were once abused or not. The latter information would provide us with a base rate against which the findings on the abused children could be compared. However, many retrospective studies lack such base rates, thereby limiting the conclusions we may reasonably draw from them about the continuity of problems from childhood into adulthood.

Prediction as a causal statement requires that a prospective analysis be carried out. Such an analysis is the one of choice as it avoids the pitfalls of a retrospective analysis by allowing us to study the course of development of individuals, only some of whom will develop mental health problems. Such analyses require longitudinal studies which are very costly to implement and therefore seldom used. When they are used, however, they provide powerful evidence for the continuity of certain behavioural and emotional patterns over time.

Prediction, then, is a complex matter which is confounded by the methodological difficulties commonly encountered in the studies which attempt to trace continuities throughout the lifespan. Notwithstanding such problems, the question of prediction has continued to engage the interest of both researchers and clinicians.

The intergenerational context

In addition to the continuities which have been suggested between childhood difficulties and mental health problems in adulthood, continuities across generations within the same family have also been traced. Indeed, one of the most prevalent assumptions in the field of psychopathology is that mental health problems run in families and therefore that a family history of such problems has predictive value. There is ample epidemiological evidence to suggest this (Beardslee et al., 1983; Weissman et al., 1987). There is also substantial evidence that parental mental health problems are related to other types of negative outcomes in children, such as delinquency, poor social adaptation or cognitive deficits (Watt et al., 1984). Evidence of familial clustering of mental health problems has led to genetic hypotheses regarding intergenerational transmission (Egeland et al., 1987). Such hypotheses have received support from epidemiological studies as well as adoption and cross-fostering studies, where the rates of disorder among the adopted-away children of parents with psychiatric problems and adopted children reared by parents with such problems appear to relate more to biological parentage than to the environment in which children are reared (Rosenthal et al., 1971; Mendlewicz and Rainer, 1977). Although it is possible to find a host of studies which support genetic models of transmission, it has become clear that such models only explain a small portion of variance in the development of pychopathology.

While many more children with a family history of psychopathology are likely to experience similar difficulties themselves, the vast majority of adults with a variety of psychiatric problems do not have a demonstrable family history of such problems. Although a family history may be a strong predictor of psychopathology, in no study do we find that every family member is affected (Rende and Plomin, 1993). Furthermore, even though there appears to be some tendency for particular problems to run in families, many, if not most, of the children of parents with psychiatric problems will not share the same type of difficulty with their parent (Downey and Coyne, 1990). Adoption studies have also come under close scrutiny, revealing a number of methodological flaws which bring into question their validity. Issues such as selective placement, contact with biological parents and the problem of generalising beyond the homogeneous Scandinavian cultures where most of this research has been carried out, have been cited as some of the limitations of these studies. Taken together, the evidence available from these various sources is not as strong as it might at first appear.

One interesting approach which has found much favour is to study the appearance of particular psychiatric problems in genetically identical twins either reared together or apart. When the problems occur in both twins we speak of a concordance: when there is a high concordance rate in a statistically significant sample of such identical twins this has been considered to be real evidence that there must be a genetic basis for the problem in question. However, even though, for example, the concordance rate for schizophrenia in identical twins is reported to be in the order of 40 per cent, it is clear that the remaining 60 per cent are discordant. On the basis of such data, it is therefore not possible to draw any firm conclusions regarding the genetic basis of schizophrenia. All that the research allows us reasonably to conclude is that if genetic factors are involved they only *partially* account for psychopathology. Such rates of discordance suggest that, while genetic factors may predispose individuals to particular types of psychopathology, environmental factors also play a key part. Moreover, the relevant environmental influences appear to be specific to each child and not general to an entire family. Plomin and Daniels (1987) suggest that it is those environmental variables which are unique to the person rather than those which are shared by others in the same family, such as siblings, that are the critical ones. Most of the environmental variation which affects a person's psychological development lies in the so-called 'non-shared' environment of siblings. This includes, among other factors, birth order, gender, adverse events, differential interactions with parents and siblings and extra-familial experiences (for example, schools, friends).

By contrast to genetic models, environmental models then posit that differences in the social and psychological environments in which children develop account for the presence of problems in childhood and adulthood. Factors such as parenting behaviour, family coping, experience of abuse and lack of a supporting social network have all been invoked as explanations at one time or another. Although environmental factors most certainly play a part, as highlighted in studies which have looked at the impact of life events on adult psychiatric problems (Brown and Harris, 1978), as well as in childhood psycho-pathology (Goodyear, 1990), it has none the less proved difficult on the basis of such variables to predict specific outcomes. Not only do some individuals appear to be more resilient than others in the face of similar stresses and similar developmental histories, but also it is by no means clear whether there are specific developmental paths from single markers in childhood (for example, loss of a parent) to individual outcomes in adulthood. For instance, if children are insecurely attached to their parents are they more likely to become depressed as adults? Some do but many do not show any problems at all and others still present a quite different clinical picture from depression.

This unpredictability when it comes to specific outcomes suggests that developmental relations may be non-specific and predictive of varied adverse outcomes. For example, insecure attachment in childhood may predict problems in a variety of domains, such as mental health, peer relationships or family functioning. Indeed, Graham and Stevenson (1985), when discussing their twin data, indicate that while there is evidence that temperamental traits are inherited and that certain traits such as aggression or greater impulsivity are associated in children with increased rates of emotional and behavioural disturbance, the specificity between particular temperamental traits and psychiatric symptoms is not high. In their study, identical twins who displayed similar tempera-ments developed quite different problems.

Research in the field of child psychopathology suggests that mental health problems in young people are likely to be caused by a configur-ation of social factors rather than by any single experience from the child's past or present (Goodyear, 1990). It has also become apparent that the effects caused by such configurations of social experiences derive from different physiological and psychological pathways. In addition, many life events and circumstances that influence develop-ment, and which may exert a causal influence on psychopathology, are seldom circumscribed events but more continuing processes where delineation of a beginning and an end stage is not feasible. Finally, the significance of events during development is an important consideration as events may have different impacts at different life stages reflecting the individual's cognitive and emotional development. The difficulty of predicting outcome on the basis of the presence or absence of certain risk factors should be clear by now.

Risk and protective factors

The study of psychopathology has traditionally concentrated on the question of why individuals who are at risk develop problems. Risk refers to elevated probabilities of undesirable outcomes ...mbers of a group who share one or more characteristics. The ...oncept of risk highlights those innate and situational factors that might be expected to enhance the probability of developing particular forms of impairment in psychosocial functioning and affecting the individual's adaptation. These are typically regarded as enduring or long-standing life circumstances or conditions that contribute to maladaptive processes. Research has focused on identifying such risk or vulnerability factors. They are subdivided into *external factors*, such as the family and social environment, and *internal factors*, such as biological predispositions and psychological functioning. It is clear that the distinction between external and internal factors is to an extent an academic one, as these sources of influence are likely to interact with one another to produce particular outcomes for each person. For example, development and life experience may alter the impact of genetic predisposition.

Risk factors act as sources of vulnerability as they detract from the achievement of successful adaptation and competence. For example, parental psychopathology and drug abuse, marital conflict, divorce, child maltreatment and parental hostility have all been shown to contribute to adverse outcomes for the developing child in their striving for adaptation (Hetherington, 1989; Toth et al., 1992). In addition, factors such as low socioeconomic status, unsupportive social or familial networks, inadequate schools, life events, may all adversely affect an individual's coping capacity and hence affect his development. It is the interaction of multiple risk factors, along with personal and collective misfortune, that appears to be especially critical in the development of psychopathology (Werner and Smith, 1992). Only small portions of variance in child behaviour and adult outcome are explained by any single risk factor. Rather, it is the cumulative nature of the risks which seems best able to explain the developmental outcome of the experience of adversity in early life. Recent models of developmental psychopathology therefore consider multiple sources of risk, concentrating on the number of risk factors rather than their specificity (Seifer et al., 1992). Specific risks are more likely to be related to a number of different types of negative outcome given that the most important variable is the unique interaction between the individual and his environment. This serves as a further reminder of the difficulties inherent in prediction, as individuals bring to their life experiences different strengths and vulnerabilities. These interact with the environment and affect the way in which it is experienced and therefore whether the environment itself becomes a source of stress or support to the life of the individual.

More recently, researchers have concentrated less on 'why have things gone wrong' and more on the question 'why have things gone right?' or, as some authors have put it, on a study of the 'roads not taken' (Masten and Coatsworth, 1995). In any examination of risk factors for psychopathology, it becomes apparent that there are also 'protective' factors that function as buffers against the risks and which need to be borne in mind when predicting outcome. Protective factors promote adaptation to one's environment. Many of these are essentially the polar opposites of the risk factors outlined earlier and would thus include parental mental health, warmth and nurturance and effective parenting to name but a few. Protective factors are thought to lead to relative invulnerability or resilience, that is, the ability to recover from, or adjust more easily to, adversity. As Cohler (1987) has pointed out there 'is a tendency to assume that deprived backgrounds always result in suffering and increase the likelihood of developing mental health problems.' Such assumptions are not invariably borne out by observation as there are those individuals whose adjustment suggests that they have been able to overcome adversity.

An individual's resilience is said to account for the variation in outcome among those people faced with the same challenges. One impressive longitudinal study traced from birth to the age of 32 the developmental paths of a multi-ethnic cohort of children in Hawaii who had been exposed as children to perinatal stress, chronic poverty and parental disharmony and psychopathology (Werner, 1993). In this cohort of 698 babies born in 1955, one-third was designated to be high risk and one in three of the high-risk children grew into competent and confident adults. The other two-thirds developed serious learning or behavioural problems by the age of 10 and had mental health problems, delinquency records and/or teenage pregnancies by the age of 18. Several clusters of protective factors emerged in the high-risk group who had a successful outcome. These included temperamental characteristics in the children that contributed to the elicitation from infancy onwards of positive reponses from a variety of caregivers; characteristics and caregiving styles of the parents that reflected competence and fostered self-esteem in the children; and supportive adults (for example, grandparents, youth leaders) who fostered trust. When the links between such protective factors within the individuals and outside sources of support or stress were examined, a continuity was traced in the life trajectories of the high-risk children who successfully overcame childhood adversities. The study suggested that their individual dispositions led them to construct environments and to make life choices that reinforced achievement and rewarded their competencies.

Fonagy (1992) provides a concise review of the research on resilience, highlighting the attributes of resilient children when compared to vulnerable children. Resilient children tend to come from higher socioeconomic status backgrounds, are female, do not have any organic problems, have a high IQ and good problem-solving ability, have easy temperaments and have not endured early separations or losses. Fonagy also outlines the features of the child's environment which function as protective factors in the face of adversity: competent parenting, a good relationship with at least one primary care-giver, the proximity of social support from spouse, family or other figures, a network of informal relationships, better educational experience and, finally, involvement with an organised religious activity and faith. In general, findings emphasise the protective function of parenting and the importance of the quality of the parent–child relationship (Pianta and Egeland, 1990).

In addition to risk and protective factors, it is also important to consider the impact of transient influences, which may exert initial positive or negative effects depending on the timing of such events, on the pertinent developmental issues for the individual at the time as well as their socio-environmental context. For example, loss of a parent may have a far greater adverse impact when it occurs in the context of poor social support networks or if it is experienced in the first decade of life (Altschul and Pollock, 1988). The same experience may thus affect the individual differently depending on her developmental maturity (which may not correlate with chronological age). Essentially this means that the meaning of a life event may change across the lifespan and will also be affected by the person's internal and external resources at that time. For any one person the vulnerability and protective factors and the transient features interact with each other dynamically (Cicchetti and Toth, 1995). It should be remembered that risk, vulnerability and protective factors do not *per se* cause pathological outcomes but rather reflect more complex processes which contribute to the highly individual ways in which people adapt to their environments and cope with life (Rutter, 1990). Furthermore, an individual's resilience is not a constant trait. Rather, people vary in their resilience across the lifespan: some are able to ovecome early adversity and display no difficulties in childhood but succumb to problems in adulthood, often triggered by life changes.

Stability and change across the lifespan

While a continuous view of developmental functioning makes intuitive sense, this has not been borne out by empirical investigation. Clinical and epidemiological data show, for example, that parents with a conflicted past, including experiences of brutality or abandonment in childhood, do not invariably repeat similar experiences with their own children, nor do they necessarily develop mental health problems. Cycles of disadvantage, as manifested in the transmission of particular vulnerabilities, do not then appear to be inevitable. The seminal work of Clark and Clark (1976) on the effects of early deprivation showed that those individuals who were likely candidates for a life of institutionalisation did not always have negative outcomes in adult life. Longitudinal studies of children reared in the absence of their biological parents tell us that the outcome is far from undesirable in all cases, suggesting that important, facilitative interactions can and do occur in later periods of life which may successfully influence subsequent adjustment (Quinton and Rutter, 1985).

For example, Rutter (1992) has pointed out that the choice of marital partner constitutes one of the most important routes by which environmental discontinuities can serve as turning points in the trajectory of lifespan development. Along these lines, a recent study by Quinton and colleagues (1993) examined the role of partner choices and the continuity between conduct disorders in childhood and poor social and psychological functioning in adult life. They found that a supportive, non-deviant partner had an effect on the transition out of conduct problems into satisfactory social functioning. There thus appear to be modifying variables which interact with predisposing factors (intrapsychic and interactionally determined) and precipitating factors (life events) to produce particular outcomes.

Given the frequently observed discontinuities between childhood problems and adult psychopathology, Sameroff (1993) advocates a developmental model which emphasises the intimate connection between the capacities of the individual and the stresses and supports of the environment: 'The contexts of an individual's development are not static . . . they are active shapers of experience that have agendas and are organised by other individuals. In this important sense development becomes the outcome of relationships between interacting individuals at every phase of life' (Sameroff, 1993: 3–4). Such a view is in keeping with the dialectical nature of development first proposed by Riegel (1978), where the actions of the individual change reality and the changes in reality, in turn, affect the behaviour of the individual. Continuity in psychopathology from childhood into adulthood cannot then be considered to be exclusively the property, or the consequence of, the child or the environment respectively. Rather, development is the product of a dynamic interaction between the individual and the environment. This, of course, includes the possibility that the individual, on account of his behaviour, may have a strong determining influence (both positive and negative) on his experiences and the environments he co-creates with others.

Vulnerability, resilience and culture

Psychopathology is a normative concept and is defined in relation to variations in human behaviour and expectations of behaviour that are culturally and historically based (see Chapter 1). However, when considering the question of vulnerability and resilience, little attention has been paid to the place of culture as a variable affecting the origin, course and outcome of psychological problems across the lifespan (Cohler et al., 1995). Cultural perspectives add to our understanding of the vicissitudes of personal adjustment over time by focusing our attention on the significance of culture in enhancing or reducing resilience in those individuals facing adversity. Risk factors, such as family conflict or social change, have an impact because of the way in which these events are understood by members of a given cultural group. The better outcome for schizophrenia which has been reported in the developing world (see Chapter 9) appears to be related to the different ways in which certain cultures respond to a psychotic breakdown and the opportunities for reintegration that such cultures offer to the afflicted individual. Transitions across the lifespan, along with the ways in which adversity associated with these transitions is managed, reflect shared symbolic meanings constituting culture. Within cultures where the extended family is important, family adversity (for example, illness or death of a parent when the child is young) has quite different consequences for the development of the child than in cultures which emphasise the nuclear family unit (Cohler et al., 1995). As Cohler et al. (1995: 786) point out: 'the very concept of resilience must be understood within a cultural perspective that takes into account symbolic constructions of self and others, values and the personal significance of particular life experiences as reflected in the personal narrative or life story.'

Predicting the unpredictable?

As we have seen in this chapter, much of the literature in the field of psychopathology has portrayed the developmental process as somewhat deterministic, resulting in maladaptive or negative outcomes for those individuals confronted with a variety of adversities in early life. Yet, work emerging from the field of developmental psychopathology affords a much needed lifespan perspective to this question. Some adults who have suffered hardship and deprivation in their childhoods not only survive but also thrive, whereas others who have been raised under more apparently 'good-enough' conditions develop psychological problems in adulthood. Such discontinuities invite us to consider those aspects of an individual's environment and their potentialities which may serve as protective factors as well as those that increase the risk of experiencing difficulties. These remind us of the complexity of causal models of development.

The identification of the mechanisms and processes that lead to competent adaptation, despite the presence of adversity, enhances our understanding of both normal and abnormal development. Underpinning such work is a view of the person as an active participant in her environment, engaged in a dynamic interaction with both intra- and extra-organismic factors. In this context, neither resilient nor maladaptive functioning is viewed as a static condition. Rather, at different developmental transitions throughout the lifespan, new vulnerabilities or strengths may emerge (Cicchetti and Garmezy, 1993). Such considerations challenge the validity of a deterministic perspective while also giving due emphasis to those aspects of our lives in which we have very limited or no choice, such as which family we are born into, a 'given' which may place some individuals at greater risk of psychopathology than others. It is reassuring for everyone to think that even with the most difficult beginnings in childhood, there may be positive outcomes in adult life. As Fonagy so aptly put it, 'history is *not* destiny' (1992: 3).

3
Assessment

What is a 'good' assessment?

Assessment has been described as an 'art' (Coltart, 1993). A good assessment is clearly not just about following a set of guidelines or covering specific areas of functioning during the consultation. It relies on other less specific, non-quantifiable ingredients which can neither be prescribed nor formally taught. A 'good' assessment is one which identifies the needs of a client so as to maximise the chance of having these needs met through an appropriate intervention. In this respect, even though the assessment may appear to the assessor to be a one-off consultation, it represents an encounter integral to the client's life as it determines where or to whom the client will be directed and what he will be offered. It also gives the client an opportunity to clarify how and what he feels; that is, to clarify his own understanding of his distress. In this respect an assessment always has a therapeutic potential. A good assessment is therefore also one that helps the client to ease a sense of chaos and confusion about himself and his predicament through a greater degree of clarity and sense of direction. It offers the client a measure of containment of feelings, which is particularly helpful if there is likely to be a long wait between assessment and intervention or if the client is seen as an emergency and may then present in a very confused or chaotic state.

In this chapter we will examine the nature of assessment as well as focus on the life circumstances and the general areas of psychosocial functioning that it is important to explore with any new client presenting with mental health problems. We will also consider broad criteria of suitability for psychological intervention.

The prehistory of assessment

Assessment and any therapy that may ensue begin before client and therapist actually meet face to face. Frequently the therapist will have received a verbal or written referral from another professional or he or she will have had telephone contact with a client if she is self-referring. Sometimes the person who makes the referral may be a relative – this is often the case with younger clients. Such contacts and the information we extract from them can be useful, but they inevitably lead to the generation of assumptions and hypotheses about the client's problems. We all make assumptions on the basis of our personal life experiences as well as the theoretical models we have been influenced by. This is inevitable but it is essential to good practice that such assumptions are acknowledged and bracketed so that we may enter the assessment interview with as few preconceptions as possible. Our assumptions may well be confirmed when we meet the client but we must not be biased by our expectations. Indeed, assessment is a most challenging enterprise as, on the one hand, the therapist needs to use his or her knowledge of psychological problems and interventions to inform his or her recommendations, while, on the other hand, he or she needs to remain open to the possibility that a client may not fit any of the familiar theories. We need to be careful with our 'knowledge', not be hostile towards our ignorance and even strive towards what Bruch (1973a) calls a 'constructive use of ignorance' so that we may appreciate the client's reality and her 'story' about her distress.

It is, however, not only the therapist who carries the baggage of preconception: the client also brings to the assessment situation a host of fantasies, hopes, expectations, fears and hidden, often unconscious, agendas shaped by his previous experiences which influence the dynamics between client and therapist. It is generally acknowledged that a strong transference exists before client and therapist meet for the first time (Budd, 1994). Some clients' hopes and expectations reveal a genuine desire to bring about change in their lives and are thus conducive to a positive working relationship. However, we must always approach the assessment situation with a degree of scepticism and not assume that just because a client has kept his appointment this is an indication of his desire to change. Freud, along with many analysts since, warned us of the perils of *naïveté* in the clinical situation and the importance of understanding the misalliances that may develop between client and therapist (Langs, 1975). Clients come for assessment for a host of reasons not all of which reflect their desire to change. For instance, some clients keep their appointments simply because they have been instructed to do so by the Courts. In other cases, consultation may be undermined by the client's ulterior motives: for instance, the need for a report to an employer or solicitor. In addition, the client's previous experiences with other mental health professionals will inevitably colour the present encounter. It is therefore important to explore any previous such experiences in the assessment.

The assessment process

As with the beginning of therapy, an assessment consultation should start with the setting of the boundaries for this meeting. This primarily involves letting the client know how long you will be meeting for and what are the aims of the assessment. Let us look at these two ground rules more closely.

Timing the assessment

Therapists vary widely in how much time they devote to an assessment, but it is generally recognised that in order to enable both client and therapist to assess the client's needs and whether they can work together, time is an important factor. In view of this it is helpful to allow at least an hour, and preferably one and a half hours, for an assessment. Alternatively, both client and therapist may decide that they need to meet again before any final decisions can be taken. Spreading the assessment over a few sessions has the advantage of allowing both client and therapist to process their experiences with the benefit of some distance. The way in which the client manages the interval between two consultations may also provide a useful source of information about her ability to contain her anxieties and how she might be able to use therapy. For instance, if the client returns for the second consultation and has clearly reflected on what had been discussed the first time, this would be a positive indication of the client's ability to use a psychological intervention.

The aims of assessment

From the outset, the therapist should emphasise the two-way process of the assessment. Assessment is as much an opportunity for the client to clarify how he feels and how he might be helped and whether the therapist assessing him is the kind of person whom he feels he could work with, as it is an opportunity for the therapist to decide how and by whom the client's needs would best be met. The ultimate goal is thus not only the development of a mutual understanding of the core problem(s) so that an appropriate intervention can be identified and planned, but also to see whether this particular intervention can be made in the context of the relationship between assessor and client. Depending on the setting in which the therapist works, it is important to explain at the outset that the person who is assessing may not necessarily be the one to carry out the work but this is usually implicit if the aims of the assessment have been clarified with the client to begin with.

The process of assessment

Having established some core ground rules, the assessment can unfold. First and foremost, assessment is based on the relationship between therapist and client. It requires openness and empathy by the therapist as well as a sensitivity to the dynamics that may transpire between therapist and client. Throughout an assessment interview it is important for the therapist to reflect on what is happening between therapist and client and to consider the following. How does the client relate to the therapist? How does the client describe her experiences? What feelings are triggered in the therapist during the interview? The answers to such questions are as important as, and often far more informative than, the biographical information we collect. They focus on *how* the client tells her story rather than on *what* the client says; on the form as opposed to the content of what the client communicates. They carry information about the client which is 'live'. An assessment interview should therefore not be carried out in a mechanistic manner where the gathering of facts about a client's life can overshadow consideration of the actual *process* of assessment. Although, as we shall see later, it is important to acquire factual information about the client, this is only one of the aims of assessment. The acquisition of objective knowledge about the client's history is meaningless if it is not considered in the context of the evolving relationship between therapist and client.

The relationship is important on practical and epistemological grounds. Practically speaking, no meaningful assessment can be arrived at without efforts to establish a positive working alliance with a client. If the client cannot trust the therapist and experience empathic concern on his or her part, the client is unlikely to engage fully in the assessment or in any subsequent treatment. The relationship between a positive working alliance and the outcome of psychological interventions is strong (see, for example, Horvarth and Symonds, 1991). A further reason for paying close attention to the nature of the emerging relationship during assessment relates to the question of what is most unfortunately referred to as 'treatment compliance'. A client who feels understood and respected by the therapist is more likely to pursue the recommendations made by the therapist than if he feels in some way blamed, intruded upon or even rejected by the therapist. For example, parents who seek help for problems they perceive to be located in their child are more likely to accept the suggestion of family therapy if, at the assessment stage, the therapist manages to give due attention to the parents' concerns and feelings, that is, to their 'reality' rather than suggesting that they are somehow to blame for their child's problem.

There are also theoretical reasons for the privileged place accorded here to the relationship between therapist and client at the assessment stage. Contemporary epistemologists argue that all knowledge is a process by which the knower actively organises and shapes what is given to perception and thought and thereby constructs what is known. Knowledge of a client then represents the outcome of a dynamic interaction between knower and known, between subject and object. The therapist carrying out an assessment thus needs to be mindful of the fact that the knowledge gathered from the assessment is inevitably subjective. This view of assessment stands in contrast with a 'medical model' approach which focuses on 'history taking'. What is being proposed here, rather, is an emphasis on 'history making' (Hirshberg, 1993), that is, the importance of addressing how the client organises and construes her account of her difficulties as she engages with the therapist. It can sometimes be helpful to comment on this explicitly during the assessment. For example, as well as commenting on any contradictions or omissions in the client's account, it can be helpful to take note of how much or how little detail is offered, whether the narrative is easy or difficult to follow, or whether the client appears preoccupied with particular relationships but relates her concerns in a very muddled or incoherent fashion. Such observations may lead to hypotheses as to their significance in terms of the client's presenting concerns, her ability to relate to the therapist and to use psychological therapy. In some instances it can be helpful to share such hypotheses with a client, or, in other words, to make an interpretation. However, such interventions should be made judiciously. Indeed, Malan (1979) cautions the therapist to guard against 'disturbing' the client by 'opening up' too much too soon. This is especially important if there is likely to be a gap between assessment and intervention. The difficulty of assessment arises precisely because of the many layers at which the therapist needs to operate.

The content of assessment

In an assessment it is important to obtain information about the client's background and his presenting concerns. The information thus gathered should always be in the service of enabling the client to organise his experience. The goal of information gathering is to develop as comprehensive a view as possible of the client *in context*. This will therefore include information about the client's perception of himself and of other important people in his life as well as of the characteristics of the cultural and social world in which he lives. It is always preferable, but by no means always possible, to learn about all these aspects of the client's experience from actual observations during the assessment and from the account given by the client rather than in response to direct questions. Allowing the client to take the lead is important as what he chooses to tell us or omits to say, what he emphasises or glosses over, all offer us a wealth of information which would otherwise be obscured through direct questioning. Having said this, there will most certainly be occasions when the therapist will need to enquire directly about, or clarify, some specific aspect of the client's story.

The assessment interview itself, then, while remaining sufficiently flexible, should cover the areas listed below. It should be remembered, however, that not everything will be of equal relevance to all clients and there will always be some unanswered questions. Moreover, the therapist's theoretical beliefs invariably direct the line of questioning and hence the content of the assessment. A psychodynamic therapist will focus far more on early childhood events than a behavioural one, whereas a family therapist will focus more on family patterns, beliefs and rules. It is because of such inevitable biases that it is helpful to enter the assessment situation with a broad framework in mind that attributes equal significance to the client's internal and external reality with regard to all the areas mentioned below so as to evaluate in detail their emotional significance to the client.

History of the presenting problem

This is an account of the client's difficulties and symptoms. The aim is to arrive at an understanding of the onset of the difficulties that bring the client to therapy. Was the onset sudden? Was there a clear trigger? For many clients the problem will have developed gradually with a succession of events contributing to their recognition that there is a problem. Others may recognise that there is a problem which is getting worse, but be unclear how it started or why it may be deteriorating. In such cases there may be stressful life events or major changes associated with the onset of the problem as well as changes in its intensity. In many cases the problem which is ostensibly the reason why the client has either been referred to, or has actively sought, therapy may not in fact be the source of their distress. The question 'why *now?*' is a most important one to clarify: it is useful to establish why the client presents for help at this particular time as this may reflect other difficulties. This exploration may also help the client to gain some perspective over her problem and hence increase its predictability and so her sense of control over her life.

The family history

The family history includes information about the constitution of the nuclear as well as extended family. The extended family is often very important and its exploration offers useful insights into how particular patterns or dynamics may be repeating themselves across generations.

The family composition typically includes information about who is in the family, their ages and occupations, births, deaths (including miscarriages, abortions and stillbirths), marriages, divorces or separations in the family, including their dates, and any major illnesses in the family. It is also important to note any family psychiatric history. The latter is relevant not only because some psychiatric problems have been found to run in families, but also because this may give the therapist an idea of the stresses the client's family may have been under and how this may have affected the client.

The personal history

The personal history should cover *major events in childhood*, particularly any separations or losses or any serious physical illnesses that may have occurred. It is helpful to get a sense of how childhood is remembered: was it felt to be a happy, unhappy, very mixed, indifferent or lost time in the person's life.

Obtaining a history of *significant relationships* is useful as it offers information about the client's capacity to form loving relationships and provides some idea of how the client manages intimacy, both emotional and sexual. If the client is in a relationship it is important to enquire about it. When did the relationship begin? Does the client feel understood, appreciated or supported by the partner? Have there been any problems? The exploration of such questions should always be carried out paying due respect to the client's reserve on these matters in an initial assessment.

The client's *educational history* is a useful gauge of the client's intellectual potential and the ways in which his present mental state may have affected this. Someone who went to university and was successful but now complains of being unable to hold down a job and cannot concentrate for long periods of time may be revealing a very significant and overall deterioration in functioning. The discrepancy between the former and present selves may also be a significant source of distress to the client. It is important to realise that such changes may nevertheless be, in some instances, only subjective changes caused by alterations in memory and concentration typically associated with severe depression (especially in the elderly).

As part of the personal history, the client's *occupational history* gives valuable information about personality as well as the range of the client's abilities. In enquiring about employment, the therapist can get some idea of the client's capacity to commit himself to a task, to bear stress, to form enduring relationships as well as allowing the therapist to assess strengths.

A history of prior *psychiatric/psychological problems* is also relevant, especially with regard to previous self-destructive behaviour (see Chapter 6) and psychotic symptomatology (see Chapter 9) as this may determine whether the client may require additional supports.

The therapist will also need to obtain information about the client's *wider context*, that is, her social circumstances. Where does the client live? With whom? Is she isolated or well supported by family or friends? Does she have any dependants? The client's cultural context and economic circumstances are also important as these may alert the therapist to particular stresses in the client's life.

A *medical history* may be relevant if the client alludes to physical problems or the use of medication or if the client suffers from a disability. The medical history should, however, not overshadow an exploration of the meaning attributed by the client to any physical problems she has and how these affect her perception of herself. Having said this, there are also a few important medical conditions which may cause significant changes in mental state. The following list, while not exhaustive, gives some of these physical conditions which may present with psychological symptoms (and require medical attention and treatment). If in any doubt about the possible organic nature of a client's symptoms, it is always advisable to consult a medical colleague or encourage the client to see her GP (for a more detailed discussion, see Lishman, 1987).

Depression

1 During and after severe infections (e.g. infectious hepatitis, glandular fever, influenza)
2 After a brain infection (e.g. encephalitis)
3 After a brain injury (e.g. following a car accident)
4 In certain dementias (e.g. Alzheimer's disease)
5 In heart disease and after heart surgery
6 With cancer (especially cancer of the pancreas)
7 In Parkinson's disease
8 In endocrine disorders:
   (a) Myxoedema: here the thyroid gland produces too little thyroid hormone leading to easy fatiguability, thinning and coarsening of the hair, thickening of the skin and changes to the heart and circulation. Paranoid symptoms may also occur.
   (b) Cushing's disease: here the adrenal gland produces too much corticosteroid hormone leading to obesity, overgrowth of bodily hair in a male distribution (called hirsutes), a red moon shaped face and hypertension with mild diabetes.
   (c) Hyperparathyroidism: here there is overactivity of the parathyroid gland with increased excretion of Calcium in the urine with the formation of renal stones.

Mania

1 As a result of intoxication with amphetamines, cocaine, ecstasy (where paranoid symptoms – hallucinations and delusions – may also occur) and alcohol.
2 As a result of medication with corticosteroids for medical conditions, such as asthma, rheumatoid arthritis, inflammatory disorders (e.g. ulcerative colitis).
   N.B. With the neurological condition of multiple sclerosis, hypomania is present in some cases whereas in others depression may occur.

Anxiety

1 As a result of withdrawal of alcohol in alcohol dependency and tranquillisers in drug dependencies.
2 In thyrotoxicosis: this is another disorder of the thyroid gland. Here there is overproduction of thyroid hormone leading to anxiety, a fine tremor of the hands (finer than in anxiety), increased pulse rate with or without a heart arrhythmia, increase in appetite with weight loss and swelling of thyroid gland (visible in the neck) and sometimes changes in the eyes (including protrusion of the eyeballs).
3 During episodes of low blood sugar (hypoglycaemia): as a result of treatment of insulin-dependent diabetes, with tumours of the pancreas secreting too much insulin.

Paranoid reactions with or without delusions/hallucinations

1 With alcohol, cocaine and amphetamine addictions
2 In hypothyroidism (myxoedema – see above)
3 With cerebral tumours
4 With dementias
5 With deafness
6 With neurosyphilis in general paresis of the insane (this is caused by the third stage of a syphilitic infection)
7 After withdrawal of barbiturates in a barbiturate addiction

Hallucinatory states

1 With psychotomimetic drugs such as LSD 25 and mescaline
2 With amphetamines, cocaine, alcohol addictions and glue sniffing
3 With brain tumours
4 With brain injury
5 In general paresis of the insane (see above)
6 In nutritional disorders (e.g. Vitamin B12 deficiency where there is a form of anaemia sometimes associated with neurological changes)
7 In Cushing's disease (see above)
8 In dementias

9   In organic confusional states (e.g. caused by cerebral infections, major metabolic disorders)

The overall aim of covering the areas subsumed under the heading of 'personal history' is to begin to build a picture of the client, of his inner as well as interpersonal resources. While one of the aims of such a personal history is to assess the client's needs, it may leave him feeling that only his weaknesses have been exposed. The art of a good assessment is also to seek with the client to emphasise his strengths.

In addition to the factual information discussed above, an assessment should aim to establish the client's 'insight' into her difficulties. 'Insight' is used here to refer to a person's acknowledgement and understanding of her difficulties. The notion of insight is, of course, controversial, as in some cases 'insight' simply means agreement with a therapist's view of the problem. Needless to say, this is no indication of insight but merely reflects compliance especially where the client has been sectioned under the Mental Health Act (see Chapter 4). Notwithstanding such problems in the definition of insight, when assessing someone for suitability for a psychological intervention, one of the most important criteria will be whether the person is motivated and able to think about her problems in psychological terms. For instance, someone who presents with a history of somatic symptoms, who is convinced that she has an organic problem and in the assessment does not acknowledge the part perhaps played by psychosocial stresses on her bodily functions, is less likely to be able to make use of a psychological intervention than someone who accepts the interdependence of mind and body. The assessment of insight also has important management implications. For example, a paranoid person who believes he is being followed, feels very persecuted but is unaware that his fears are based on a delusional belief system, may present a greater risk of harm to others. Under such circumstances a referral to a psychiatrist is indicated.

Finally, it is important to gain a sense of the client's expectations of any help he might be offered or of his thoughts about what could be helpful. Although some people may have little or no idea of what could help them with their distress, others may hold very particular beliefs about what has been helpful in the past or could be helpful in the future.

Arriving at a formulation

On the basis of what we learn in the assessment about the individual client and how she views her problem, we develop provisional hypotheses which help us to reach a *formulation* of the client's difficulties (see Figure 3.1). A good formulation is not only a summary of what has been cooperatively learned, it is ideally also an attempt to construct a

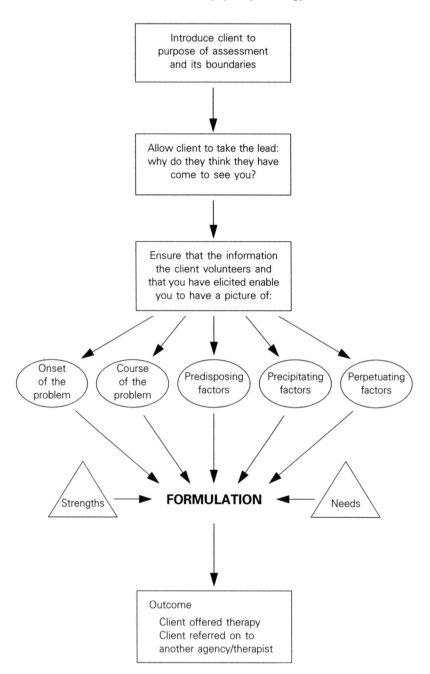

Figure 3.1   *The content of assessment*

reasoned argument for defining the person's difficulties and for future intervention and the evaluation of its outcome. The following is an example of a psychological formulation.

Reason for referral

Ann was referred by her GP because she was experiencing difficulties with her daughter, Karen. She felt that Karen had become very defiant following her father's departure from the family home, and Ann felt unable to cope with her demands. At school, Karen was said to lack concentration and told one of her teachers that she hated her mother and wanted to be adopted. The GP also mentioned that Ann was herself moderately depressed for which he had prescribed some medication.

Initial presentation

Ann presented as an attractive, well-groomed person. Her hair was immaculately styled and her clothes were fashionable. At first, she appeared to find it difficult to speak, only responding to my prompts. Her replies were succinct and I felt that she did not want to be in the room with me. When I pointed out how uncomfortable she seemed to feel, Ann said that she felt ashamed to be seeing a psychologist and quickly added that the home situation was much better now and that she would be wasting my time. I said that it seemed difficult for her to take up my time. Ann stared at me intensely for the first time and said that there was never any time for her at home. Her younger son, Mark, was constitutionally weak and he always needed her around. He was so dependent on her and she could not bear the extent of his needs. Karen was, in her words, 'just too much'. Ann felt that Karen should be able to understand that she had a lot on her mind, with Mark being so unwell and her father having left. She confessed to having physically pushed Karen away the previous day as she had simply had enough. I said that she seemed to be surrounded by what she perceived to be two very needy children and I wondered whether she also felt very needy but feared that if she told me about her needs I might feel over-burdened and I might push her away. My comment seemed to strike a chord and it facilitated our subsequent exchange. Ann began to air her concerns, including an unexpected revelation about what she referred to as her 'binges' and her belief that she was too fat. She also complained of frequently feeling depressed. She told me she often binged but I was unable to gain a very clear picture of the nature or extent of the binges. Her answers felt more like confessions of the most shameful nature and I sensed Ann's awkwardness as she spoke. By the end of this session Ann did, however, agree to come for another assessment session even though she said that she thought two sessions would be 'more than enough' as she was really feeling much better now.

Background information

Ann came from a large family of six brothers and three sisters, being the fourth eldest. She described distant relationships with her parents who were now separated and with her siblings. She alluded to complex and acrimonious family relationships and a high degree of parental disharmony and violence in her childhood. Her mother featured as a very powerful figure who had been ill throughout Ann's childhood and adult life. Ann recalled having to look after herself and never being cared for when she was ill as her mother would not acknowledge the children's problems. She recalled being sent to school once with diarrhoea but fearing that if she were to go back home her mother would have been very angry with her. Her father featured as a largely absent figure but physically punitive towards all the children.

Ann now worked as a sales assistant. She married Len when she was 19 and had two children, Karen (7) and Mark (4). She felt that she would not have married Len had it not been for the fact that she became pregnant with Karen. Len was described as a very distant man who had on occasion hit Ann. She also said he had been very concerned with appearances and obsessed with cleanliness. Three years after Karen's birth, Ann became pregnant with Mark who was born with a heart condition. This was something that was kept secret from the rest of the family and friends, as both Ann and Len had been ashamed of having a child who in their eyes was not 'normal'. However, as Mark was about to start school, Ann was concerned that she could no longer safeguard the secret.

Ann's eating problem first emerged following Mark's birth. She felt she had put on a lot of weight and decided to go on a diet. She lost a considerable amount of weight but then found herself bingeing and gradually began to make herself sick and took laxatives. The eating problem had worsened after the Christmas preceding the referral as she felt she had allowed herself to indulge too much during the festivities. She described obsessively weighing herself. Ann in fact weighed 8 stone and this weight seemed to be about average for her height.

Formulation

Ann came from a very large family where both parents had been experienced as unavailable, depriving figures so that even basic needs such as clean clothing had been consistently overlooked. The experience of having no reliable adult figures to turn to may have been further exacerbated by the demands of a very large family which had been uprooted from their local community to another city when Ann was very young so that there had not been any extended family or friends to turn to. As a result of her experiences in her family, Ann seemingly concluded that it was best not to rely on others for her needs as she was likely to be disappointed. This led to the development of a rather resourceful individual as Ann had in many respects managed to get by in her life and had found a job which she sustained throughout difficult crises. She was none the less very vulnerable to pervasive feelings of guilt and shame for having needs of any kind. This, in turn, set up a rather punitive cycle of self-deprivation and negative self-evaluation. Ann's very rigid and persecutory upbringing contributed to her tendency to evaluate feelings and behaviours in terms of their 'goodness' or their 'badness' with little room for understanding the nature and meaning of her experiences. Within this particular world-view, her need for attention and for love, her feelings of hate and envy, were all denied as they were classed as bad.

Over the years Ann developed a very convincing 'false' self – compliant and organised – which enabled her to function without having to fear other people's disapproval or retaliation. Mark's birth and the discovery of his disability, and hence his need for care, represented a significant life event for Ann which triggered her own fears associated with being needy and dependent on others. As a solution to this she found some relief in controlling her weight: by remaining slim she was able to maintain the facade to the outside world that everything was fine and that she was 'good'. Such control was alternated with periods when she felt herself to be getting out of control and giving in to her needs and to this she responded with punishment in the form of vomiting and/or taking laxatives.

Ann's marriage to Len contributed to a perpetuation of the dynamics of her own family of origin as she had to be available to meet his needs while denying her own. Ann's problems were partly maintained by a marital relationship she experienced as lacking in intimacy and characterised by poor communication. Her choice of partner suggested a need to find someone who could collude with her own need to pretend that everything was fine and to deny any difficulties as evidenced in their need to keep secret their son's disability and the occasional violence between them. Together, they seemingly lived the illusion that they were happy. However, Len's departure precipitated a crisis for Ann as the precariousness of her contrived 'happy family' was threatened by reality.

In conclusion, Ann presents as quite depressed and with a difficulty in acknowledging her needs, whatever their nature. Her feelings of depression and low self-esteem appear to be the underlying problem which has given rise to an eating problem. The disgust attached to what she eats seems more indicative of a difficulty in acknowledging needs of any kind and the shame attached to this. The bulimic symptomatology serves the function of encapsulating the problems in her life but is treated as a separate, hidden part. All the 'needy' – and in her opinion 'bad' feelings – are attached to the bulimic symptoms so that they are not directly experienced and cannot be integrated with the whole of her personality. This encapsulated bubble appears to allow Ann to lead quite a 'normal' life where she can present herself to the world as a 'good', well-organised person. However, this reinforces a dichotomy between her 'false' self and her 'true' self.

Further investigations

Following the first session, it seemed important to ascertain the extent and nature of the eating problem. Ann had been rather elusive with regard to the details of the binges and I sensed that talking about this elicited feelings of shame and guilt. I thus asked her to keep a record for two weeks of her eating, noting what, when and where she ate and in particular to note what she regarded as a binge and whether or not she had taken laxatives and/or made herself sick. In the session I encouraged her to explore some of the thoughts and feelings elicited by my suggestion as I anticipated that she may be very concerned about what I would think of her as I read her diary.

When Ann showed me her completed diary it was immediately clear that she was only bingeing once a week and that she had a rather distorted perception of how much she ate and how she looked. On most days, she appeared to be eating within a normal range. Her 'indulgences' appeared to be triggered by feelings of depression, and after eating she would then report feeling more depressed than before, labelling her behaviour as 'greedy'. There was no evidence of the use of other methods of weight control and Ann made it clear that she had not vomited or taken laxatives for some months. Her eating problem did not fulfil either the diagnostic criteria for bulimia or anorexia, although it was clear that she experienced difficulties around eating.

Recommendations and intervention

The assessment helped to confirm the preliminary hypothesis, namely that while the eating problem may have been a more pressing issue in the past, by the time Ann was assessed her eating was more under control and this did not seem to require any direct intervention. Rather, the underlying feelings of depression and her need to keep up a 'false' self appeared to be more appropriate targets for psychological intervention.

I decided to opt for a focused psychodynamic approach in view of Ann's high degree of ambivalence and resistance to engaging in therapeutic work and the underlying anxieties that this suggested. Within a psychodynamic approach such issues could be addressed more productively. Furthermore, I anticipated a very strong transference reaction given her difficult relationship with her mother. In the context of a psychodynamic approach, I could use my relationship with her to bring to the fore some of her conflicts with her mother so that she may explore these and be able to make a more realistic appraisal of herself and her relationships in general.

A convenient way of constructing a provisional formulation of the client's predicament is in terms of predisposing, precipitating and perpetuating factors. *Predisposing* factors are those that relate to the client's personal history: they are the psychosocial factors that may predispose the client towards experiencing psychological difficulties. *Precipitating* factors are those situations and events that appear to have triggered the presenting problem. *Perpetuating* factors refer to the factors that now maintain a problem. For instance, there may be some secondary gain from having a particular problem.

The formulation is the basis on which decisions for intervention can be made. These may be communicated there and then to the client if the therapist works privately or they may need to be discussed first with a supervisor or other team members, depending on the setting in which the client is seen. If the therapist who has carried out the assessment decides to work with the client him or herself, the assessment interview should conclude with a discussion of the practical arrangements and setting the boundaries for therapy. Particular attention needs to be given to:

- considerations of time, place and frequency of sessions
- the nature of the contract (for example, whether an open-ended or time-limited contract)
- fees (if applicable); if fees are to be paid, specify clearly whether the client will be charged for cancellations and holidays
- whether the GP or any other professional needs to be contacted; if so, then clarify with the client the limits of confidentiality

Assessing the appropriateness of psychological interventions

In a general sense it could be easily argued that to offer people in emotional distress a structured space where they can share their feelings and concerns is appropriate for everyone irrespective of their presenting problems. It is, however, clear that not everyone is inclined to talk about their problems nor that such an intervention brings about the change, for instance in mood or anxiety, that the client desires. Moreover, depending on which theoretical model we subscribe to, the type of therapy we offer may be more or less appropriate in specific circumstances. For example, someone in the grip of psychosis and whose grasp on reality is very weak, may not be helped by a more classical psychoanalytic approach. Even where such an approach has proved useful, it has usually been only so with considerable psychiatric back-up (see Chapter 9). While supportive therapy is unlikely ever to be counter-therapeutic, more exploratory, insight-orientated approaches need to be carefully considered in particular circumstances. Moreover, as we shall see in later chapters, there are certain problems, such as phobias, which appear to respond better to more structured approaches which contain a behavioural component.

Given the variety of theoretical models which therapists subscribe to, it is beyond the scope of this book to list the specific assessment criteria for each one. However, notwithstanding their differences, certain core aspects of the client's functioning and attitudes need to be borne in mind when considering the suitability of any form of psychological therapy as follows:

1 An acknowledgement by the client that she has an emotional life and that how she feels and thinks affects her behaviour towards herself, others and life more generally.
2 The motivation to reflect on problems or concerns rather than a desire to seek symptomatic relief (for example, through drug or alcohol abuse) or a pronounced tendency to act on feelings rather than reflect on them (for example, instances of self-harm or suicide attempts).
3 A willingness to accept some responsibility for herself and her development.
4 A recognition that even where organic factors are undisputed, psychological factors may none the less exert an influence on the experience of physical symptoms.
5 The ability to make contact and to establish rapport with the therapist.

Such factors can be subsumed under the more general heading of 'psychological mindedness', an attitude which is a prerequisite for psychological interventions. None of the above factors in isolation should be taken as an indication that therapy is appropriate as a way of helping the person. However, difficulties in any of the above areas should be borne in mind and considered alongside other aspects of the person's history and presenting concerns before therapy is offered.

Conclusion

Frameworks and guidelines hold a certain appeal when we are faced with clients who are in distress, who are confused about their experiences and who perhaps even frighten or disturb us in some way. The framework is our way of imposing some structure where we may perceive chaos. History taking, though an important aspect of the assessment process, can be used as a defence against establishing emotional engagement with the client. However, frameworks are not necessarily used defensively. Rather, by offering a more coherent sense of a meaningful story about the client's emotional distress, they serve to allay the anxieties of the client, whose sometimes quite conflicting feelings and experiences can be reflected back to them in the assessment in such a way that they feel understood and contained. However, guidelines and frameworks are only beneficial to the client if they can be used flexibly and sensitively. The ultimate goal of assessment is to form a relationship with the client through which the therapist can observe, and at times explicitly elicit, a range of psychological functioning on the basis of which the client's distress can be understood by both client and therapist.

One should never underestimate the clinical responsibility of the assessor for his or her client in assessment. Not only is this meeting designed to arrive at a decision and possible plan for therapy but it will also inevitably lead to legitimate expectations of the assessor in the client. At the end of the interview these expectations must be carefully considered. If a referral to another source of help is indicated (see Chapter 4), then the potential feelings in the client of rejection and abandonment by the assessor must be allowed for.

4

The Management of Referrals

Nowadays therapists are employed in a variety of settings within the public and private health care systems. Each setting, with its dynamics and culture, will determine how referrals are managed. Depending on the priorities and/or constraints of a given setting, the individual therapist may not have complete responsibility over the management of referrals. This is in contrast to private practice where the therapist is free to determine how to manage his or her own practice. Although working for an institution and having to abide by policies with which we may disagree can be frustrating, at other times the knowledge that we are not alone in making a decision about a client, or that there are clear procedural guidelines in cases of emergency (for example, what to do with a highly suicidal client), may be experienced as containing and supportive by the therapist and also the client. Having sole responsibility for the decisions we make on a given referral may provoke anxiety and may lead to 'knee-jerk' reactions which are not always in the client's best interests.

This chapter will examine some of the issues which arise once a referral is received. The aim is not to provide answers to clinical dilemmas, which should always be assessed on their individual characteristics, but rather to raise awareness of the practical, ethical and legal aspects of working with people with mental health problems.

What happens once a referral is received?

Typically, referrals are made by other professionals who are already involved in the care of the client (such as a social worker or doctor), a relative who may be concerned about a family member, or by the individual himself. When a referral is made by another professional, it is good practice to acknowledge the referral in writing both to the referrer and to the client. The initial acknowledgement letter should be followed later by a letter or report to the referrer outlining your assessment and the decisions arising from it. If the referrer is not the client's general practitioner (GP) it will be important to discuss with the client at the assessment stage, whether the GP can be contacted. GPs act as the gatekeepers to health care generally and carry medical responsibility for the clients registered with them and, as we shall see later, liaison with the GP may be very important and beneficial to the client, even if it places some limitations on the confidentiality of the therapeutic sessions.

If the referral is made by a relative it will be important to encourage a self-referral or even, where appropriate, to suggest to the relative that they may themselves like to see someone to share their own concerns. In some cases, relatives present another family member as their concern and consequently the individual in question is presented, in a sense, as a symptom of the relative's anxiety. This is often the case when parents refer their children for help. In such situations, the suitability of a family-orientated approach needs to be seriously considered and an initial family meeting may well be the most productive way to assess what other individual interventions, if any, are indicated.

The majority of referrals in private practice are self-referrals, while the opposite will be true in public mental health services, although there will be exceptions to these general trends in both settings. In many respects, self-referrals present the least difficulty as they circumvent the issues of motivation and of confidentiality. Someone who takes the trouble to refer herself is more likely to engage in therapy than someone who has been told by another person that it would be in her best interests to see a therapist. Self-referrals are also uncontaminated by the perceptions and assumptions of the third party who makes the referral. However, self-referrals will not have been screened by another professional. This presents a challenge to the therapist who may be faced with a potential client who is not suitable for his or her approach but may none the less be very needy and react negatively to being referred on, as well as those clients who may represent a risk to the therapist because of their potential for violence.

Once a referral is received, this is no guarantee that the person will keep his initial appointment. This may reflect fear, ambivalence, lack of motivation or misunderstanding about the nature of counselling and psychotherapy as well as practical problems (for example, the client could not arrange child care). In a few cases the client's psychopathology itself leads directly to an avoidance of help as the person may have little insight that he is suffering and needs help. In such instances it is likely that the person will only come to the attention of mental health professionals when and if his actions overstep the limits of social tolerance.

For therapists working in busy practices with long waiting lists, such as those employed in primary health care settings, the non-attendance rate can become a very real problem. One way of minimising the time spent waiting for clients who do not keep their initial appointments is to invite them to confirm their appointments either in writing or by telephone and to make it clear that if they do not confirm you will assume that they do not feel it would be useful to meet with you at the present time. This, of course, raises problems for those clients who are intimidated by formality – which may well have become equated by them with authority figures – as well as those who are simply unable to read or write and who may therefore not confirm and not take up an appointment they in fact need. There is no foolproof solution to this but it certainly helps to ensure a higher rate of response if your letter is accompanied by a tear-off slip and/or a stamped self-addressed envelope.

As with any system, the overall approach to the management of referrals has to be sufficiently flexible to give due consideration to individual needs. For example, if a client is referred for depression and because she has a long history of overdoses, it would be wise to offer a second appointment even if she fails to confirm the first. A more proactive approach is often required with people with a long psychiatric history. Problems of engagement with mental health services are not uncommon with this particular client group.

Guidelines on report writing

By the time a comprehensive assessment has been carried out, the therapist will have developed a comparatively clear, if inevitably provisional, formulation of the client's problems (see Chapter 3). This should first be shared with the client who can then comment on it so that both client and therapist can come to some agreement about the formulation. This shared understanding of the problem is then fed back to the referrer with the client's consent. The letter to the referrer should contain the following information however concise:

- client's name, address and date of birth
- reason for referral
- date(s) of assessment
- description of client's behaviour and affect on initial presentation (e.g. appearance, mood)
- history of the problem
- formulation of the problem
- treatment goals or reasons for referring on to another agency/ therapist

Figure 4.1 gives a sample letter to the referrer of client 'Ann' whose assessment was presented in Chapter 3.

Dear Dr Hyde,

Thank you for referring Ms Goodman whom I have now had the opportunity to meet on two occasions.

Ms Goodman presents as a very organised person who has her life under control. However, my meetings with her suggest that this is far from the case. Rather, Ms Goodman is preoccupied by a number of family matters but experiences considerable difficulty in sharing her concerns with others. Her preoccupation with being in control and giving the appearance that she has no needs has manifested itself in problems around eating.

While Ms Goodman first told me that she frequently binged and would occasionally take laxatives and/or vomit, further investigations have confirmed that her eating is presently more controlled but she has a rather distorted perception of how much she does eat and subsequently of how she looks. With respect to the other means of weight control, I understand from Ms Goodman that she has not been taking laxatives or vomiting for a couple of months.

Ms Goodman's concerns about her eating are very real to her and are a source of distress. However, I think that a more fundamental problem is her difficulty in acknowledging that she has any needs or wishes at all and hence their relentless denial. This has led her to live her life according to what she believes or imagines other people want. Her constant appraisal of herself in terms of whether she is 'good' or 'bad' has left little leeway for an exploration of how she feels about herself and her life.

In view of this, I think that Ms Goodman would benefit from some individual sessions to offer her an opportunity to examine some of her assumptions about herself and how these influence how she feels and behaves.

I shall keep you informed of any developments.

Yours sincerely,

P. Morgan

Clinical Psychologist

Figure 4.1   *Sample letter to client's referrer*

Writing back to a referrer raises the thorny question of confidentiality, to which we shall return later in this chapter. However, it is clear that letters to referrers can be as superficial or as detailed as the individual therapist deems appropriate. It is as well to remember that long, detailed assessments are seldom read thoroughly by their recipients! The decisive consideration here is really whether it will benefit the client if the referrer is aware of certain details about the client's predicament. Generally speaking, it is unnecessary to disclose intimate details about a client's history or present circumstances. It is more useful to summarise the assessment in terms of general, broad themes or patterns which are relevant to the client's presenting complaints.

Let us take as a hypothetical example, Ms M who is referred by her GP because she has recently been feeling very tearful, complains of poor appetite and an erratic sleep pattern. The GP also says Ms M has recently had a miscarriage. During the assessment, Ms M tells her therapist in some detail about early traumatic sexual experiences which represented for her the loss of a part of herself and which she also feels now affect her sexual relationship with her husband. How much detail does the GP need to know? I would suggest that it would suffice to say that Ms M has become depressed following her recent miscarriage which has triggered earlier unresolved feelings of loss. In such a case, it seems highly unlikely that the knowledge of Ms M's experience of abuse and her sexual difficulties would help her GP to provide her with a better quality of care. However, it will be important for the GP to have the reactive nature of the depression confirmed by the assessment as this will guide his or her prescription of medication which may in fact not be necessary if Ms M is motivated to see a therapist.

The referral network

At the outset, the therapist does not know whether what he or she has to offer could be of any benefit to the client. It is therefore important to set clear boundaries for the initial consultation and to have some links with or awareness of other professionals or agencies to which the client may be referred on. A therapist's appreciation of his or her own personal limitations, as well as those of his or her chosen therapeutic approach, is integral to a good assessment. This may sound so obvious as not to deserve mention, yet time and again we all succumb to our omnipotent feelings which may lead us, for example, to work with a client we are not experienced enough to manage or to assume that therapy is a panacea for all ills. In order to manage our omnipotent feelings and to rein in the enthusiasm for one particular therapeutic approach, it is helpful to be familiar with other approaches and their suitability for particular clinical problems, as well as developing an understanding of other services and of allied professionals working in the mental health field. Although each locality may offer a particular resource which is not available elsewhere, most areas provide some core services such as the following:

1 *Hospital casualty department* For a number of people with mental health problems a hospital casualty department may be their first port of call if they are feeling very distressed or if they are picked up by the police because of their disturbed behaviour. However, the situation could well arise where a client who is in some form of

therapy is very seriously intent on killing himself and may need to be brought to such an emergency service for admission to hospital.

2 *Social service departments* In most public health service settings, liaison with Social Services is an integral part of day-to-day work as so many of the clients referred for psychological help are socially disadvantaged in a number of ways. Social Services help with accommodation, financial problems and have access to other services, such as day centres or respite care, which may be an essential adjunct to the therapist's one-to-one work with a client. A single mother who is very depressed, expresses suicidal ideation and says she feels unable to care for her children requires help besides therapy. In such a case a referral to Social Services may be appropriate not only to support the mother through her difficult times but also to ensure that the children are being adequately cared for.

3 *Outpatient psychiatric and psychological services* These vary considerably in what they offer but usually provide a range of clinical services such as psychiatric assessment, individual or group therapy and family therapy. The advantage of such services is that they have close links with the hospital and more specifically the department of psychiatry.

4 *Crisis centres* Where available, these represent a most valuable resource for clients who require an urgent consultation. This is a particularly useful service in those instances where a client contacts the therapist for the first time and expresses high levels of anxiety and wants an appointment very quickly which may not be possible.

5 *Women's centres* These offer a variety of services specifically for women and provided by women, including family planning, assertiveness classes, groups and counselling or psychotherapy. Some may be very active in fostering self-help groups for women which can be very useful for clients who are themselves quite isolated and would benefit from establishing links with other people.

6 *Self help groups* These represent a very useful contact resource for both clients and professionals alike as they disseminate information on the particular problem they are concerned with (for example, rape, addictions). They sometimes also offer helplines where distressed clients may turn for support during non-working hours.

7 *Alcohol and drug services* These offer specialist help and advice to clients who are dependent on drugs, alcohol or both. The help may take the form of individual counselling, group work or self-help groups.

The above list is by no means exhaustive but gives some idea of the types of service a therapist may liaise with. The nature and extent of liaison between the therapist and the services listed above will depend on whether the therapist is employed in the public health service or works privately. Knowing of their existence and their role is an essential prerequisite for any therapeutic endeavour. While one of the therapist's tasks is to give due attention to the client's internal reality, an acknowledgement of the client's external reality, which may need to change if significant psychological change is to take place, is also important. There are numerous 'real' stresses which impinge on people's lives and their psychological well-being: poor housing, unemployment and racism to name but a few. The stresses facing clients lend content and form to, or may reinforce, their fantasies about themselves and the world they live in. Conversely, client fantasies also affect how they manage such stresses and the inferences they draw about themselves in the process. The interaction between external and internal reality is a highly complex one and an overemphasis on one to the comparative exclusion of the other is unlikely to be helpful. At the practical level, this means that the therapist may need to refer on to other agencies which can offer the assistance the client needs. Those therapists working on the 'frontline' in public health service settings are often faced with clients with multiple needs, of which psychological therapy may be but one.

When referring on to another therapist or agency the client should be consulted as to whether she would like you to give the new agency some background history. Some agencies will not accept self-referrals and you may therefore have to make a referral on behalf of your client. Here the content of your referral can be as detailed as you think appropriate and should clearly state your reasons for referring the person to a particular agency. To avoid disappointment, when referring on to colleagues, it is good practice to check first with them if they have any vacancies before you give the client their contact number.

Liaison with other professionals

Unlike private practice, work in the public sector invariably involves far more active liaison with other professionals – an aspect of work which can be enriching and supportive as well as frustrating. As the practice of counselling and psychotherapy is generally understood to be one where respect for boundaries and confidentiality is a key feature of the work, liaison with other professionals has been viewed by some therapists as a very real problem. For instance, difficulties may arise if there is an expectation in a multi-disciplinary team that clients will be reviewed and therefore that the therapist will report back on the progress of the work, or the therapist may feel uncomfortable about writing back to a referrer. However, it is clear that for therapists who work in the public sector the clients they will see are likely to present with far more complex problems than those encountered more typically in private practice. The complexity of the problems often means that the clients will have a variety of needs and hence will be involved with more than one professional or service. Although there is often no reason why, say, a social worker or a GP needs to know the details of a client's therapy, it is important that professionals are at least aware of the various inputs a client is receiving. This helps to circumvent the possibility of splitting of the different agencies by the client.

Liaison with other professionals over such matters as the client's medication or her general management may also be important. For example, in the case of clients who are chronic somatisers and who present a complex picture, limit setting and a consistent approach to the management of requests for GP consultations is essential at the outset. Liaison with a GP in such cases is in the client's best interests as the GP plays a crucial role in the final outcome of any psychological intervention depending on how he or she manages his or her own boundaries, whether he or she prescribes unnecessary medication or instigates excessive investigations (Bass, 1992). Communications between the GP and the therapist could therefore avert unnecessary medical interventions. Such communication does lead to inevitable breaches in confidentiality and the meaning of this for the client needs to be worked through with the client.

In considering the question of confidentiality, we need to bear in mind that what our clients tell us is never, strictly speaking, totally confidential as it will be at least shared with a supervisor. Indeed, what we as therapists mean by confidentiality is unlikely to correspond exactly with what most clients understand by the term. This was highlighted in a study by Weiss (1982) who compared the understanding of confidentiality held by doctors and patients. He found that the expectations of medical patients about the ways in which information about them would be treated were very different from those of the doctors. It seems reasonable to suggest that we would find a similar discrepancy in the interpretation of confidentiality between therapists and their clients.[1] Most clients do have an expectation that their discussions with a therapist will be private.

The issue of confidentiality and the desire to protect the privileged therapeutic space form one of the challenges posed by working alongside other professionals. Such work presents other frustrations which often result from misunderstandings and rivalries between core professional groups whose priorities and perspectives on the nature of psychopathology itself may well differ. In addition, the increasing popularity of 'counselling', and the claims made by various mental health professionals for the role of therapist, has led to situations where professional boundaries may feel threatened by other colleagues perceived to be doing, or at least claiming to do, a similar type of work. Working with other professionals therefore raises a number of issues which will be considered under the following headings proposed by Tollinton and Grinsted (1992).

Authority and power

Authority within an organisation has been referred to as the power vested in a person by virtue of their role to use resources to meet the aims of a given organisation. Therapists may experience frustration and dilemmas which arise from an awareness that they have the required knowledge and skill without the power or the authority necessary to allow their implementation, such as the authority invested in approved social workers or psychiatrists. This issue is especially pertinent to the developing professions of psychotherapy and counselling, the status and career structure of which is still precarious within the public health sector. Traditionally, such interventions have been offered by other core mental health professionals, such as psychologists or psychiatrists, who have specialised in particular therapeutic interventions. Moreover, therapists employed in the public health sector may be supervised by professionals with whom they do not share training, such as clinical psychologists. While this can often result in a productive exchange of ideas and perspectives, it is clear that the training undergone by counsellors and psychotherapists differ in content and in their overall culture from that undergone by psychologists or psychiatrists. This may lead to misunderstanding and a clash of values.

Accountability and responsibility

It is important to any professional to be clear about his or her own accountability and responsibility in the course of his or her work. The notions of responsibility and accountability are closely connected where responsibility comes to mean that we have a duty as a result of our professional role to perform a particular task. Someone who has such a duty may then be expected to account for the manner in which the given task is performed. As Fairbairn (1987) points out, the responsibilities of different professionals may well conflict with one another and lead to ethical conflicts both with employers and with members of other professional groups. In such situations it is important to strike a balance between the responsibility to do what is best for a client and the need to sustain working relationships with colleagues. When several professionals are involved in the care of one person, responsibility is, on one level, shared by all concerned; but, depending on the setting, the ultimate responsibility may rest with one particular person, for instance a team leader or a consultant psychiatrist to whom the individual therapist is accountable.

It is reasonable to expect that practitioners should be accountable for what they do. However, as Fairbairn (1987) rightly points out, accountability tends to be mainly construed in terms of the possibility of being blamed when things go wrong. In the current climate in Britain, where media attention has focused on the dangers of community care, therapists may be understandably concerned about the possibility of accusations being levelled against them if, for example, a client endangers the life of another or takes his own life. While instances of actual harm to others may seem far removed from the everyday practice of many therapists, many practitioners are likely to be confronted with a suicidal client. Depending on the therapist's response to this, the client may either see his suicidal plan through to its conclusion or he may be prevented from doing so. In such cases, therapists are presented with a scenario where they may well be held in some way accountable and responsible.

Allocation of blame depends on decisions about the causes of an event. If it can be demonstrated that a therapist, for the sake of argument, was causally responsible for bringing about the death of one of his or her clients, then it would of course make sense to ask whether he or she should be held accountable for its occurrence. However, ultimate responsibility for a client may not necessarily rest with the individual therapist but with some other more senior clinician. This is a complex area, particularly since causality is rarely a simple thing and, returning to the example above, a client's decision to take his own life is invariably overdetermined so that the attribution of responsibility and even blame in such matters poses a problem. An important consequence of the tendency to construe accountability as blame is that, as Fairbairn highlights, 'in the health and welfare services [it] is likely to have the result that caring professionals respond by becoming less willing to make "high risk" decisions because they fear that if a bad result follows they will be attacked and accused of irresponsible action even where this results in poorer standards of care and even harm to clients' (1987: 266). At a practice level, the conservative tendency fostered by the fear of being blamed may limit not only the freedom of the therapist but also that of the client in taking responsibility for their own actions.

Values and belief systems

The greatest challenge when working with other professionals arises from the need to acknowledge and respect other ways of conceptualising and responding to mental health problems. Essentially this is about the management of difference. Just as any family may encounter difficulties if its members hold incompatible beliefs and values, multi-disciplinary team work can also run into difficulty if very different value systems coexist without opportunities for their exploration and the resolution of differences. For example, therapists working in GP practices may find that the doctors do not readily appreciate the importance of boundaries in counselling or, while acknowledging the importance of counselling more generally, the doctors none the less retain a fundamentally 'medical' approach to the care of their patients which may conflict with the aims of the therapist, for instance through the prescription of medication. Similarly, different disciplines may well have very different opinions on how best to advise for particular problems, ranging from medication to long-term analytic therapy. Such divergence of opinion should not be discouraged as it acts as a reminder that there is not one single way of understanding or inter-vening in mental health problems. The differences are thus potentially enriching and stimulate us to clarify why we think our preferred approach may be more appropriate for the individual in question. However, difference which is not acknowledged and spoken about can lead to splits, projections and rivalries which are not only stressful for the professionals involved but are ultimately also unhelpful for the client who may get caught in a theoretical crossfire. Team meetings may offer a helpful forum for the exploration of such difficulties.

For multi-disciplinary work to be successful there needs to be opportunities for communication. This requires a commitment by all parties to understand the roles and fundamental aims and assumptions of the various disciplines. It also places demands on each of the disciplines to educate colleagues about their own roles and responsi-bilities. Therapists working in medical settings frequently complain about the unsatisfactory working conditions and the lack of under-standing about the nature of counselling or psychotherapy. While there are often limitations imposed by certain settings on how far we can safeguard a good enough therapeutic frame, there is often scope to communicate with medical colleagues about why the conditions are far from ideal, thereby explaining the nature of the therapeutic work itself.

Therapists working in public mental health service settings are likely to work with a variety of other professionals. The most common core professional groups are described below.

1   *Psychiatric social workers (PSWs)* receive a special training in the management of people with mental health problems. Nowadays they are, however, largely social workers who have received a generic training. They contribute to the social aspects of assessment and treatment with regard to such issues as social welfare (e.g. housing), sources of social support and the impact on the family of

a family member with mental health problems. Some PSWs have 'approved social worker' (ASW) status which carries special responsibility with regard to the Mental Health Act 1983. ASWs are expected to have expertise in mental health and in this role they are responsible for bringing a client with severe mental health problems to the attention of a psychiatrist if it is felt that the person needs to be hospitalised.

2 *Psychiatric nurses* have undergone specialised training in mental health and play a very important part in the care of individuals who present with quite severe or chronic difficulties. Nurses, by virtue of their presence on wards, have the opportunity to observe clients over extended periods of time as well as developing close relationships with them which, because of their comparative informality, are often experienced as less threatening by the client. Nurses can thus provide a rich source of information and understanding about the client. Community psychiatric nurses (CPNs) have received specialised training to provide nursing care in the community.

3 *Psychiatric occupational therapists* (OTs) have special skills in the management of disability in those individuals with mental health problems and in helping clients to re-enter the world of work. They have an input in cases where the individual may lack self-confidence or social skills, as well as helping clients to cope with disabilities secondary to their psychiatric diagnosis. OTs may be involved in the assessment of activities of daily living which include self-care skills, such as washing and cooking, as well as the assessment of work and leisure activities.

4 *Clinical psychologists* specialise in clinical health problems and community care. They draw on a broad range of theories and psychological approaches which reflect an appreciation of the multi-dimensional nature of people's experiences. While clinical psychologists often see clients for individual or group therapeutic work, they also play an important role in assessment and in providing support and consultancy to other professionals.

5 *Psychiatrists* are medically trained practitioners who have subsequently specialised in the assessment and treatment of psychopathology. While they are responsible for assessing and monitoring mental state, prescribing and monitoring medication, some have also undergone further training in psychological therapies and may see clients for therapeutic work.

All these professionals will use counselling skills as part of their interactions with clients. A recent survey in one British NHS Trust suggested that the utilisation of psychological theory in interactions with clients is high, and that out of a range of psychological interventions 'counselling' is most frequently practised, but that the actual rate of formally contracted psychological therapy is lower (Cureton and Newnes, 1995). A proportion of core mental health professionals will employ a range of specific psychotherapeutic skills which are typically acquired through further training. A smaller proportion still will offer formal psychoanalytic psychotherapy (Nitsun et al., 1989). The extent to which mental health professionals overlap in their provision of counselling and psychotherapy opens the possibility for rivalry and defensiveness. While it would be unhelpful to prescribe in the abstract how the individual therapist should deal with such situations, it is none the less useful to bear in mind that counselling and psychotherapy as psychological interventions are quite different from the application of psychotherapeutic skills (empathic listening) and understanding in interacting with clients. Nurses or occupational therapists who make use of such skills in the course of their work are likely to be delivering a far better standard of care to their clients (Davis and Fallowfield, 1991). However, the provision of formal counselling and psychotherapy, consisting of a clearly defined contract, represents a different service and one which may conflict with the responsibilities and priorities of an occupational therapist or a nurse.

The provision of services to people with mental health problems requires all concerned to be clear about their own role as well as that of colleagues so that the power to use available skills and knowledge is legitimated appropriately and each worker's potential contribution is well used and delineated.

Legal aspects of psychiatry

Working in the mental health field entails operating within a specific legal framework, one which is likely to affect the practitioner in the public health services more than the therapist practising privately. However, it remains encumbent on all therapists to have some awareness of the legal system and how it deals with people whose mental health problems are assessed as placing them or others at risk.

Punishment once characterised the most common approach to the treatment of 'mental illness', the aim being to drive out or kill evil spirits which were thought to be responsible for the affliction. During the nineteenth-century, reforms were introduced with the primary aim of improving the care of those labelled mentally ill. The 1890 Lunacy Act in England and Wales prescribed that admission to hospital and treatment would be governed by statute. This marked the beginning of the relationship between the law and the medical profession. Diagnosis and admission are now seen primarily as the concern of the medical profession. This is the view underpinning both the 1959 Mental Health

Act and the current British legislation, the 1983 Mental Health Act, on which we shall focus in this section. The Mental Health Act of 1983 reduced the period of time a person could be compulsorily detained in hospital and increased access for appeal against detention. The conditions of care were also safeguarded by the establishment of a new body, the Mental Health Act Commission. This comprises part-time commissioners drawn from the various professions involved in the mental health services.

The majority of people in psychiatric units or mental hospitals are 'informal' patients, that is, they are in hospital on a voluntary basis and have the same rights as any other person being treated for physical problems. The large number of informal patients has been upheld by some, mainly medical, professionals as evidence that mental illness is now being treated just like any other illness. However, this optimistic stance has been criticised by others who suggest that, as long as there is legislation authorising compulsory detention, it is not possible to speak of genuine voluntary admission (Pilgrim and Rogers, 1993). Indeed, while patients may be admitted voluntarily, should they wish to dis-charge themselves or should they refuse treatment which the psychiatric staff consider necessary without placing themselves or others at signifi-cant risk, the psychiatric staff may invoke the powers of the Mental Health Act formally to detain an originally informal patient. Once someone is admitted, the person's voluntary status is therefore inevit-ably precarious. Section 5 of the Mental Health Act allows for an application for compulsory admission to be made for those already in hospital on an informal basis. About 5 per cent of the population in psychiatric hospital settings are compulsorily detained under a section of the Mental Health Act 1983 (see below).

The Act's main concern is with the care and treatment of 'mentally disordered' people detained in hospital and those placed under guardianship. Compulsory admission is only possible when the person is said to be suffering from one of the four forms of 'mental disorder' specified in the Act: mental illness, mental impairment, severe mental impairment and psychopathic disorder. Mental illness, perhaps unsur-prisingly, is undefined and remains a matter for clinical judgement. Mental impairment and severe mental impairment refer to states of arrested or incomplete development of mind, including significant or severe impairment of intelligence and social functioning which are associated with abnormally aggressive or seriously irresponsible conduct. Psychopathic disorder is defined as a persistent disorder or disability of mind which results in abnormally aggressive or seriously irresponsible conduct. None of the qualifying terms is operationalised in the Act. Promiscuity, sexual deviance, other immoral conduct and dependence on alcohol or drugs alone are not considered by the Act to be forms of mental disorder.

Sections 2 and 3 of the Act are the main sections authorising civil compulsory admission. Section 2 is a 28-day order allowing admission for the purposes of assessment which may be followed by treatment. Section 3 is a 6-month order permitting admission for the purposes of treatment. An application for invoking either of these orders rests upon the written medical recommendations of two doctors, typically an approved specialist and the person's GP. Under section 5(4) an approved nurse can detain a person for up to 6 hours where it is not possible for a doctor to attend immediately in order to detain an originally informal patient. In addition to the Act, the current legislation in Britain accepted by the House of Lords is that a private individual has a common-law power to detain, in a situation of necessity, a person of unsound mind who is a danger to themselves or others. Such common-law power is restricted to the short period of confinement necessary before the person can be handed over to a proper authority such as a doctor.

Patients, whether voluntarily admitted or compulsorily detained, are deemed capable of giving informed consent to treatment if they understand its nature, purpose and likely effects. The question of whether people have 'insight' into their difficulties and therefore their need for treatment is central to the issue of consent. 'Insight', however, as Pilgrim and Rogers (1993) point out, is frequently defined in a circular manner as 'sanity and madness are socially agreed notions and where agreement breaks down in a psychiatric encounter between doctor and patient, then the more powerful party has their view upheld' (1993: 110). In other words 'insight' all too frequently means sharing the same point of view as the person who has the power to detain you – a typical *Catch 22* situation.

In certain cases, treatment may be given even though the person refuses or is incapable of giving consent. This is the case where urgent treatment (which is neither irreversible or hazardous) is given without consent to a detained patient when it is immediately necessary to save life, prevent serious deterioration of health, alleviate serious suffering or prevent the person from behaving in a manner which is dangerous to himself or others. General treatments, such as nursing care and medication, do not require consent to be given if the patient is detained under sections 2 or 3 of the Act for up to 3 months; the patient can then request a review. Those who are compulsorily detained have a right under the Act to appeal against their section. Their case is heard by a review tribunal which hears evidence from the individual, his or her relatives and the professionals involved. After considering all the information available, the tribunal can either uphold or revoke the section.

Whether working privately or in the public health service setting, it is important to be familiar with the referral procedure should a client's mental state deteriorate to the point that an admission to hospital needs to be considered. In the UK if a person needs an urgent assessment of their mental state the therapist will need to contact an approved social worker (ASW) in the first instance. Each local Social Services Department will have one. They will then arrange for the person to be assessed along with a doctor. Together, these people will make a decision as to whether the person is sectionable under the Mental Health Act. Alternatively, if the person has a good relationship with his or her GP, it might be less traumatic for the person to arrange to see the doctor as a matter of urgency and to allow the GP to take the final decision as to whether an ASW needs to become involved.

Conclusion

The practice of counselling and psychotherapy takes place in a moral, ethical and legal maze. Depending on the level of disturbance of the clients who are seen by the individual therapist, he or she may manage to avoid having to address some of the dilemmas facing those therapists working with people whose behaviour may place them or others at significant risk. In such instances, the difficult questions, for example, of whether the individual has the right to take her own life or whether the therapist is responsible for the client's death through suicide should he or she decide to take no action on this matter, need to be confronted. Admission to hospital under the Mental Health Act in turn raises a number of ethical issues: involuntary patients have no one to act as their advocate to retain their freedom at the time of admission but can only put their case forward once they have been admitted. Moreover, people can be involuntarily admitted on preventative grounds on the basis of their *potential* rather than their actual behaviour.

The more typical dilemmas facing practitioners will be those of how to preserve confidentiality when working in multi-disciplinary settings and how to manage the conflicts with other professionals arising from differing value systems and philosophies of care. All the issues raised in this chapter may give to private practice a special appeal as some of the dilemmas and challenges that have been addressed here can be circumvented or managed more easily by the private practitioner who has more scope to determine how he or she manages the referrals received. Private practice is none the less challenging in a very different way: it requires practitioners to set their own rules and to bear alone the burden of responsibility for the rules they abide by and the decisions they make.

Working solely in private practice, however, not only restricts the range of clients we may work with but can also shelter us from the reality of people's lives and the systems which affect all of us. It may also feel more lonely and we are more vulnerable. Working in the public mental health services makes explicit the moral, ethical and legal dimensions of the practice of counselling and psychotherapy. This provides a constant stimulus to what we think we do when we see someone for therapy and why we think we do it. Irrespective of the work setting, the therapist is invariably confronted with decisions about who they will work with, how they will work with them and, if not, who they will refer them on to.

Note

1. In recent years clients have been given more rights in Britain relating to access to their own health records under the Access to Health Records Act, 1990. The Act allows clients the right to see their records and to correct inaccurate records. Confidentiality may also be challenged in legal proceedings. Should a case go to court, for instance, where allegations of abuse are made by a client, the police may apply to the Court to gain access to a therapist's notes. Confidentiality is not a legal prerogative and is ruled on by the judge in individual cases.

5
Depression

The nature of the problem

I have been in bed all day . . . I slept very badly last night and I woke up early this morning wih that same old sinking feeling. I just can't see any point in getting up. When I do get up I am just faced with what a failure I have been. I don't seem to be able to do anything right . . . [long silence]. I was a failure at school, couldn't read or write well and the teacher always made me sit at the back of the class. I felt so alone, just like I feel now. I guess I'm just a loner . . . there is something wrong with me, something which cannot be put right. So what's the point in coming to therapy even. All I do here is cover old ground [long silence]. One day the pain will stop because I will succeed in killing myself. You see I have not even managed to be successful in doing that yet. Instead I find myself in a hospital and I don't feel there is any way out of here because there is nothing left for me out there.' (Terence, aged 32, diagnosed as suffering from a 'major depressive episode')

Terence, aged 32, has suffered from recurring depression since his early teens. He was first hospitalised when he was 16 following a serious overdose. He had subsequent admissions as he found it increasingly difficult to cope on his own. He attempted suicide several times. The excerpt from the session reported above dates from a time when he had spent eight months as an inpatient where he failed to respond to any antidepressant medication. While in hospital, Terence spent most of the day and night shut away in his room, in bed. He did not want to participate in any of the activities in or off the ward. He had a very poor capacity to take care of himself.

Terence is the second of three children. His older brother and younger sister appear to have been successful in their careers and lead independent lives and have established their own families. This has been a source of great distress for Terence who has always compared himself unfavourably with them. At school he struggled considerably as he was dyslexic, although this was not picked up by his teachers. He describes cold and unresponsive relationships with both his parents with whom he now has very little contact. Little is known of his developmental history but he has recollections of frequent visits to the hospital as a child because of various physical problems (deafness and asthma). Terence feels he has always been a 'loner', finding interaction with others very difficult as he invariably felt rejected.

Definitions and clinical features

Depression

Depression is one of the most common psychological conditions and is a normal part of living in view of the losses and disappointments that we all encounter at different stages of the life-cycle. Moreover, as Rippere (1994) points out, because most people who are referred for therapy are depressed to a degree, the dividing line between a depressed and a non-depressed client is largely hypothetical. The term 'depression' itself refers to a heterogeneous set of phenomena, ranging from a normal mood, which is common and probably affects most of us at some point in our lives, to a more severe affective state. Whereas most people may become mildly depressed in response to certain events in their lives only a few react with a severe depression (Gotlib and Hammen, 1992). Diagnosable depression may thus be related to some underlying vulnerability of a biological and/or psychological nature which may be triggered by external factors.

The central features of all depressive conditions include emotional, motivational, cognitive and psychomotor changes as follows:

Emotional manifestations
- sadness
- anhedonia (loss of pleasure from one's usual activities)
- tearfulness
- hopelessness
- feelings of guilt
- feelings of worthlessness

Motivational manifestations
- increased dependency
- low energy
- fatigue
- apathy
- poor concentration
- loss of interest

Cognitive manifestations
- negative expectations

- negative self-concept
- exaggerated view of problems
- attribution of blame to self
- difficulty making decisions
- suicidal ideation
- thoughts about death itself
- abnormal preoccupation with bodily illness

Psychomotor manifestations
- disturbances in appetite and/or weight (increased or decreased)
- disturbances in sleep rhythm (difficulty in 'getting off' to sleep, frequent waking or hypersomnia)
- reduced libido
- early waking
- diurnal variation in mood (worst in the morning)

Bodily manifestations
- irregular menstrual cycle
- amenorrhoea (cessation of menstruation)
- constipation

The syndrome of depression (i.e. the cluster of symptoms associated with depression) is defined in DSM-IV as depressed mood along with a set of additional symptoms, persisting over time and leading to disruptions and impairments in functioning. DSM-IV gives the following criteria for a major depressive episode. Five or more of the following symptoms need to be present during a two-week period (at least one of the symptoms is either depressed mood or loss of interest or pleasure).

- depressed mood
- loss of interest or pleasure
- poor or increased appetite/weight loss or gain
- insomnia or hypersomnia
- psychomotor agitation or retardation
- loss of energy/fatigue
- feelings of worthlessness, guilt or self-reproach
- poor concentration/indecisiveness
- thoughts of death or suicide attempts

Psychotic depression is a severe manifestation of depression characterised by a pervasive depressed mood along with depressive delusions (for example, ideas about being wicked or having a disease or believing that one is a nothing) as well as hallucinations (usually voices speaking in the second person in an accusatory manner). Ideas of guilt and unworthiness are prominent. Suicidal ideas with definite plans are likely, as well as murderous plans (for example, a psychotically depressed mother who plans to kill herself and her children). Another feature of psychotic depression is that the person may be extremely agitated and restless (so-called 'psychomotor agitation') or may be very slowed down (so-called 'psychomotor retardation') and speak with very long pauses. The person is also likely to neglect themselves. Sleep disturbance is characterised by early morning wakening with diurnal mood variation in which the mood is typically worse at the beginning of the day. In the middle-aged and the elderly, concentration and memory may be so poor that a dementia may be considered to be the cause of the marked cognitive deficits.

Organically induced depression refers to a depression which is the presenting symptom of an organic condition, in particular when the thyroid is underactive or when the client is on exogenous steroids and the dose is suddenly reduced (for example, in the treatment of an asthmatic episode), or as a rare presentation of brain tumour or cancer in some other part of the body. The commonest organic cause of depression is a viral illness followed by the use of certain drugs including alcohol and tranquillisers (for example, Valium).

Depression as a reaction to physical illness may be real and understandable but may also be confused with symptoms of fatigue produced by the illness itself. In the past people spoke of 'masked depression' where one or other physical symptoms (for example, backache, headache) overlay a significant depression. *Neurotic depression* no longer exists as a diagnosic entity and is now replaced by the concept of *dysthymia* which refers to chronic mild depression of two years' duration at least (DSM-IV). This is usually thought to be reactive to events in the person's life.

Mania

Depression has typically been further divided into the *unipolar*, that is depression experienced in the absence of manic episodes, and the *bipolar* types; the latter is also known as *manic-depressive psychosis*. Some people present with episodes of severe depression with particular psychotic features which alternate with periods of psychotic excitement, referred to as *mania*. The DSM-IV criteria for a manic episode are as follows:

1. A period of persistently elevated, expansive or irritable mood, lasting at least one week, severe enough to disrupt work and social activities.
2. At least three of the following symptoms:
   • increased activity or restlessness
   • pressure of speech (speech is rapid)
   • inflated self-esteem or grandiosity
   • flights of ideas or subjective experience that thoughts are racing

- distractibility
- disinhibited behaviour (e.g. unrestrained buying sprees, sexual disinhibition)
- decreased need for sleep

Mania represents approximately 10 per cent of all depression. When this mood is not so intense and unaccompanied by the other features of mania it is referred to as *hypomania*. In mania, delusions and hallucinations are often observed and these tend to be congruent with the person's mood. The delusional ideas are grandiose and the hallucinations may consist of first-person voices telling the person that she has special powers. In a manic state the client is characteristically hyperactive and speaks with considerable pressure of speech. They may be aggressive and violent and at gross risk to themselves and other people. Their disturbance may lead them to do reckless deeds (for example, taking all their money out of the bank and giving it away to passers-by in the street). In such a state the person is in urgent need of specialised care but is very likely to lack insight into her difficulties. In such instances, a referral for a psychiatric assessment should be seriously considered.

The unipolar–bipolar dichotomy rests on the proposition that depressions with and without manic episodes should be viewed as distinct disorders but such diagnostic distinctions are not always easy to make as the features of the depressive episode may be very similar for some individuals with unipolar or bipolar disorders. In addition, the unipolar depression may be just as severe and psychotic as the bipolar depressive mood.

Other classifications

It is confusing for those new to this subject to come to grips with the different classificatory systems, the simplest of which is based on the severity of the depression and the presence or absence of mood swings (i.e. the unipolar–bipolar distinction). It is none the less helpful to be familiar with other classificatory systems.

Primary depression is said to occur in someone with no prior history of any other psychiatric diagnosis. *Secondary depression*, on the other hand, refers to depression arising subsequent to the onset of, or superimposed upon, other psychiatric or medical conditions. In practice, it is very difficult to clarify the timing of symptoms in relation to one another. Indeed, while this appears to be an operationally cogent distinction within the category of unipolar depression, there has not in fact been any convincing evidence that the subtypes differ in phenomenological response to treatment or in any other way.

An *endogenous depression* is said to arise without any obvious external precipitating factor and is therefore thought to be biological in origin, whereas a *reactive depression* is believed to arise in response to external factors (for example, bereavement). There is, however, little evidence to support this distinction. Depressions that appear to be triggered by external stressors do not necessarily differ in symptoms from those that do not. Moreover, it is rare for any depressive episode to be totally devoid of external precipitating factors (Keller, 1988). There is also no convincing evidence to support the distinction from the standpoint of the response to treatment (Gotlib and Hammen, 1992), even though it is believed by some that endogenous depression responds better to somatic treatments.

The postpartum period has been associated with an increased risk of depression. *Postnatal depression* (PND) usually refers to the depressive state, the severity of which falls roughly between the so-called 'baby-blues' (fleeting in nature) and puerperal psychosis which affects one or two per thousand women (Murray and Stein, 1989). Recent epidemiological research suggests that approximately 10 per cent of women suffer from non-psychotic depression following childbirth (O'Hara et al., 1990). While there is good evidence that following childbirth women are at an increased risk for puerperal psychosis and periods of mild depression, there appears to be insufficient evidence to support the notion that women are at an increased risk of non-psychotic depression following childbirth. Furthermore, there seems to be no convincing evidence that PND refers to a discrete clinical entity even though the postpartum period may be accompanied by some deterioration in psychological and social adjustment (for example, problems in the marital relationship). It is, however, possible that childbirth may act as a stressful life event in combination with certain other vulnerability factors in some individuals.

A number of psychiatric problems are frequently accompanied by depressive symptoms or syndromes (for example, eating problems, personality disorders, alcoholism and schizophrenia). Anxiety and depression often overlap. The association between depression and suicide is strong (see Chapter 6). Besides suicide, depression is also associated with increased mortality due to medical conditions. In some cases this may be because depression impairs immunological functioning thereby decreasing resistance to illness.

Epidemiology

Prevalence

There are several pitfalls in the epidemiological study of depression, not least because the term 'depression' describes, as we have seen, an appropriate mood state as well as symptoms of a more severe problem.

Bearing such difficulties in mind, the prevalence of major depression in the general population appears to be approximately 6 per cent (Angst, 1992).

Age and gender

Trends suggest that rates of depression are increasing and that young people are particularly at risk. Rates of depression are highest in young adults. This finding has been accounted for by some authors as a consequence of changes, for example, in family composition and mobility which may contribute to increased stress and reduced social supports (Klerman and Weissman, 1989). Others view it as a possible artefact of young people's greater willingness to admit to mental health problems.

There now exists considerable evidence to suggest that women are twice as likely to experience clinical depression than men (Nolen-Hoeksema, 1990). Such gender differences are not found in younger children who are depressed, but in adolescence levels of depressive symptoms and diagnoses in girls are higher than for boys (Allgood-Merten et al., 1990). The gender differences have received various interpretations. Some investigators view them as reflecting real aspects of different psychological and biological vulnerabilities, while others have argued that they are artefacts of the differences between men and women in respect of income, status, employment opportunities, support, the early socialisation of girls to be more helpless and power-less than boys and the greater acceptability for women to express depression than men. With respect to the latter explanation, it is of interest to note that men are twice as likely as women to become alcohol or drug abusers, behaviours which may reflect attempts at 'self-medication' for depressive symptoms.

Cross-cultural factors

Most studies fail to find any significant differences in the rates of depression or symptoms between ethnic groups. Rather, they point to important similarities in depression that outweigh cultural variation. For instance, Sartorious et al. (1980) suggest that anxiety, tension, loss of energy, sad mood, difficulties in concentration and feelings of low self-worth constitute core depressive symptoms and are relatively culturally invariant. A similar finding emerged from a study of the Asian community in Britain (Fenton and Sadiq, 1990). However, it has been suggested that ethnicity and cultural background may strongly influence the experience and expression of depressive symptoms.

Although it has often been said that in some cultures, for example in people from the Indian subcontinent, depression may be experienced largely in somatic terms, there is contradictory evidence for this. One study in England found no significant differences in the reporting of somatic symptoms between Asian and white British groups of patients (Bhatt et al., 1989). The white patients were, however, found to be more likely to attribute their complaints to psychosocial causes.

The use of somatic symptoms to express a depression appears to be more a reflection of social class and educational background rather than ethnic background. However, it may also be that, when physical symptoms are presented, this is not an indication of a lack of understanding by the person of the connection between the mind and the body but rather may reflect the perception that doctors are there to treat physical symptoms only.

Social class

Community surveys have tended to find a higher rate of depression among working-class people. The seminal work of Brown and Harris (1978) found a greater prevalence of depression in working-class women. This difference was accounted for in terms of the greater likelihood of certain vulnerability factors being present among working-class women: loss of mother before the age of 11, lack of paid employment, three or more children under 14 years of age living at home, and lack of an intimate and confiding relationship. All these were understood to be markers of deficits in social and material resources. However, as many community studies identify milder depression, it may be that the latter shows an understandable relationship to the increased social stress that would be expected in a more socially disadvantaged group. Studies of admission rates to hospital do not show a significant departure from the distribution of the general population.

Theoretical approaches

Genetic models

In a review of studies, McGuffin and Katz (1986) highlight a consistent finding which suggests that the average lifetime risk of depression is just under 10 per cent in the first-degree relatives of those with a diagnosis of unipolar depression and about 19 per cent in the first-degree relatives of those with a diagnosis of bipolar disorder. The evidence from adoption and twin studies for a genetic factor has been stronger in bipolar than unipolar disorder. However, familial tendency does not necessarily imply that a disorder is genetic. Moreover, there has been no discovery of a linkage marker of a genetically determined aetiological factor and no mode of inheritance has yet been established.

Biological models

These models have been advanced to account for the action of drugs used in the management of depression. In the early 1950s, reserpine, a drug long known to deplete all of the major brain monoamine (noradrenaline, dopamine, 5HT) from presynaptic stores, was found to produce depressed symptoms in people taking the drug to alleviate hypertension. Depression was thus conceptualised as a monoamine depletion state. The monoamine theory which followed such observations proposes that a deficiency of noradrenaline and serotonin causes depression whereas excess results in mania. Antidepressant drugs are thought to exert their effects by increasing the levels of these monoamines by inhibiting their natural breakdown in the brain. However, this theory fails to account for the fact that some depressed people do not respond to antidepressant medication, and our current understanding of brain biochemistry suggests more complex mechanisms underlying depression and mania.

Psychoanalytic models

Psychoanalytic accounts of depression do not reflect a single theory but a multitude of theories with different emphases. In his classic paper 'Mourning and Melancholia', Freud (1917) drew a distinction between grief and depression where grief was understood to be the conscious reaction to a loss, while in depression the true feelings of loss remain unconscious. Freud added that in depression the ego is weakened and there is loss of self-esteem. Depression was seen to result not simply from a real loss of a loved person but could also stem from some phantasised or symbolic loss. After a loss, Freud suggested that the individual regresses to an emotional stage in which loss of a loved person is managed by attempting to incorporate them into the self. The problem in depression, as in pathological grief reactions, is that hidden away in the past the depressed person has experienced powerful, ambivalent feelings towards the loved person which were not expressed at the time and are hard to resolve and work through. The self-accusations and denigrations characteristic of depressed people were understood by Freud as not being directed at the self but at the lost person. He theorised that the anger and disappointment previously aimed at the lost person are internalised and so lead to a loss of self-esteem and a propensity for self-criticism. The idea of 'anger turned inwards' is still assumed by modern theorists to be central in the aetiology of depression.

The Freudian formulation was essentially an elaboration of an earlier theory by another psychoanalyst, Karl Abraham (1911). He proposed that depressed people harboured ambivalent feelings of love and hate towards the loved person that is experienced as lost. The ambivalence gives rise to anger towards the loved one because he or she is perceived to have rejected or deserted the individual. This destructive wish in turn gives rise to feelings of guilt. Abraham further suggested that the loss of appetite so often observed in depressed people is a defence against the hostile wish to 'incorporate' the loved person.

The emphasis in more recent psychoanalytic formulations has shifted towards focusing on the idea that people experiencing depression have an exaggerated ideal of what they should be like (the ego-ideal) which contrasts sharply with their equally false perceptions of how they in fact are. Another recent trend is the effort to relate depression to actual loss. This flows from the views of Bowlby (1981) on the importance of early attachments and the effects of early separations and losses. The death of a parent does appear to have a bearing on the development of depression (Harris and Bifulco, 1991).

Cognitive models

These models are the most recent and represent a major development in psychological accounts and the treatment of depression. Such models are predicated on the assumption that behaviour and affect are mediated by cognitive processes. The pioneer of this work is Beck (1979) who proposed that negative cognitions form part of a causal sequence of events in the onset of depression. The critical dividing line between a clinically depressed person and a so-called normal person is not whether they have negative thoughts about themselves or the world but how such thoughts are managed. Normal and pathological syndromes are conceptualised as being mediated by primary cognitive processes which contribute to an interpretation of situations in global and crude terms. In normal reactions, such initial perceptions are refined and tested against reality, correcting the earlier global and primary conceptualisation. However, in psychopathology, these corrective functions are impaired and emotions become exaggerated.

According to Beck, depression is characterised by a cognitive triad reflecting the person's negative view of the self, the world and the future – hence negatively biased thinking is a core process in depression. The predisposition to focus on the negative is thought to arise early in life through personal experience and identification with significant others. The attitudes and beliefs internalised in childhood may thus persist and influence future cognitive processing. The constructs used subsequently to classify, evaluate, interpret and assign meaning to events are called schemata – the latter may be maladaptive. Events are thus not considered to produce depression unless the person is predisposed by cognitive schemata to be sensitive to the type of event that he or she is confronted with. Schemata are conceptualised here as trait-like persistent characteristics.

It is precisely this latter point that has spurred further theorising and research in this area as it has been argued that vulnerability to severe depression is related to differences in patterns of thinking that are activated in the depressed state rather than persistent cognitive differences among people (Teasdale, 1990). Teasdale understands the increased accessibility of negative constructs and representations as a consequence of the depressed state reactivating the negative constructs that have been most frequently and prototypically associated with a previous experience of depression. Depressed mood increases the accessibility of representation of depressive experiences and of negative constructs which makes it more likely that an experience will be interpreted as highly aversive, uncontrollable and persistent and will thus produce further depression.

While cognitive models have become very influential at both a theoretical and applied level, it is debatable whether depressed people are genuinely biased or in fact realistic in their perceptions. Indeed, as Rippere (1994) observes, some people's depression seems entirely appropriate to their depressing circumstances – people are not necessarily suffering from a pathology of affect or cognition but from a 'pathology of circumstances' (for example, ill health, racial prejudice, poverty).

Bradley and Power (1988) argue that the possibility of a negative social/familial milieu contributing to the maintenance of depressed mood is problematic for cognitive theories of depression since many cognitive accounts of onset and maintenance emphasise the distorted or erroneous nature of negative cognitions. Cognition as a primarily intrapsychic variable characterised by individual bias in processing information takes little account of those occasions, for example, when depressed people have been found to be more accurate than non-depressed controls in evaluating the effects of their behaviour on others. Depressed people deal with distressing experiences that often do not yield to their efforts and they frequently do so in the face of rejecting and critical significant others. Negative verbalisations about the self in such a context do not require the postulation of intractible cognitive processes. In the light of such considerations, it becomes important in clinical work to take into account the possibility of a depressive feedback from the environment. At a theoretical level, this demands a more complex conceptualisation of depression than one explaining its phenomena with reference to the isolated depressed person alone.

Other cognitive models have also been proposed. The learned helplessness model (Abramson et al., 1978) postulates that individuals with a 'depressogenic' attributional style have learned through early experiences to believe that previous events in their lives were uncontrollable and they expect that future outcomes will be similarly out of their control. The problem-solving theory of depression (Nezu et al., 1989) implicates ineffective problem-solving skills (for example, how problems are defined, how decisions are made) in the onset and maintenance of depression.

Behavioural models

Less attention has been devoted to depression by behavioural theorists than other psychiatric problems. In its simplest form the behavioural theory of depression is that it is a function of inadequate or insufficient reinforcers. Once positive reinforcement is withdrawn and behaviours are no longer rewarded, the person ceases to perform such behaviours and becomes withdrawn and inactive and hence depressed. While the reduced rate of reinforcement can be due to various factors, most behavioural theories focus either on the overt behaviours of depressed individuals as ineffective in eliciting reinforcement or on the behavioural reaction of others in the social environment as offering low rates of reinforcement to the depressed individual (Lewinshon, 1974; Coyne, 1976). The aphorism 'smile and the world smiles with you' does have a certain truth to it; the depressed person gradually drives people away by his unresponsive self-absorption.

Social models

As feelings of depression are common following traumatic experiences, research has focused on the aetiological significance of adverse life events. Most studies show that, compared with control groups, those individuals with a diagnosis of depression report more life events prior to the onset of depression (e.g. Brown, 1989). The most common events are those termed 'exit events', such as a relationship break-up, which are related to loss but not all depressions are related to such events. It would appear that the events in and of themselves are not sufficient to produce a clinical depression but rather that they interact with other vulnerability factors (Bebbington and McGuffin, 1989).

Social models have also focused on the effects of other social factors on depression such as racism and unemployment. It has been argued that the effects of racism can result in depression because it confronts the individual with an experience of rejection and loss. However, the results of studies addressing the question of whether race and the experience of migration place people at an increased risk of becoming depressed have been inconsistent: once age, gender and social class are taken into account, there appear to be few ethnic risks for depression. Unemployment, however, particularly among men, represents a clear risk for depression (Warr, 1982). The picture is more complicated for women. This may be because family-based work can provide them with a socially legitimised alternative to paid employment.

Current interventions

Course and outcome

Depressive episodes are generally considered to be time-limited with the majority recovering in a few months whether treated or not. For a substantial number of individuals, however, the depression is a recurrent problem: between 50 per cent and 85 per cent of people with one major depressive episode who seek treatment will experience at least one additional episode (Keller, 1985). The period immediately after recovery is the highest risk period for relapse. Those individuals with more previous episodes are more likely to experience recurring problems: the best predictor of future depression is past depression. There is some evidence that earlier age of onset of depression predicts a more pernicious course but this is not a consistent finding.

Medication

The use of drugs in the treatment of depression is widespread. Antidepressants appear to be effective in the treatment of major depressive episodes but have not been found to be effective in clinical trials with people in the very mild end of the clinical range (Paykel and Priest, 1992).

Tricyclic antidepressants ('tricyclic' refers to the molecular structure of these drugs) are many, with fewer differences than similarities between them. Amitriptyline and imipramine are the most widely prescribed. The onset of their antidepressant action is relatively slow (two to four weeks may elapse before there is any noticeable change in mood), and because the side-effects of these drugs are unpleasant many people do not continue taking them as there is no apparent reward for doing so in the short term. Such antidepressants are highly dangerous in overdose. Although they are not addictive, many people will experience withdrawal effects when they stop taking them (for example, nausea, headache, chills, vomiting). In view of this, people should be encouraged to reduce the dosages gradually rather than stopping abruptly. Common side-effects include dry mouth, tiredness, nausea, constipation, weight gain and blurred vision, all of which may deter the person from taking them. These drugs will cause glaucoma in predisposed individuals as well as heart arrhythmias. The relapse rate is also high: 30–50 per cent relapse in 12 months.

Another set of drugs used in the treatment of depression are the *monoamine oxidase inhibitors* (MAOIs) which act by inhibiting monoamine oxidase enzymes which are responsible for the intracellular breakdown of monoamines within the central nervous system. Their prescription is less common as conflicting evidence exists of their effectiveness. In addition, these drugs can only be taken with certain foods or drinks, otherwise the person may experience a serious (but seldom fatal) reaction. Withdrawal from MAOIs is also more difficult than from tricyclics because of their side-effects, which include dizziness, dry mouth, drowsiness, insomnia, increased appetite, constipation and feelings of weakness.

There has been considerable publicity about *serotonin re-uptake inhibitors* which act at the synapse preventing the re-uptake of serotonin by the postsynaptic nerve terminal. These drugs include Prozac and Seroxat which are said by some people to have less disagreeable side-effects than the tricyclic antidepressants. *Lithium Carbonate* is frequently prescribed in the treatment of mania and is very effective in stabilising mood and preventing both the depressive 'lows' and the manic 'highs' of bipolar conditions. Prescription of this drug requires regular blood tests to check the concentration of lithium in the blood. One of the main problems with lithium is that its therapeutic window is narrow: overdosage can lead to very unpleasant toxic effects (particularly kidney and nervous system damage) and so blood levels have to be monitored. It also takes several weeks to become effective. The mode of action of lithium in its anti-manic effect is not clear. Side-effects include nausea, mild stomach upset, increased thirst and urination, trembling hands, dry mouth and muscular weakness.

This section on medical treatments would not be complete without a consideration of one of the most controversial treatments in depression, namely electroconvulsive therapy (ECT) which was originally introduced for the treatment of schizophrenia. Nowadays, ECT is administered following a short-acting general anaesthetic and muscle relaxant by placing two small electrodes on the scalp either unilaterally or bilaterally (the former is more common). An electric current of very low voltage is passed between the electrodes for a few seconds to induce a fit. Its mode of action has been poorly understood. The most favourable response to ECT appears to be in cases of severe depression characterised by early wakening and speech retardation. The problems with ECT, besides its unacceptability to some people, is that it requires several administrations to be effective. This led in some cases to amnesic effects which are now not as prevalent if unilateral ECT is given to the non-dominant hemisphere. The relapse rate is also high and in some cases lasting structural damage is caused.

Psychological treatments

The two most prominent psychotherapeutic approaches in the treatment of depression have been cognitive therapy and dynamic exploratory therapy. Cognitive therapy has been applied extensively to the treatment of depression with encouraging results. Cognitive therapy and antidepressant medication are virtually indistinguishable in their effectiveness, and cognitive behavioural treatment appears to be superior to less structured forms of psychotherapeutic intervention. Dynamic therapy is not favoured in any one study over other approaches and a number of studies actually suggest that it performs more poorly. The best studies in the field indicate, however, that interpersonal therapy (which is broadly based on psychodynamic principles) and cognitive behavioural therapy are equivalent in their efficacy (Barkham et al., 1994; Shapiro et al., 1994).

Although psychological treatments are often offered alongside some kind of antidepressant medication, there is little evidence to support treatments combining pharmacotherapy and psychotherapy. However, long-term pharmacological treatment is the only method shown to date to be unequivocally effective in the prevention of relapse. The superiority of psychotherapeutic treatment over pharmacological treatment is small and unreliable across studies (Roth and Fonagy, in press).

Practical considerations in assessment and management

Assessment

Depressive feelings and thoughts are very common themes and preoccupations of clients in therapy, if not the presenting complaint. As the earlier sections of this chapter have highlighted, 'depression' as a clinical entity refers to an heterogeneous set of experiences with differing presentations. It is quite clear that for the milder forms of depression verbal therapies are indicated and often very beneficial. The nature of the therapeutic work with depressed clients does not present any special features. The vast majority of therapeutic approaches, while differing in their emphases and techniques, most probably share the following aims: to accept the person while trying to understand his negative view of themselves and the world and to draw attention to and foster the person's strengths.

As long as the individual at the assessment stage is able to establish a rapport with the therapist and accepts that his depression may be caused by psychosocial factors, there is no reason why he could not benefit from therapy. However, very severely depressed clients, who present with the more 'biological' features of depression (for example, loss of weight, pronounced sleep disturbance, diurnal variation in mood) and where social functioning is severely impaired, may benefit in addition from seeing a doctor and this needs to be considered with the client. It is usually less intrusive to the therapeutic relationship if the client consults the GP with the therapist's prompting.

Although medication, as we have seen, is not helpful to everyone, it is certainly beneficial to some people and may help them to cope with a very entrenched depressive state which prevents them from even making use of an exploratory therapy which may itself be prohibitively painful to them. As therapy progresses and the clients feel stronger within themselves, they often begin to reduce their medication with a view to eliminating it altogether. It is important not to collude too readily with clients in stopping their medication prematurely; it is normally recommended that a person started on antidepressants should continue to take them for a period of some months unless the side-effects are too disagreeable.

Where the person presents with both depressive and manic episodes, a referral to a psychiatrist is often advised, especially where there is evidence of delusional thinking or very disinhibited, impulsive behaviour. The task of the therapist is to assess the extent to which the mania places the individual at risk; for instance, the client who, when in a manic phase, incurs large debts. Such behavioural excesses are quite different from the more common use of manic defences (for example, denigration of someone or something experienced as lost to the self; overinvolvement in work) as a way of diverting oneself from depressive feelings. In the latter case, the use of such defences can be explored in the therapy. At the assessment stage, it may well be difficult to know whether the client is prone to manic episodes, especially if the client is interviewed while in a very depressed state. It is therefore helpful to enquire whether they are aware of sudden changes in their mood states and if so to elicit examples of how their behaviour actually changes. It is also worth checking with clients to see whether their depression has led to addictive behaviour in the past or in the present, especially to alcohol.

Depression and suicide risk

If a client presents as severely depressed, it is important to enquire whether they have had thoughts about killing themselves or whether they have in fact attempted this in the past. These themes usually emerge quite naturally in the course of an assessment. The question of the assessment of suicide risk is dealt with separately in Chapter 6.

Depression and social adversity

When we engage in therapeutic work with clients most approaches all too readily assume an intrapsychic perspective where the focus is on the clients' cognitions or the nature of their internal world or on their biology. While it is important to explore such aspects, it is equally relevant to pay due attention to the sometimes very 'real' social problems which may precipitate or exacerbate depression. The effects of unemployment, poverty, housing and racism all have an impact on mental health and this needs to be acknowledged and worked with wherever possible. It is not uncommon for therapists working with a depressed and socially disadvantaged client to be asked, for example, for a letter of support to the housing department. Some therapists are reluctant to become involved in such matters and it is indeed unhelpful to be prescriptive about the appropriateness or otherwise of such interventions by the therapist. It is none the less important to consider these issues as the environment in which people live exerts powerful effects on their well-being. While unequivocal causal links between social adversity and major depression have not been established, it is clear that people interact with an outside world as well as an internal one. The outside world, in turn, can provide the person with feedback which confirms their low self-esteem or increases their sense of hopelessness. Once the therapy session is over, all clients have to return to their respective environments. If the therapist can practically help a client to change his or her environment by writing a supportive letter, say, to the housing department, this is not necessarily counter-therapeutic. However, as with any intervention a therapist makes, this one also needs to be carefully considered in terms of its implications for the therapeutic relationship.

6
Suicide and Self-harm

The nature of the problem

Susan is crouched on the floor in the hospital ward – she stares blankly at the floor, initially immobile. I remind her that it is time for our session but there is no response, verbal or otherwise. I kneel by her for a few minutes and we are both in silence. I tell her that she looks as if paralysed and that what she is feeling seems just too difficult to put into words but that perhaps it would be helpful if she could find some words. Susan gets up very, very slowly and, though not looking at me, she follows me into the room. Once in the room she crouches again against the wall and starts crying inconsolably 'This time it has all gone too far, I don't see the point in going on. It is all meaningless. There's no turning back, I have gone too far . . . I just want to die, there is nothing left to live for. Nothing helps, talking doesn't help. I don't know why I'm seeing you . . . being run over by a car might help more . . .'. She continues in a similar vein for a large part of the session. (Susan, aged 28, diagnosed as suffering from 'schizo-affective disorder').[1]

Susan is the youngest of three children. She was received into local authority care when she was six years old because her mother committed suicide. She was repeatedly sexually abused while in care. It later emerged that she had also been abused by her father, brother and uncle. From the age of 15 onwards, Susan has made a total of 20 suicide attempts – two have been very serious ones and because of this she spent several years in a locked secure unit. Once discharged she fell pregnant by a man who was physically abusive towards her. Although she very much cares for her little girl Tracy, who had to be taken into care, she has found motherhood very difficult as it has triggered unresolved feelings deriving from her disturbed and highly abusive childhood. She now feels unable to care for Tracy and this has precipitated a very severe depressive state with psychotic symptoms, as Tracy has been her only reason for living. A few days after the session reported above, Susan cut her wrists but was found by the nurses.

Definitions and clinical features

Fatal and non-fatal suicidal behaviour

A common distinction in the literature has been drawn between those who complete suicide and those who attempt suicide but for whom the outcome is not death. The latter is usually referred to as 'para-suicide'. Typically, the two are said to be distinguished by the seriousness of the suicidal intent: those who do not actually complete suicide are believed to want to survive and to have made a suicide gesture for psychological ends (for example, manipulation, a cry for help). Such distinctions, however, fail to reflect that not all persons who engage in non-fatal suicidal acts actually wish to survive; conversely, not all suicidal deaths are intended. As Taylor observes 'most suicidal acts are undertaken with ambivalent intention' (1984: 143). However, the idea of ambivalent intention should not be used to trivialise what is a very serious and meaningful act even when death is not the outcome. When considering suicidal behaviour it is thus more helpful to define it in terms of outcome (i.e. fatal or non-fatal) so as to avoid making assumptions about the individual's suicidal intent and the personal significance of the suicidal behaviour (Canetto, 1994).

Fatal and non-fatal suicidal behaviours have been linked respectively to a number of factors which suggest differences between the two. Fatal suicidal behaviour is more common in men, in those over 40 years of age, living alone, widowed or divorced, and is associated with alcohol problems and physical illness. It also tends to be carefully premeditated. Drug overdosage is the cause of death in approximately 50 per cent of completed suicides and other violent methods, such as hanging, drowning, shooting, gassing, jumping from buildings or in front of vehicles or trains, account for the remainder. The methods of committing suicide appear to be influenced by cultural and historical circumstances. For example, in the US, guns are the method most frequently used in fatal suicidal acts, especially among men, perhaps reflecting the fact that men in the US are more likely to have been exposed to the handling of firearms.

Non-fatal suicidal behaviour, by contrast, is more common in young women (two-thirds are women under 25 years of age), tends to occur in response to an acute personal crisis and is a more impulsive act. It remains one of the commonest reasons for admission to a general hospital. The method most frequently used in acts of non-fatal suicide is an overdose of medically prescribed psychotropic drugs. According to Jack (1992), every year in the UK as many as 215,000 people deliberately poison themselves with drugs; this represents the most common method of suicide among women. This is not surprising given that in many countries women are more likely than men to be prescribed and to follow through their prescriptions of psychotropic medication (Fidell, 1982).

Whereas those who commit suicide are less likely than those who attempt it but survive to have sought help from a mental health professional, in the UK 45 per cent of those who commit suicide have been in touch with medical help in the three months preceding the attempt (Williams and Morgan, 1994). However, only 7 per cent of those who commit suicide are in treatment for mental health problems at the time of their death (Clark and Horton-Deutsch, 1992). Those who attempt suicide have been further differentiated into 'single episode' and 'repeat attempters'. Compared with the former, the latter show more symptom chronicity, worse coping histories, more frequent histories of substance abuse and suicidal behaviour in the family, and higher depression scores. They are also more likely to kill themselves in the end.

The 'self-harm syndrome'

In the literature a distinction has been drawn between non-fatal suicidal behaviours where the intention, at some level at least, appears to be to kill oneself and those instances where the individual engages in self-harm as an end in itself. Such behaviour has been variously referred to as 'deliberate self-harm syndrome' or 'wrist-cutter syndrome'. It may involve, for example, individuals cutting their wrists or any surface of the skin, burning themselves with cigarettes or scraping their skin with graters. Repeated self-harm only rarely results in suicide. It may none the less be associated in some people with other more lethal behaviours (for example, hanging, self-poisoning).

Repeated self-harm is commonly associated with borderline personality disorder (see Chapter 10). Some authors, however, prefer to see self-harm as a diagnostic category in itself, including other impulsive and destructive behaviours (Tantam and Whittaker, 1993). The motivations ascribed to those individuals who self-harm repeatedly include the desire to reduce tension; a means of restoring a sense of being 'real' following depersonalisation; a substitute for suicide which allows the individual to expiate guilt; and a means of controlling relationships and the ambivalent feelings they arouse as self-harm has the effect of both distancing others and allowing individuals to protect themselves against rejection. There is general agreement that self-harm is an intentional behaviour primarily aimed at expressing and relieving feelings which the individual feels unable to manage in any other way (Favazza, 1989).

Suicide and hopelessness

As we saw in Chapter 5, suicide and depression are often linked. Among psychiatric patients who commit suicide, depression is the most common diagnosis (Hirschfeld and Davidson, 1988). Notwithstanding such a correlation, there is accumulating evidence to suggest that hopelessness – itself often a sympton of depression – is the key variable in depression determining suicidal behaviour (Beck et al., 1985b). A high level of hopelessness, whether rated on a scale or assessed clinically, is among the best predictors of eventual death by suicide (Beck et al., 1989). At a practical level, this means that when faced with a client who expresses suicidal ideation it will be important to assess their degree of hopelessness, for example, whether they can envisage any solutions to their problems or even a future. Verbal expressions of hopelessness by a client are often suggestive of suicidal intent and this needs to be explored with them. Focusing on the possibility of suicide, even if this has not been explicitly mentioned by the client, does not incite people to kill themselves nor does it exacerbate a crisis. Rather, clinical experience repeatedly shows that making such thoughts explicit is helpful as it helps the client to feel that she is being taken seriously.

Suicide and psychopathology

The correlation between psychopathology and suicide (fatal and non-fatal) reflects a widespread assumption among mental health professionals, namely that suicidal behaviour is symptomatic of underlying psychopathology. Indeed, several psychiatric problems are associated with an increased risk of suicide, particularly depression, schizophrenia and personality disorders. In addition, alcoholism and other addictions are frequently associated with a heightened risk of suicide. The association between suicide and psychopathology carries important implications for practice because if the person who wants to kill himself is thought to suffer from a psychiatric disorder, this could be used to justify compulsory admission to a hospital. Because of these implications, it is worth taking a closer look at the statistics which support such an association.

In a review of studies which looked at the presence of psychiatric disorders in those who had completed suicide, Hawton (1987) highlights the problematic nature of such studies and hence the conclusions we may reasonably draw from them. First, such studies include only cases where an official verdict of suicide was recorded. Such a verdict might well be more likely in someone with a known psychiatric history, leading to an overestimation of the prevalence of psychiatric problems among those who commit suicide. Secondly, the reports of informants (which were used in all the studies) may well have been biased in favour of an over-reporting of psychiatric symptoms in an attempt to make sense of the suicidal act. Suicide as a rational act is difficult to accept for many people. Indeed, this is reflected in the fact that punishment for attempted suicide was only abolished in England by the Suicide Act of 1961. In view of these considerations, we can really only reasonably conclude that the risk of suicide is heightened in those individuals who are experiencing certain psychiatric problems. However, the majority of people who harm themselves have no diag-nosable psychiatric problems even though in most cases an attempted suicide is an indication that the person is in distress and may need professional help.

Epidemiology

Any review of epidemiological research into suicide needs to be con-sidered in the context of the problematic nature of the official statistics in this field. A verdict of suicide can only be made if there is evidence that the death was self-inflicted and that the deceased intended to end his life. The coroner has to be convinced beyond reasonable doubt of these two 'facts' before passing a verdict of suicide, otherwise an 'open' verdict will be returned. In practice this means that the official statistics may actually underestimate the true rate (O'Donnell and Farmer, 1995).

Suicide is the second most common cause of death in the age range 15–34 years after road traffic accidents. Although the suicide rate decreased in the 1960s and early 1970s partly, it is thought, due to a general reduction in the prescription of barbiturates, it appears to have risen again. Suicide represents a serious problem in Europe. According to 1990 statistics from the World Health Organisation (WHO), mortality rates for suicide for men are highest in Hungary, followed by Finland, Austria, Denmark and Switzerland. For women, Hungary ranks first, followed by Denmark, Austria, Switzerland, France and Finland (WHO, 1991).

Fatal suicidal behaviour is the least common. Whereas the lifetime prevalence of attempted suicide in the general population in North America is estimated at 3 per cent, that for completed suicide is 0.5 per cent (Kral and Sakinofsky, 1994) According to the Samaritans, the average suicide rate over the past ten years for England and Wales is 7.8 deaths per 100,000. For the UK, the total number of suicides in 1992 was 4,673, of which 72 per cent were male and 28 per cent were female. This percentage by gender is also reflected in the American statistics. In the UK, the incidence of non-fatal suicides is in the order of several hundred thousand cases per year and seems to be increasing, especially in the younger age groups (15–24-year-olds).

Whereas the lifetime risk for suicide is low in the general population, it is higher in particular groups. For example, the lifetime probability of suicidal death is estimated at 45 per cent for individuals with a major mood disorder and at 10 per cent for those with a diagnosis of schizophrenia (Klerman, 1987).

Age and gender

The suicide rate increases with age for adolescents, particularly males. It is very rare in childhood, especially under 12 years of age. Attempted suicide is a far more frequent phenomenon in adolescence, where young women are affected about three times more commonly than young men. In England and Wales, along with most other countries, the suicide rate is at its highest in the elderly population, where elderly men feature in the highest rates of all age groups (Diekstra, 1989).

On the whole, women commit a greater number of suicidal (fatal and non-fatal) acts than men (Lester, 1990). However, fatal suicidal behaviour is more common in men by a factor of about 2 : 1. In the US, men are three times more likely than women to die from suicide (McIntosh and Jewell, 1986). Men's suicide mortality rate reaches its highest level in late life, whereas women's suicide mortality rate decreases after midlife. The gender differential is therefore most pronounced in late adulthood and smallest in midlife (45–54 years).

Women's suicidal behaviour is typically non-fatal. A multi-centre study of non-fatal suicidal behaviour in selected European catchment areas in 1989 revealed that women were more likely to engage in acts of non-fatal suicidal behaviour than were men in all areas except one (Platt et al., 1992). Women's patterns of suicidal behaviour do appear to differ from those of men. The reasons for suicidal behaviour are also often assumed to vary by gender. Women's suicidal acts are often conceptualised as symptomatic of individual psychopathology and believed to arise frequently in response to relationship difficulties. By contrast, men's suicidal acts are typically described as understandable, rational responses to social or physical problems. However, Canetto (1994) argues that the recurring themes in suicidal women's lives do not appear to be love, dependence or individual psychopathology; rather, they relate to socioeconomic disadvantage, unemployment and hostile, often physically violent, relationships. She further argues that those who label suicidal behaviour as manipulative ignore that suicidal people – often women – find themselves in relationships in which their ability to negotiate becomes so restricted that suicide can be understood as the only culturally sanctioned behaviour open to the person.

Social class

Fatal suicide is commonest in people from higher socioeconomic backgrounds, whereas non-fatal suicide is over-represented in people from lower socio-economic backgrounds.

Theoretical approaches

> There is but one truly serious philosophical problem and that is suicide. Judging whether or not life is or is not worth living amounts to answering the fundamental question of philosophy.
>
> (Camus, 1955: 11)

Central to any psychological approach to the question of suicide is an attempt to understand why some people choose to take their own lives. In the above quote, Camus firmly locates suicide as a philosophical concern. His perspective is all too often missing from psychological accounts of suicide. There are some cultures, the best known of which is the Japanese, where the act of suicide is considered a noble deed under certain circumstances (for example, the kamikaze attacks of the Second World War). It is also sometimes the case that we find it quite difficult to decide in individual instances when we look at the quality of life of the person who has committed suicide whether there might not have been some justification in this ending of life. However, this point of view is fundamentally opposed to the ethics of the caring professions which are dedicated to preserving life. Indeed, far more common in the psychological/psychiatric literature are studies linking suicide to psychopathology as we saw earlier. Rational, existential and political suicides no doubt occur, but they have not received as much attention and represent very few of the reported suicides. The majority of recorded completed suicides are those associated with psychiatric disorders.

Biogenetic models

Proponents of biogenetic theories argue that suicidal behaviour has, in many instances, a neurochemical basis. For example, Slaby (1994) has studied the changes in the metabolism of the indoleamine serotonin. His results suggest that impulsive violent behaviour (both self- and other-directed) is associated more with disturbances in serotonin metabolism in the brain than in mood disorders. Such disturbances have been reported in suicide, homicide, assaults, rape and eating problems (Cohen et al., 1988). However, as many so-called healthy people also reveal such abnormalities, it is clear that no firm conclusions can be drawn regarding the biogenetic basis of suicidal behaviour.

Psychological models

Cognitive models have focused on specific patterns of thought commonly identified in suicidal individuals (Williams and Wells, 1989). Neuringer (1988) found that suicidal people are prone to dichotomous thinking. They tend to be rather rigid in their thinking and this impedes the resolution of problems as it prevents them from entertaining flexible, alternative options. It has also been observed that suicidal people have quite polarised views about themselves and their problems.

Freud (1917) understood the suicidal act as the result of unconscious forces. He viewed the urge to self-destruction as an attack against a loved one with whom the individual had identified and towards whom he or she harboured hostile wishes. Such views have been greatly developed since Freud's time and modern *psychoanalytic models* in this area converge on the central importance of unravelling the fantasy underlying the suicidal behaviour as the key to understanding the motivation to kill oneself; for instance, the attempt may reflect the person's need to punish another or the self or to merge with another through death (Campbell and Hale, 1992). Such approaches suggest that the suicidal act reflects a conscious aim of killing oneself and more specifically of killing the body; and a less conscious aim of surviving. Killing the body is understood to be the means to an end – the end paradoxically being to survive, albeit in another dimension. According to Campbell and Hale (1992), the suicide fantasy is rooted in childhood and more specifically in the mother–infant relationship and the mother's previous incapacity to accept the infant's projections. We shall return to the question of the suicide fantasy in the final section of this chapter.

Vulnerability to suicide

This brief overview of theoretical approaches to suicide suggests that suicide is frequently understood to be symptomatic of some other core disturbance. Research has shown that certain factors are typically associated with, and perhaps even causally related to, suicidal behaviour. Such background factors alert us to the likelihood of increased risk of suicide in a person who expresses suicidal ideation. But knowing that a person belongs to a high-risk group does not necessarily imply that she will commit suicide. This knowledge should be used as part of an overall formulation of the likelihood of risk: risk increases as the factors accumulate for any given person who is suicidal. The background factors listed below should always be considered alongside subjective risk factors; that is, the individual's feelings, thoughts, idiosyncratic meanings and her general emotional state at the time of assessment. Factors associated with an increased risk of suicide include:

1 *Social status* (male, single, divorced or widowed, living in a deprived urban area, age over 40)
2 *Family psychiatric history* (especially suicide, alcohol dependence and depression)
3 *Previous psychiatric history* (especially depression, alcohol abuse and previous suicide attempts)
4 *Broken homes* (adults who kill themselves more often come from broken homes, death of at least one parent in childhood is common)
5 *Precipitating factors* are likely to vary according to the individual's social environment and what is considered stressful by the person, the more common appear to be
   • physical illness
   • recent loss (e.g. divorce, bereavement)
   • disharmony with a key other which may lead to social disruption

Current interventions

As suicidal behaviour is frequently observed in clinical settings in the context of other psychological and psychiatric disturbances, therapeutic intervention cannot be said to be specific to it, even though suicidal ideation and suicide attempts may be the focus of particular interventions as they frequently occur in people without any formal psychiatric diagnosis. In view of the latter, pharmacotherapy is of questionable value and psychological approaches need to be considered.

Suicidal clients pose a tremendous challenge and can arouse considerable anxiety in us. Consequently, there has been interest in how best to manage and help them. The general trend running through the literature on the treatment of suicide is a remarkable unanimity about the ineffectiveness of various psychological and psychosocial treatments in affecting outcome. Hirsch et al. (1982) reviewed treatment outcome studies of non-fatal suicides and concluded that (a) suicide prevention centres do not decrease the incidence of fatal or non-fatal suicides; (b) even though those who attend outpatient psychiatric treatment following a suicide attempt appear less likely to repeat the attempt, they are a self-selected group and this confounds the results; (c) behaviour therapy is no better than insight-orientated psychotherapy when offered intensively over a 10-day inpatient period; and (d) antidepressant medication does not affect the repetition rate. More recent reviews on suicide crisis centres confirm the apparent ineffectiveness of such centres on suicide rates (Frankish, 1994). Cognitive-behaviour therapy has been used with suicidal clients. Treatment involves the therapist teaching clients to deal in a more systematic way with stresses and crises in their lives by using problem-solving techniques, but there are few prospective studies to support the effectiveness of this particular approach over any other and those available tend to involve relatively small samples (Salkovskis et al., 1990).

Outcome of attempted suicide

Generally speaking, it is not the norm for non-fatal suicidal acts to produce a change for the better in a person's circumstances, even though in individual instances it may represent a significant life event with a positive outcome. Research has consistently shown that approximately one out of every 100 people who attempt suicide will die by suicide within the year following an attempt. The more typical picture following a suicide attempt is that approximately 25 per cent repeat the attempt within a year, the risk being heightened within three months of the index attempt.

Practical considerations in assessment and management

Assessment of risk

Therapists may be faced with two possible assessment tasks: (a) that of assessing the potential risk of suicide in someone who has not attempted suicide (or is in between episodes); and (b) that of asssessing suicidal intent following an attempt and risk of further attempts. The initial assessment with a client following a suicide attempt is very important because for many this assessment is the only contact with a mental health professional that they are likely to accept. The overall aims of the assessment interview in such cases will be:

1   To establish a working alliance which will encourage the client to engage with therapeutic help. Although one of the aims of the assessment is to gather information about the attempt and the psychosocial situation of the client, the primary aim is to establish a

relationship where the client can feel understood, not blamed and where painful thoughts, fantasies, wishes and feelings towards self and others can be thought about.

2 To understand the circumstances of the attempt and the intentions behind it.

3 To assess future risk.

4 To work with the client towards formulating a plan of action of which individual therapy may form a part.

While some therapists may be faced repeatedly with the task of assessing someone who has just attempted suicide, far more common in clinical practice is the question of how we manage clients' expressions of suicidal thoughts. Suicidal ideation is not uncommon and occurs in people who have no formal psychiatric problems. Passing thoughts, for instance, of killing oneself or wishing one would never wake up again, can occur in people who are only feeling mildly depressed or simply low in mood. When such thoughts are expressed either directly or indirectly (for example, 'I can't see any point anymore') in the context of a therapeutic session, they should *always* be taken seriously and followed up with a sensitive assessment of the level of intent. In such a situation the therapist may need to engage more actively with the client even if their usual therapeutic stance is a more passive, silent one.

Suicidal intent can be elicited by asking the client whether he has any thoughts or actual plans about killing himself ('Does it sometimes all feel so pointless that you feel like ending your life?') and if so invite him to share these with you. While it is important to elicit a suicide plan if the client expresses suicidal ideation, failure to disclose a plan does not mean that the client does not have one in mind. In some cases where a suicide plan has been worked out, the person may experience a kind of inner peace. A client who expresses suicidal ideation in one session and is deeply distressed but who returns the following session in a very relaxed state may not be indicating a resolution of the previous week's turmoil. Rather, this may simply reflect that the person has found a measure of comfort through entertaining a suicide plan which he may well feel protective of and hence reluctant to share. Suicidal ideation, along with actual suicide plans, can be understood not only as a product of despair or a communication but also as a form of self-soothing. Above all, they always serve a purpose. As Joffe (1991) observes in relation to adolescents, where they feel out of control and helpless the idea of suicide may give them a sense of power over their own lives and may help them to nurse a fantasy where the parent or even the therapist is seen as the one who is helpless. In light of these considerations, if suicidal ideation has been expressed, any sudden changes in the client's affective state towards calm and relaxation should be taken seriously (Campbell and Hale, 1991). An important group of clients to be especially concerned about comprise those who are being treated with pharmacotherapy or ECT for severe depression at the point when they begin to feel more energetic and active. It is just at this point that they may decide to take action on their previous intention to kill themselves as they now feel more able to act.

The assessment of the client's degree of hopelessness is also critical. The aim is to gain a sense of whether the client can envisage any solution, besides suicide, to her present predicament and whether she can in fact imagine the future at all. If the client does express clear suicidal ideation an exploration of reasons for living and reasons for dying has been found to be helpful in specific instances. In so doing, the therapist needs to caution against focusing more on reasons for living – such an emphasis can be experienced as alienating by the person who is in the grip of very strong suicidal ideation as she will not feel heard. In such circumstances, it can be tempting for the therapist, who feels overwhelmed by the client's expression of very strong emotions and the desire to die, to try to reassure her. Reassurance comes in many guises and, no doubt, most of us would agree that reassurance seldom reassures. When we take a closer look at our interventions in such situations, a more pernicious form of reassurance becomes evident and that is reassurance in the form of a premature offering of a pre-packaged meaning of the client's distress. From the client's point of view, the expressed concern of the therapist may be the most vital ingredient in preventing them from taking action.

Assessment of suicidal intent

The assessment of suicidal intent is best inferred from the circumstances surrounding the attempt, such as:

1 The behaviour of the person just before and after the attempt.
2 The expected lethality of the drugs used (if an overdose) *as believed by the person* as people vary in their knowledge of the effects of drugs. Suicidal intent does not always correlate with actual bodily harm inflicted.
3 Whether any effort was made to seek help after the attempt.
4 The degree of hopelessness.
5 An exploration of whether the client actually wanted to die.
6 An exploration of the motivations and intentions behind the act.

The characteristics of a suicide attempt which suggest serious suicidal intent are as follows:

- act carried out in isolation
- timed so that intervention by others is unlikely
- precaution taken to avoid discovery

- preparation made in anticipation of death
- extensive premeditation
- suicide note left
- failure to alert others following the attempt.

When faced with a client who has just attempted suicide, it will be important to assess the probability of his doing it again. The greater the probability the more difficult it may be to continue seeing the client in therapy without psychiatric/medical back-up. Deciding about hospitalisation is a complex matter as there are advantages and disadvantages to this. A psychiatric unit will certainly provide a safe place for those people who do not have a supportive enough home environment. However, an admission will entail a loss of freedom. Moreover, when the admission is organised by a therapist and is against the client's wishes, the therapeutic alliance is often seriously, and at times irrevocably, compromised. In such circumstances some therapists, wishing to avoid a hospital admission, negotiate verbal and even written 'no-suicide contracts'. The use of such contracts, however, is controversial and there has not been much research into their effectiveness. In many instances, such contracts seem to do little more than just reduce the therapists' anxiety as they feel they have achieved something concrete with the client.

The characteristics associated with increased risk of repeated attempts are as follows:

- previous attempt (those who have attempted suicide once represent a 27-fold greater risk of subsequent successful suicide compared to the general population (Hawton and Fagg, 1988)
- psychiatric problems
- abuse of drugs or alcohol
- social isolation
- middle or old age
- male sex
- antisocial personality
- unclear reasons for previous attempt.

While it is important to cover all the areas listed above, the exploration of the motivation behind the suicide attempt is central to therapeutic work following an attempt. In this respect a psychoanalytic perspective affords us important insights. Psychoanalytic practitioners have focused on the violence inherent in the suicidal act. This exposes an even less acceptable face of suicidal behaviour as it leads towards an understanding of such behaviour in light of the person's own aggressive wishes which, though ostensibly aimed at the person's own body, may in fact reflect the person's need to retaliate against or punish another. If we can accept that unconscious processes underlie suicidal behaviour, then it becomes important in the course of therapeutic work to examine the inner fantasy world of the individual where we may find some clues as to the destructive and/or vengeful nature of the suicidal behaviour. For example, the body of the person who attempts suicide may have become identified with a person who is experienced as ungiving or even 'poisonous' in some way and which therefore needs to be destroyed. The body may also be attacked because it is experienced by clients as containing their sexual identity or sexual needs which they have been unable to integrate or come to terms with and which may lead them to wish to punish their own body. It is through an understanding of the *suicide fantasy* that we may begin to help to defuse the person's need to act out their fantasy (Campbell and Hale, 1991).

Susan, who was mentioned at the start of this chapter, presented a very high risk of suicide. The exploration of her own need to kill herself highlighted her desire to punish her body because it had become associated with her experiences of being sexually abused. Her fantasy, however, was also that if she killed herself she would be able to re-join in some purer, innocent form, her mother who had herself committed suicide and so, in some way, repair the damage she had believed from a young age she had done to her mother, thereby causing her death. Although Susan did continue to cut herself superficially while in therapy, she did not make any further suicide attempts.

Ethical issues

On the whole, as therapists, we are trained to help people to manage their lives in more constructive ways which expand their possibilities for choice and action in the world. Where faced with clients who want to exercise their choice to kill themselves, many therapists are reluctant to view this as a reasonable, rational choice. In practice, it can be difficult to assess how much the person's mental state has impaired his judgement. Clinical experience teaches us that a proportion of those who attempt suicide are in extreme states of despair, at times compounded by psychiatric problems, when it may well be difficult to envisage any solution to their problems other than suicide. Those in the grip of psychotic delusions and hallucinations, where voices are telling them to kill themselves, are particularly vulnerable to acting on such feelings. In such circumstances it is hard to see suicide as the outcome of a rational process.

Tony is a 20-year-old man with a diagnosis of schizophrenia. As a child, he was sexually abused by a man who befriended him and drew him into a paedophile circle where Tony was exposed to drugs and multiple sexual relationships with other men. As an adolescent, Tony presented a challenge to those who were responsible for him. He was rebellious, became involved in delinquent behaviour, abused a variety of illicit drugs as well as engaged in repeated self-harming behaviour. At the age of 18 he began to hear voices in the third person. These voices were critical of him, accusing him of being a homosexual and telling him to hurt others. Before his latest admission to hospital, Tony was alone in his flat where the voices told him to kill himself by throwing himself out of his window as he was 'bad'. The only way to redeem himself was through death. Tony proceeded to jump out of the fourth-floor window and sustained moderate injuries.

When we follow-up people such as Tony through their crises we *sometimes* observe that as their mood lifts, or their hallucinations subside, they are relieved not to have been successful in killing themselves. With such clients the aim of the work is to contain their distress and their urges to kill themselves – in short, to keep them alive and to create a space for 'thinking about' feelings as opposed to 'acting out'.

Work with suicidal clients challenges us to think about the question of the individual's responsibility for his or her life. The therapist who is dominated by a determination to prevent suicide at all costs may risk taking over the client's life, so that the client, now deprived of sufficient autonomy, may in fact respond by becoming more demanding and increasingly regressing into a pattern of suicidal threats and attempts. As Maltsberger (1994: 201) observes, 'when we see that continued monitoring, vigilance and pre-emptive anti-suicidal intervention is leading to the development of coercive bondage and psychotherapeutic stalemate, giving responsibility back to the patient for the decision whether to live or to commit suicide becomes not only ethically defensible but therapeutically necessary.' Hillman (1965) goes one step further when he suggests that we can only treat suicidal people when we give up the notion of prevention altogether.

Management of self-harm

Managing clients who repeatedly harm themselves also presents a challenge to the therapist. Such behaviour is not only highly distressing but may also lead therapists to feel personally attacked as their therapeutic efforts appear thwarted when faced with a client returning to a session with multiple cuts. Under such circumstances it may be difficult for the therapist to retain a compassionate attitude. Many authors have reflected on the fear, anger and anxiety that clients who deliberately harm themselves provoke in therapists or those who care for them.

Self-harm which appears to be in response to an acute personal crisis may be easier to manage. However, for some it becomes the primary, if not the only, vehicle for expressing and relieving intolerable psychic pain. In such instances, the behaviour acquires an addictive quality and is therefore more resistant to change. Such behaviour is best understood in the context of persistently disordered relationships. Psychoanalytic clinicians have emphasised the importance of translating the self-harming behaviour into the feelings which it is believed to express indirectly, typically feelings of anger and hostility as well as fears of dependency and of being out of control.

The client who repeatedly engages in self-harming behaviour may require admission to hospital as a means of containing the behaviour. Admission to hospital is, however, not always helpful. Rather, as Feldman (1988) points out, restriction may in fact lead to an increase in self-harm. It is not appropriate to be prescriptive about the management of such behaviour in the context of a therapeutic relationship as each individual demands a very particular understanding of the meaning of his or her self-harm and a correspondingly individualised approach to its management. However, an admission to hospital should not be dismissed outright as one possible way of containing the client. Where the self-harm results in significant wounds, medical assistance should be sought. The therapist needs to convey to the client the message that the expression of distressed feelings will evoke appropriate concern, while making it clear that self-harm will be met with whatever medical treatment is needed. This 'matter of fact' attitude to the self-harming behaviour itself is an attempt to convey a clear message to the client about the more adaptive ways of communicating feelings, thereby not reinforcing the self-harming behaviour. It is, however, important to remember that being 'matter of fact' does not mean that one should be insensitive to the person who will be very distressed.

Countertransference and suicide

Losing a client through suicide is invariably a painful experience for the therapist. It is not only painful because it involves the loss of a person with whom we have engaged emotionally but also because a client's suicide can be experienced as a narcissistic injury. In our work we sometimes bring unrealistic expectations and aspirations for care-giving which render us particularly vulnerable when working with clients who display self-destructive behaviour. Such vulnerabilities were termed 'narcissistic snares' by Maltsberger and Buie (1974), who pointed out that the three commonest snares are 'heal all, know all and love all'. Such high expectations of the help we can offer may leave us feeling helpless and guilty and lead us even to wishing that we no longer had to see a particular client if the client does not get better but actually harms or kills herself. As Watts and Morgan (1994: 13) point out: 'the mute, suicidal patient is particularly likely to become the target of projected counter-transference hate. To sit for hours with such rejecting patients can evoke hateful fantasies.' Such unacknowledged feelings in the therapist may alienate further the suicidal or self-harming client who cannot find any other ways to express her need for help and may heighten the risk of self-destructive behaviour. Rejection of the therapist by the client through suicide attempts or suicide threats may precipitate a number of countertransference responses in the therapist, for example separation anxiety, depression and frequently rage and hate. Indeed, McGhinley and Rimmer (1993) observe that suicidal clients challenge us with our own dread of abandonment and our despair. In addition, death by suicide attacks our own reparative strivings and 'brings reality to bear on our omnipotent phantasies of rescuing and making good damage that is irreparable' (McGhinley and Rimmer, 1993: 55).

It is worth bearing in mind that not all suicides are preventable. Hospitalisation may at times even reflect the therapist's unconscious retaliation towards the client because they themselves feel so attacked. The anxiety elicited in the therapist may also contribute to premature decisions to hospitalise on the basis of little evidence of the need for this, reflecting more the therapist's inability to contain the client's despair and his attacks on both himself and the therapist. Awareness of such countertransference issues is critical for work with suicidal clients who often experience considerable difficulty in managing their own hostility and sadism.

Finally, working with suicidal clients is especially taxing because it requires us to face head on our own feelings – often fear – about death. This difficulty may lead us to hold steadfastly to our theoretical models and to slot the suicidal client into a particular mould, keeping them and what they arouse in us, at a safe distance. However, we must not forget that each suicide attempt tells a very unique story. While this chapter has reviewed some of the main research findings related to suicide, it is important to resist the temptation to hide behind such facts but to remain open to the pain, anger, hopelessness and sometimes even hope that is contained and expressed through a suicide attempt.

Note

1. Schizo-affective disorder is said to be characterised by both affective and schizophrenic symptoms simultaneously or within a few days of each other.

7
Anxiety

The nature of the problem

"You fucking bastard go kill yourself, you are useless". You asked me what was going through my mind and this is it. All the time I have these thoughts telling me to kill myself. Right now I have the thought that I want to have sex with you and my daughter . . . [cries]. You know I would never harm you or my daughter but I just can't get rid of my thoughts. When I was talking to my daughter on the 'phone last night I just kept thinking "have sex with her" and then the thought is to throw myself under a car. The thoughts just keep on repeating "kill yourself, you don't deserve to live". I'm afraid that one day I will kill myself or act on any one of these thoughts. I feel constantly apprehensive, I can't relax ever. I feel I am mad. (Mark, aged 49, diagnosed as having 'obsessive-compulsive disorder')

Mark was a successful businessman until seven years ago. He recalls waking up one morning, experiencing what he now refers to as his 'intrusive thoughts'. These thoughts were suggesting to him to have sex with his daughters, with strangers and to kill passers by in the street as well as to kill himself. These recurring, repetitive, obsessional thoughts continue to preoccupy Mark seven years on. Mark is aware that the obsessional thoughts are the product of his own mind and that they are not imposed from without as in psychosis (see Chapter 9). In the meantime, however, he has lost his family, his job and his home. He now lives in a run-down council flat, has developed an alcohol problem and is at risk of severe self-neglect. He seldom leaves his flat because he is afraid that he might act on his thoughts. The fact that he has lived with these thoughts for seven years but never acted on them provides little reassurance to Mark. On the contrary, he continues to experience heightened anxiety in response to his obsessional thoughts which he manages by drinking heavily in order to knock himself out. Although Mark does not perform any overt compulsive behaviours (e.g. checking, washing) as a way of reducing his anxiety, his repetitive thoughts about killing himself do appear to serve the function of relieving some of the anxiety triggered by his sexual thoughts of which he is very ashamed. Mark suffers from what is referred to as obsessive-compulsive disorder (OCD). OCD is one of the 'anxiety disorders' that we shall be reviewing in this chapter. In common with the other disorders, the experience of anxiety and attempts to avoid it are its central features.

Definitions and clinical features

The nature of anxiety

We are all familiar with the experience of anxiety to a greater or lesser extent. Anxiety is, of course, a part of everyday life and what it means to be human. Indeed, existential thinkers view it as a given of existence. It is an emotion that is principally characterised by feelings of dread, worry, apprehension or fear. The experience of anxiety lies on a continuum from a normal, adaptive response in the service of survival to a more severe form which can lead to the disruption of a person's life. The fearful reaction which is a part of anxiety has functional value in evolutionary terms as it drives us to avoid potentially dangerous situations. In existential terms it is the understandable response to the givens of existence, particularly the inevitability of death, and our freedom, and consequently the responsibility we each have to assume for the choices we make.

Anxiety may be triggered in response to particular situations, people or events (for example, going to the dentist, taking an exam). It can also be triggered in anticipation of an event. The stimuli capable of eliciting anxiety may be both external and internal (for example, negative evaluations of the self). Anxiety is often accompanied by feelings of being out of control. In addition, the individual experiences physical symptoms which reflect increased sympathetic nervous system activity (increased heart rate, respiration and desire to urinate, sweating, nausea, muscular tension, diarrhoea). The unpleasantness of this experience is such that the person attempts to avoid it by avoiding the stimuli associated with it.

The term 'anxiety' is used in quite different ways, at times to refer to a relatively enduring characteristic of a person which remains constant across situations, as well as to refer to a situationally specific characteristic. These are respectively called *trait anxiety* and *state anxiety* (Spielberger et al., 1970). Such variations in the use of the term can be traced in DSM-IV where generalised anxiety disorder (GAD), for example, appears to refer to an enduring trait of a person, while post-traumatic stress disorder (PTSD) refers to a classification where the anxiety is experienced in response to a particular situation. The notion of trait anxiety has, however, not received unanimous acceptance. Mischel (1973), for instance, argued that in order to understand any type of behavioural response it is essential to consider the complex interaction between the person and the environment. Notwithstanding such considerations, in clinical practice we do come across individuals who appear typically to respond to many, if not most, situations in an anxious manner and whom we might generally describe as being 'worriers'. According to Spielberger's model (1970), such individuals would score highly on trait anxiety. The model allows us then to distinguish between more common anxious responses which are situation specific and more intense, pervasive anxiety. It does not, however, provide an explanation for individual differences in trait anxiety.

Theories of anxiety

Biological models

As mentioned above, psychophysiological changes are characteristic of anxiety states. The finding that panic attacks can be provoked by infusions of lactate or voluntary hyperventilation in those with a history of panic in contrast with people with no such history, led researchers to propose that certain biochemical changes have a direct panic-inducing effect and that those individuals who are vulnerable to such pharmacological or physiological agents have an underlying biochemical disorder. This, in turn, has led researchers to identify biological markers which are capable of distinguishing anxious from non-anxious individuals. The findings in biological psychiatry are partly founded on animal experiments and partly on the selective workings of various drugs in humans. Such studies have focused on the disorders in different neuro-transmission systems, namely the GABA-system and the noradrenergic system.

In biological accounts of anxiety, attention has also been focused on the nervous system and its degree of reactivity. Eysenck (1967), for example, proposed a theory of personality which was principally based on individual variations in intensities of cortical arousal, and this was believed to be biologically determined. Within this model, anxious individuals are said to have high resting levels of cortical arousal (that is, when not emotionally or physically aroused) and high autonomic nervous system activity.

The results from biological research are mixed, to say the least, and reflect a far too narrow and oversimplified approach to understanding anxiety, where social and other environmental factors are likely to play an important part in aetiology. Moreover, such models fail to account for individual differences in the varied types of situation which provoke anxiety.

Behavioural models

In 1920 Watson and Rayner successfully attempted to condition fear of a white rat in a 14-month old baby by pairing presentation of the animal with a loud noise. Extrapolating from this experiment, they postulated that any neutral stimulus could elicit fear if it is paired with a threatening stimulus. This is what is known as 'classical conditioning'. Replication of this original experiment has, however, been unsuccessful. Furthermore, the most powerful evidence for the conditioning theory of fear acquisition has been derived from laboratory studies using animals. The problems of generalising from animals to humans are clear. However, this model is also problematic on other grounds. Contrary to the prediction one would make on the basis of this model that people exposed to fear-provoking situations would acquire a particular fear, real-life experiences suggest that this is by no means invariably the case. Rachman (1977, 1990), for instance, illustrates this latter point with examples of people exposed to air raids who did not develop anxiety reactions in spite of repeated exposure to a frightening situation. Moreover, in everyday clinical practice, it is far from uncommon to assess people who present with severe anxiety but where it is not possible to identify a clear aversive experience acting as a trigger. Indeed, between 40 and 80 per cent of people presenting with fears and phobias cannot recall any traumatic experiences associated with onset (Brewin, 1988).

If we take the example of naturally occurring phobias, the shortcomings of the conditioning model will become even more apparent. According to the basic learning theory model, any neutral stimulus paired with an unpleasant stimulus is capable of developing into a phobic stimulus. If this were so, then we would expect phobias to be evenly distributed across a whole range of stimuli but, as Seligman (1971) points out, phobic stimuli are not evenly distributed. On the contrary, they consist largely of a limited and non-arbitrary set of situations and stimuli whereas more probable genuine traumatic associations seldom act as phobic stimuli. In light of these limitations, the conditioning models have undergone revision. Seligman has challenged the notion that one stimulus is as good as any other in a conditioning paradigm (the equipotentiality assumption). He proposed the notion of 'preparedness' to explain the non-random distribution of phobic stimuli. According to Seligman, as a consequence of evolutionary history, our organism is innately prepared to learn certain 'conditioned stimulus–unconditioned stimulus' associations. While this notion helps to account for the selectivity of phobias and the speed of their acquisition, the potential circularity of the concept of preparedness presents a problem. As Matthews and MacLeod (1988) point out, researchers have typically defined stimuli as being 'prepared' depending on whether or not they represent common phobias. In addition, there are limited clinical data to support this notion.

Although it is the case that for some people a past personal experience with a phobic stimulus helps to account for the genesis of a phobia, there is also evidence that fears may be transmitted indirectly by modelling. Strong evidence for this comes from studies which have shown that exposing phobic patients to non-fearful models reduces levels of fear. Pinto and Hollandsworth (1981), for example, used videotaped displays of a coping model to reduce anxiety in hospitalised patients. Furthermore, there is considerable correspondence between the fears of mothers and their children and between children in the same family.

Cognitive models

Conditioning models have been criticised by cognitive theorists who have argued for the central role of cognition in anxiety. Bandura (1977) has focused on the role of expectation. He proposes two kinds of expectations: *self-efficacy expectations* which refer to the beliefs people hold about their capacity to control potential outcomes, and *outcome expectations* which refer to beliefs about the likelihood of an aversive outcome. Within this model, a person who is phobic of snakes is afraid because he envisages aversive outcomes which he perceives himself powerless to control. This theory, while contributing to our understanding of the maintenance of anxiety, does not, however, provide an adequate account of its development.

The notion that cognitions cause anxiety was put forward most comprehensively by Beck et al. (1985a). The central tenet of this approach is that it is not events *per se* which are responsible for making people anxious, but rather it is the person's interpretation and expectation of events which gives rise to anxiety. They suggested that clinical anxiety arises through the overactivation of schemata which are predominantly concerned with the encoding and elaboration of threat-related information. It is argued that the activation of these cognitive structures leads to processing biases which generate danger-related thoughts in anxious people. In anxiety, the important cognitions relate to perceived physical or psychosocial danger.

Such a theory has received support from studies looking at processing biases in anxious people by comparison with non-anxious controls. For example, Matthews and McLeod (1985) found evidence of an attentional bias towards threat-related stimuli. In their study, clinically anxious people but not controls were differentially disrupted on a colour-naming task when they were required to ignore threat-related rather than neutral distractor words. Such findings have since been replicated.

The important role of cognition in anxiety has also been highlighted in panic attacks. The latter can be induced by a range of physical agents such as carbon dioxide. At first, these effects were understood as evidence of biological vulnerability. However, more recent work suggests that people differ in the way they experience the same physiological reactions depending upon their expectations and interpretations of their reactions. Those people who interpret the physiological changes as signs of an impending heart attack, for example, are more likely to experience a panic attack.

Psychoanalytic models

Broadly speaking, such models propose that anxious feelings stem from internal conflicts or impulses which are unconscious. Anxiety is conceptualised as a response to inner danger as opposed to fear which is a response to external threats. However, inner danger can be projected into the outer world and may therefore manifest itself as a phobia.

Freud proposed two theories of anxiety. In the first theory instinctual energy was said to be directly transformed into anxiety. Then he understood anxiety as primarily the outcome of undischarged sexual tension. The inadequacy of the first theory lies primarily in its inability to explain how dammed up sexual feelings can account for all experience of anxiety. This led Freud to propose his second theory of anxiety in 1926. Here he suggested that it is the ego rather than the id which is responsible for producing anxiety. One of the functions of anxiety is to warn of a potential danger situation which calls forth defensive mechanisms. Emerging thoughts and feelings engendered by instinctual wishes lead to what Freud termed 'signal fear'. The fear activates the defence mechanisms which serve to keep the emerging thoughts or feelings unconscious. If the defence mechanisms fail, then anxiety is experienced.

The second theory focused particularly on the importance of loss as Freud argued that the ego feels threatened by abandonment, separation and loss of love, all of which may give rise to anxiety. The first anxiety experience was thought to occur at birth when the baby is separated from the mother's body. The role of trauma in the aetiology of anxiety was thus central. Freud did also speak about actual neuroses that resulted from external stress producing massive anxiety as, for example, in victims of shell shock and other war neuroses.

Anxiety disorders

The so-called 'anxiety disorders' listed in DSM-IV, include agoraphobia (with and without panic disorder), panic disorder, specific phobia, social phobia, post-traumatic stress disorder (PTSD), generalised anxiety disorder (GAD) and obsessive-compulsive disorder (OCD). Although DSM-IV lists a further four anxiety disorders, we shall only concern ourselves here with the ones listed above as these represent some of the most common anxiety-related problems encountered in clinical practice.

While the core experience in all the disorders we shall review is that of anxiety, its source varies and this is reflected in the variety of anxiety disorders. Anxiety is, of course, also experienced by people who are depressed or psychotic or have an eating problem. Clinical anxiety disorders, however, refer to states where anxiety is the main feature.

Agoraphobia

Agoraphobia refers to 'anxiety about, or avoidance of places or situations from which escape might be difficult (or embarrassing) or in which help may not be available in the event of having a panic attack or panic-like symptoms' (DSM-IV). The term itself originates from the Greek words *phobos* (fear) and *agora* (marketplace) and thus literally means a fear of public places. However, the central theme in agoraphobia is of not being able to leave, of feeling 'stuck' and this is far more important than the mere fact of finding oneself in an open, public space.

Agoraphobia is commonly preceded by a high degree of general stress and it is this which may provoke the first experience of panic. Subsequent avoidance of a situation appears to be an attempt to avoid the experience of panic, a phenomenon referred to as the 'fear of fear'.

A comprehensive summary of epidemiological catchment area survey (ECA) data from US sites suggests that 2.9 per cent of the US population are agoraphobic (Boyd et al., 1990). If the figures are applicable to the UK, this would suggest that between 0.3 and 3 per cent of people in the UK are agoraphobic. A very consistent finding has been the gender skew in agoraphobia where women predominate, usually representing not less than two-thirds of the agoraphobic population. This has been accounted for in terms of sex-role stereotypes whereby women tend to be seen as helpless and dependent, rendering them more vulnerable to fear and avoiding a wide range of situations. The mean age of onset is the mid-twenties which is significantly older than for other anxiety states.

Although in the literature there are descriptions of an 'agoraphobic personality', characterised as soft, emotionally immature, infantile, passive and anxious, studies of personality characteristics have produced very mixed results, thus providing meagre support for a specific agoraphobic personality type (Emmelkamp, 1988). Some authors have argued that agoraphobics have a history of traumatic separations. Although this is borne out clinically in specific instances, such generalisations do not hold true for the majority of agoraphobic people.

The quality of the marital relationship of agoraphobic people has also come under scrutiny, with some authors suggesting a close connection between agoraphobia and relationship difficulties. It has been noted that improvement in the agoraphobic spouse is not always welcome by the partner who may in fact behave in such a manner as to impede treatment. This led to the hypothesis that agoraphobic symptoms serve to maintain the marital status quo. The results from studies which have investigated such questions suggest that agoraphobic people do not significantly differ from normals in their overall interpersonal difficulties, even though the interaction between personal characteristics and marital dissatisfaction may be an important variable in the development and maintenance of agoraphobia in some cases. However, it is the case that those agoraphobic people who are in a 'good' relationship seem to sustain treatment gains. In addition, it is a universal clinical observation that the amount of anxiety that agoraphobics experience in a phobic situation depends heavily on whether they are accompanied by someone they can trust to help them. The interpersonal context is less relevant to simple phobias and seems to operate in a different way. A spider phobic, for example, may find it helpful to have someone else around to remove the spider but would not look to that person to help them in coping with their anxiety in the way that an agoraphobic would. Such considerations are relevant to clinical practice as they underscore the importance of addressing the interpersonal context of the agoraphobic person even when the primary mode of treatment may be a behavioural one.

Panic disorder

Panic disorder refers to the presence of recurrent, unexpected panic attacks (that is, they do not occur immediately before or on exposure to a situation that typically causes anxiety as would be the case, for example, in a phobia of spiders) which usually last minutes, and in some cases, hours. Following Freud's (1894) seminal paper on anxiety neurosis, panic attacks have long been recognised as a central feature of certain types of anxiety states. Panic attacks are a not uncommon experience. Prevalence figures vary, with some studies reporting up to 59 per cent of a sample of students having experienced a panic attack in the past year (Margraf and Ehlers, 1988). In the UK between 0.5

and 1.5 million people are likely to meet the clinical criteria for panic disorder without agoraphobia.

Typically, a panic attack begins with the sudden onset of intense fear and is accompanied by the following somatic and psychological symptoms: palpitations or accelerated heart rate; sweating, trembling or shaking; sensations of shortness of breath or smothering; feelings of choking; feeling dizzy or faint; chest pain or discomfort; nausea or abdominal pain; derealisation (feelings of unreality) or depersonalisation (feelings of being detached from one's body), numbness or tingling sensations; flushes or chills; fear of dying and fears of going crazy or of doing something uncontrolled. The fear of losing control (somatically, psychically, behaviourally or socially) is a central experience in panic. In DSM-IV only attacks involving four or more of the above symptoms are termed 'panic attacks'. Some panic attacks appear to be triggered by a clearly identifiable event or short period of anxious rumination. Others, however, are perceived by the individual as occurring 'out of the blue' and consequently can be experienced as even more frightening and uncontrollable.

As panic attacks are such a common experience in non-clinical populations, this begs the question of what differences if any there are between clinical and non-clinical panickers. Research in the field of cognitive psychology has repeatedly highlighted that the most striking difference between the two groups lies in the way people respond to the physical sensations associated with a panic attack. Clinical panickers are more likely to respond with anxiety to the sensations because of the catastrophic misinterpretation of the sensations, leading the person to perceive them as much more dangerous than they really are. For example, dizziness and palpitations are more likely to be construed as signs of an impending heart attack (Clark, 1986). Anxiety may form the basis of many of the less severe hypochondriacal symptoms presenting in general practice.

Specific phobia

This refers to the persistent and irrational fear of a specific object or situation. The individual typically attempts to avoid the object or situation and this may lead to considerable restrictions in day-to-day life. The most common specific phobias include fear of heights, animals, blood, enclosure and of medical surgery (injections, dentists). At first it was believed that it was possible to be phobic about any object. However, phobic stimuli, as indicated earlier, span a rather limited range. It is a theory that the things which we are most likely to fear are ones which may have been or are potentially dangerous to the human race (for example, heights, strangers, water). However, in some cases the phobia may be about an object which cannot be accounted for in these terms; for example, a client who was phobic of triangular shapes and had to avoid coming into contact with any pattern which displayed this shape.

Fears in young children are very common and pertain to varied objects and situations but by and large such fears naturally subside with age (Ollendick et al., 1985). Epidemiological studies carried out with adults in the US, Canada and Germany suggest that phobias are common, with a lifetime prevalence of 13 per cent compared to 2.3 per cent for panic disorder (Emmelkamp et al., 1989). As with other phobic disorders, specific phobias occur more often in women than in men.

Social phobia

This is described as a persistent fear of social or performance situations in which embarrassment may occur (DSM-IV). The fear tends to be of being in the centre of other people's attention and of being judged. Confrontation with the feared situation usually elicits an anxiety response thereby leading to avoidance of the particular situation.

Feelings of discomfort in social situations (social anxiety) are quite 'normal' (Arkowitz et al., 1978). Social anxiety, as reflecting a concern about social encounters, is reported by up to 40 per cent of the general population. However, in social phobia the experience of anxiety is so overwhelming that in many instances the avoidance behaviour interferes with social and occupational functioning. This affects a far smaller number of people, with prevalence rates of about 2 per cent of the general population. The most commonly avoided social situation is fear of public speaking which is reported by over 70 per cent of socially phobic people (Pollard and Henderson, 1988). This is followed by eating in public and writing in public. Unlike other phobias where women have been found to predominate, social fears do not follow this gender skew (Solyom et al., 1986) but are present in roughly equal numbers in men and women. Age of onset is typically between 15 and 20 years (Turner et al., 1986).

Although people who are socially phobic are often perceived to lack social skills, there is little evidence to support this even though they are more likely to underestimate their own level of social skill in social situations. Moreover, while they may possess adequate skills, they are often inhibited to use them in real-life situations as a result of their anxiety. There is convincing evidence to suggest that social phobics are especially preoccupied by fear of negative evaluations or fear of blushing (Edelmann, 1990) and that they are more likely to generate negative cognitions in stressful encounters.

Post-traumatic stress disorder

PTSD refers to the development of particular symptoms following exposure to an extreme traumatic stressor which is beyond the range of usual human experience (for example, witnessing a death, being the victim of a natural disaster). The characteristic symptoms include persistent re-experiencing of the traumatic event (nightmares, hallucinations, intrusive recollections called flashbacks); persistent avoidance of stimuli associated with the trauma and a numbing of general responsiveness (psychogenic amnesia, diminishing of interest in important activities); persistent symptoms of increased arousal (difficulty in falling asleep and in concentrating, hypervigilance) as well as survivor guilt.

PTSD is probably the only anxiety disorder in which the onset is clearly demarcated. Essentially, PTSD differs from the other anxiety disorders with respect to its more specific aetiology, such as a traumatic event. PTSD is common in war veterans and after involvement in a traumatic event such as a major disaster (McFarlane, 1989) or an assault incident (rape, sexual abuse). General population surveys reveal a prevalence of 1–2 per cent (Helzer et al., 1987). It tends to be associated with other psychiatric problems, particularly depression and anxiety.

Obsessive-compulsive disorder

OCD is characterised by recurrent obsessions (persistent ideas, thoughts and impulses or images that are experienced as intrusive and inappropriate and that lead to marked anxiety) and/or compulsions (repetitive behaviours, the goal of which is to prevent or reduce anxiety) that are severe enough to be time-consuming (that is, they take up more than one hour per day) or that cause marked distress or significant impairment in functioning (DSM-IV). The obsessive preoccupation may be total, occupying the person's mind constantly and thereby also preventing any other thought process. This observation has led psychoanalytic practitioners to view this as a displacement activity, distracting the person from essential concerns (Salzman, 1995).

The most common obsessions tend to be repeated thoughts about contamination and dirt; thoughts about violence or harm to another person and doubting (for example, asking oneself if one has made a serious mistake). Frequent compulsions are cleaning, washing hands, counting and touching objects. The obsessive thoughts are often alien to the individual's usual attitudes and are experienced as strange, outrageous, disgusting and frightening. Their presence, as indicated in the clinical example at the start of this chapter, is embarrassing for the person and very distressing. While compulsions often take the form of overt behaviours, in some instances compulsions can involve covert neutralising thoughts (for example, thinking to oneself a particular word or sentence). In addition, though compulsions often serve the function of reducing the anxiety triggered by the obsessional thoughts by creating the illusion of control, they sometimes also increase the anxiety. Obsessions may occur in the absence of compulsions but this is less common. Research findings tend to indicate that obsessions and compulsions are closely related (Emmelkamp, 1987).

Normal and abnormal obsessive thoughts are similar in form and are considered by people as being ego-dystonic, that is, not acceptable to the self. However, clinical and non-clinical groups differ in important respects: clinical obsessions last longer, are judged as being more intense and frequent, and they are less acceptable and therefore more strongly resisted.

The relationship between depression and OCD is strong. Studies of co-morbidity suggest that up to 80 per cent of people with OCD may also be concurrently depressed. In such cases, treatment appears to be less effective, although the evidence for this is mixed. In most cases the depression appears to be secondary to OCD. This is unsurprising given the distressing nature of OCD and its significant interference with daily life. Also found in the literature are reports suggesting a link between OCD and obsessive-compulsive personality disorder but the evidence for this is weak.

OCD appears now to be far more common than it was first believed to be, probably reflecting the low presentation rates for treatment. The six-month prevalence rate from the ECA survey is 1.5 per cent, with similar rates reported in other studies. The representation of men and women is roughly equal, but some studies report a slightly higher incidence among women. Women are over-represented where compulsive cleaning rituals are concerned, while compulsive checkers are more likely to be male. This suggests that sociocultural pressures and expectations may play some part in influencing the development of specific types of OCD.

The age of onset tends to be late adolescence or early adulthood, with a mean age of onset between 20.9 and 25.4 years (Karno et al., 1988). OCD in childhood is rare. A common primary antecedent of obsessive thoughts is stress. Studies suggest that about two-thirds of people with OCD report significant life events associated with the onset of their problem (Rachman, 1985).

Generalised anxiety disorder

GAD refers to an unrealistic or excessive fear and anxious concern about two or more aspects of life (for example, worries about health, family, finances) occurring more days than not for a period of at least six months (DSM-IV). The person finds it difficult to push their worries to one side. In one study, the most frequently reported focus of anxiety was related to family issues, followed by excessive or unrealistic concerns about finances, work and illness (Sanderson and Barlow, 1991 quoted in Edelmann, 1992).

Given the comparatively recent specification of GAD as a distinctive anxiety disorder, prevalence rates are difficult to establish. However, the available evidence indicates that GAD is comparatively frequent in the general population and may be three to four times more prevalent than panic disorder (Edelmann, 1992). It will be apparent that GAD is a difficult category. It refers to a condition which could just as readily be understood as a residual category of the phenomenon of anxiety. However, distinguishing GAD from other anxiety disorders is the focus of worry which is less specific in the former and generalises to various aspects of a person's life.

Current interventions

Anxiety disorders tend to be chronic and persistent with a considerable proportion of people continuing to experience significant degrees of anxiety even following treatment. The research findings from outcome studies for each of the anxiety disorders listed above will now be briefly summarised. This focuses virtually exclusively on cognitive–behavioural and medical treatments as there is a paucity of literature addressing the effectiveness of either dynamic or humanistic approaches to psychotherapy. On the basis of the available empirical evidence, the use of such approaches in the treatment of anxiety only appears warranted where anxiety is only one part of the presenting problem or in cases where other approaches have failed (Roth and Fonagy, in press). In addition, it is always important to remember that cognitive-behavioural approaches are not congenial to everyone. Some clients are motivated to understand what they believe to be the underlying cause of their anxiety and are therefore not purely seeking symptomatic relief. This is more likely to be the case where the anxiety, though possibly the source of considerable discomfort, does not significantly interfere with day-to-day life.

Agoraphobia

In the early 1960s agoraphobia presented a treatment challenge. While systematic desensitisation had been effective in the treatment of specific and mixed phobias, with agoraphobia alone its success was limited

(Gelder and Marks, 1966). By the late 1960s, however, studies appeared which lent considerable support to *in vivo* exposure to the feared situation as a treatment method, involving, for example, the person entering a crowded shopping centre as part of the therapy. Such methods have met with far more success and *in vivo* exposure is now widely considered to be the treatment of choice. Overall improvement rates lie in the region of 50 per cent (Barlow and Wolfe, 1981), but individuals differ markedly in the extent to which they benefit from such treatment. There are few studies which include long-term follow-up of *in vivo* exposure treatment and those which are available are limited by methodological flaws. When cognitive therapy is compared with *in vivo* exposure, the latter emerges as more effective. The studies evaluating cognitive interventions have on the whole yielded mixed results.

Panic disorder

Until recently, panic was largely considered from a biological perspective and hence medical intervention was the treatment of choice. Benzodiazepines and other minor tranquillisers have been moderately successful in reducing anticipatory anxiety as well as in the treatment of panic symptoms. While such drugs clearly have an effect on anxiety, their use is controversial as they not only lead to physical and psychological dependency but relapse rates following withdrawal are high. In addition to the use of tranquillisers, antidepressant medication has also been prescribed, particularly tricyclics such as imipramine, but the results of studies evaluating their effectiveness are mixed. Studies comparing cognitive, behavioural and pharmacological treatments confirm the high relapse rates for the latter by contrast to psychological treatments. Overall cognitive techniques are the treatment of choice (Roth and Fonagy, in press). Treatments offering a combination of medication and psychological interventions show only a small improvement in efficacy.

Specific phobia

The first behavioural treatments of phobias relied on the application of imaginary procedures, such as systematic desensitisation (SD) and flooding. SD was found to be more effective than other therapeutic interventions such as dynamic therapy. *In vivo* exposure treatment was introduced in the 1970s and in virtually all studies it emerged as the most successful treatment. No fundamental changes have occurred since then with now as many as 70–85 per cent of phobic people being successfully treated by this method. The combination with cognitive techniques does not appear to improve efficacy. In the most up-to-date and thorough review of psychotherapy outcome, the authors unequivocally state that 'there is little justification for using anything other than exposure treatment for specific phobias' (Roth and Fonagy, in press).

Social phobia

Cognitive interventions have received some degree of support in the treatment of social phobia but only in conjunction with an exposure component in the treatment package. The effects of social skills training are less clear. For those who present with strong physiological arousal in social situations relaxation methods may be helpful.

Post-traumatic stress disorder

Research in PTSD has been hampered by a lack of clear diagnostic criteria as well as control groups against which to judge the efficacy of any professional intervention. Studies evaluating the treatment of PTSD beyond the circumscribed area of PTSD following the experience of war are relatively recent (Scott and Stradling, 1992). The treatment of PTSD consists predominantly of cognitive-behavioural interventions, including stress management/stress inoculation training and exposure. Less-structured approaches, including psychodynamic therapy, have been found in some studies to be as effective. The evidence for the efficacy of psychodynamic therapy is nevertheless mixed, and given the small number of participants in these studies it is not possible to draw any firm conclusions. Overall it would appear that the most effective interventions involve combinations of various treatments (Roth and Fonagy, in press).

Obsessive-compulsive disorder

Over the past 20 years the treatment of choice for OCD has been exposure and response prevention. This involves exposing the person to their obsessional fears and preventing them from performing the compulsive ritual which serves to maintain the obsession. Reports indicate that up to 75 per cent of people thus treated improve. However, such figures mask the fact that many people refuse treatment, drop out or relapse. Poor outcome is associated with the co-occurrence of depression, with a greater conviction in the plausibility of the content of the person's worries and with the severity and duration of the complaints. In view of this, cognitive-behavioural interventions have been applied. Cognitive therapy has been found to be an effective adjunct to exposure in the treatment of intrusive thoughts and ruminations.

Medication such as clomipramine (which is a tricyclic antidepressant) is an effective treatment for some people with OCD but relapse rates are high. On the whole drug treatments are as effective as behaviourally based interventions involving exposure and response prevention. While such treatment methods are clearly the ones of choice, consideration needs to be given to those individuals who report continuing levels of distress even following treatment and for whom their lives may have been significantly adversely affected by OCD. In such cases supportive therapy may be indicated (Roth and Fonagy, in press).

Generalised anxiety disorder

The use of benzodiazepines in the treatment of GAD has been widespread. Most investigators recognise that, while these drugs can be useful in the short term, they seldom are in the longer term. Their side-effects have also been a cause for concern as they typically lead to dependence, sedation, impairment of cognition and performance. Withdrawal symptoms include rebound anxiety and panic.

Until recently, there were few outcome studies and those that were available involved mainly analogue populations. Now cognitive-behaviour therapy has been evaluated with good results at six months follow-up. Such improvements are greater than those following analytic therapy, non-directive counselling and other behavioural interventions such as relaxation training (Roth and Fonagy, in press).

Practical considerations in assessment and management

It is beyond the scope of this chapter to give consideration here to each of the anxiety disorders which have been reviewed. However, some general guidelines will be useful when assessing people who present with anxiety.

Neurotic and normal anxiety

Anxiety takes many forms and stems from different sources. The mere fact of being alive and confronted with some of the harsh realities of existence is enough to trigger considerable anxiety in the vast majority of people. Indeed, existential therapists speak of 'existential anxiety' when referring to the normal experience of anxiety resulting from a confrontation with what it means to be human. Within an existential framework, anxiety is therefore considered an unavoidable aspect of existence.

People who seek professional therapeutic help at times present with anxiety as being their main concern. They may describe themselves as being unusually anxious and report the somatic manifestations of anxiety. The focus of the anxiety of course varies. Many people are anxious about health-related issues and this tends to be presented as the problem (see below). Further questioning reveals that such people are not suffering from an anxiety disorder as such. Rather the anxiety they report is an understandable, even unsurprising, response to a life crisis which has challenged their belief in an orderly, stable world which they had perhaps believed themselves to be able up until that point to predict and control. Anxiety states are usually related to stressful life events which act as triggers. In many cases the anxiety represents the somatic manifestation of emotional and existential concerns. For some people the connection between their somatic experience of anxiety and emotional problems will not be obvious, and part of the task of assessment and of subsequent therapeutic work will be to make these links explicit so that the underlying concerns can be addressed. In other cases, the anxiety may be one manifestation of a conflict which can now no longer be denied. For such people, counselling or more exploratory psychotherapeutic approaches are often indicated.

Although there is no clear boundary between so-called normally anxious people and those with anxiety disorders, it is the case that for some people the experience of anxiety is so overwhelming that it interferes significantly with day-to-day life. It is in instances marked by the severity of the anxiety that more structured therapeutic approaches have a role to play and have been shown to be effective. The severity of the problem can be estimated by enquiring the extent of interference with the individual's life, including relationships, work and hobbies. To elicit such information it is helpful to ask about the ways in which life would be different if it were not, for example, for the phobia. In the case of Mark who suffered from very severe OCD (see the beginning of the chapter), it was clear that his life had been dramatically affected by his symptoms. Although therapeutic work with him revealed significant events from his early childhood which could help to account for the development of OCD and its symbolic significance, the severity of the symptoms was such that these needed to be addressed in their own right to alleviate some of the distress they caused him. Only once the symptoms were alleviated could a more exploratory approach be considered.

Assessment

Given the consistent finding that by and large cognitive-behavioural and behavioural interventions are the treatment of choice for anxiety disorders, the assessment session will need to establish the severity of the problem in order to make a decision about referring on to a suitably qualified practitioner. However, where clients present with severe problems which have not previously responded to such treatment methods, other therapeutic approaches need to be considered.

The assessment session should aim to gather as much information as possible about the nature of the anxiety. This will include an exploration of situations when the anxiety is most pronounced as well as situations when it is less marked. It will also involve the identification of any avoidance strategies as well as strategies which modulate the experience of anxiety. An attempt should be made to identify any maintaining factors, particularly where the problems have been long standing. This will lead to an exploration of the interpersonal as well as intrapersonal context so as to identify the secondary gains which might be playing a part in maintaining the problem.

Resistance to psychological treatment

At initial presentation some clients, though clearly anxious, do not view their problem as being one of anxiety or, even if they view it as such, are far less enthusiastic about the suggestion that psychological factors may be involved. This is often the case where clients present with anxiety related to physical health concerns and where they may hold the belief that there is truly something physically wrong with them. Such referrals are quite common for those mental health professionals working closely with general practitioners. It has been estimated that between 25 and 30 per cent of general practice attenders are 'somatisers', with what really amount to insignificant differences between ethnic groups. People who somatise are those who give expression to their emotional distress through bodily manifestations which may lead to seeking medical help. Most people who somatise also experience symptoms of anxiety and depression, but do not complain about these symptoms unless directly asked about them.

The body has a language of its own. Psychosomatic expressions are the most elusive of a group of phenomena characterised by what a psychoanalytic theorist, Joyce McDougall (1989), refers to as 'expression in action', that is, a means through which 'one disperses emotion rather than thinking about the precipitating event and the feelings connected to it' (p. 15). It is as if individuals who somatise are expressing their reluctance to reflect on their inner emotional experiences. Indeed, psychoanalytic practice with somatising clients often reveals them as having few neurotic symptoms as though they are obliged to maintain a camouflage of what McDougall has termed 'pseudo-normality' in order not to think or feel too deeply about inner pain and conflict that might otherwise be experienced as overwhelming and psychically disorganising. In referring to psychosomatic problems, I have in mind not only the classical picture of hysterical conversion which is quite rare nowadays, but I am also thinking about everything that concerns the 'real' body where there may well be real damage or ill health in which psychological factors nevertheless play an important role.

The field of psychosomatic medicine has its own categories and, although nowadays it is fashionable to regard all physical disorders as potentially psychosomatic, that is *in part* stress related, many still distinguish between those disorders in which there is true physical pathology that are partly induced by stress (for example, inflammatory bowel diseases, bronchial asthma, eczema, essential hypertension, peptic ulceration) and those disorders in which the physical symptom is functional and not resulting in anatomical disturbances (for example, tension headaches, hyperventilation, fatigue syndrome, irritable bowel syndrome, hypochondria, conversion hysteria). In these disorders, stress plays a far more significant role, if not a primary role in causation – these are properly referred to as the 'somatisation disorders' (DSM-IV). Whereas with somatisation disorders, anxiety, and to some extent depression, may play a direct role in the production of the physical symptoms, the role of these two effects in the more truly psychosomatic conditions is much less clear and the neurobiological mechanisms are still not worked out and are probably various.

Psychosomatic problems may come to acquire secondary gains. Psychotherapeutic work of more exploratory nature often uncovers the fantasy that the physically attacked body is at the same time a way of attacking the body of a 'bad' internalised significant person in the client's life. In other cases, communicating a state of despair through organic illness may also give greater access to care-taking people. For other people still, physical illness may be paradoxically experienced as a reassuring proof that one's body is alive: the self, through the medium of the sick body, here is reinforced against a feeling of inner death that frequently stems from a disturbed infancy (McDougall, 1989: 29). Let us not forget that psychosomatic expressions, in by-passing language, mirror the most primitive modes of communication that we can observe in infants.

Assessment with these clients requires being able to guide and manage the interview if they become too circumstantial. It involves repeatedly summarising and reflecting back where the client discloses information about somatic complaints that might be linked to life events and recognising the client's *feelings* as soon as they appear. Wherever appropriate, as Bass suggests, 'an attempt should be made to link the physical and psychological symptoms to relevant life events or setbacks, using judiciously timed summarising statements inviting comment from the patient' (1992: 110). For example, 'you told me that the tiredness and headaches began about three years ago soon after you lost your job and at about that time you were also feeling very tense, anxious and tearful. Have I got that right?' The aim here is to help the client recognise that each physical complaint is being taken seriously; physical and emotional symptoms sometimes co-exist and both might be related to specific psychosocial stresses – in the above example the loss of a job. This encourages the client to make links between her emotional state and somatic symptoms.

Medication

People who have suffered from long-standing anxiety-related problems may have been prescribed minor tranquillisers. The most commonly prescribed are the benzodiazepines (for example, Valium) which are labelled as 'anxiolytics'. Such drugs have been over-prescribed, creating considerable dependency problems for many people. Although there are some cases where the short-term prescription of anxiolytics may be helpful to the person in managing an acute personal crisis, there is little evidence to support their long-term use.

When clients enter psychological treatments they may express the desire to stop taking the medication. While this should be encouraged, given the dependency problems associated with such drugs, this should always be done in consultation with a medical practitioner as the withdrawal effects are unpleasant.

8

Eating Problems

The nature of the problem

When I wake up in the morning there is always the feeling of dread. The dread that I will have put on some weight. No, I can't even bear the thought but I know that I will have to face the scales and then my day will be ruined if I have put on any weight at all. Sometimes I weigh myself repeatedly because I just cannot believe that I have put on weight – not after trying so hard. When I look at myself in the mirror all I can see is fat and it disgusts me. You can all tell me as much as you like that I am only 6 stones and thin but I know that I am fat. Can't you see it? No one understands really even if they say they do. I can't face another day. I feel so depressed, nothing seems right and I just don't know how to put it right. I feel terrible – I drank half a pint of beer yesterday. I didn't mean to but my friend forced me saying I was being stupid. I had to make myself sick later that day. Do you realise how many calories there are in half a pint of beer? I also took some laxatives. I hate taking these, they always make me feel bad but I had to. I had really overdone it. I hate myself for it. Why am I so weak? I hate this flab. I just wish I could get rid of it. I don't think I can face anyone today. I just don't see the point. (Lucy, age 17, diagnosed 'anorexic')

Lucy's feelings are by no means uncommon among people with an eating problem. Nor are they particularly extreme by comparison to the stories you might hear from other clients with a similar problem. None the less, they sound extreme when we compare them with how most of us feel about our bodies. While we might share with Lucy a preoccupation with body weight and shape, Lucy's feelings may be difficult to appreciate fully. She is not only describing feeling trapped in a body she perceives as fat even though it is clearly emaciated, but she is also trapped in her thoughts which revolve obsessively around food, shape and weight and which, in turn, are intimately linked with how she feels about herself.

Uniting anorexia nervosa and bulimia nervosa are their character-istic, and extreme, concerns about shape and weight. These concerns, or 'overvalued ideas', are peculiar to eating problems. In such instances, the individual's belief in an idea is seen to be more emotional than rational. Both anorectics and bulimics attach a great deal of importance to the pursuit of a thin body shape and the success or otherwise of this pursuit often determines how they will feel about themselves and their lives. Cognitive therapists and researchers have gone as far as to argue that these overvalued ideas concerning shape and weight constitute the core psychological disturbance in eating problems and that the main aim of psychological intervention is to alter the individual's beliefs regarding the importance of shape and weight (Fairburn and Cooper, 1988). Although it is debatable whether this is indeed the core problem, it none the less remains true that one of the tasks of any therapeutic endeavour is to facilitate individuals' exploration of their beliefs and assumptions regarding weight gain and control and how these relate to their sense of self.

This chapter is concerned with the two major eating problems, anorexia nervosa and bulimia nervosa (which from now on will be referred to just as anorexia and bulimia), but will not address obesity as only the first two refer to psychiatric problems. Obesity is at times, however, also associated with psychological problems. As bulimia is a comparatively recent diagnostic category, it has not been researched as extensively as anorexia and this chapter will inevitably reflect this fact.

Definitions and clinical features

Anorexia nervosa

The term anorexia nervosa is in many ways inappropriate as it implies that anorexia is rooted in a 'nervous loss of appetite'. This in turn suggests a loss of interest in, and desire for, food. However, those who have become anorexic report having a strong interest in food. More importantly, they feel that their appetite is too powerful and they attempt to control it by exerting constant vigilance and observing the most rigid rules about what they may or may not eat. Sufferers feel that if their control lapsed, even momentarily, and they ate food beyond their pre-established daily allowance, they would lose control and 'go to pieces'.

These observations have led some clinicians to point out that it is the preoccupation with weight control and the all-pervasive fear of weight gain which represent the most important and most characteristic symptoms of anorexia. Such definitions of anorexia are largely the result of an acknowledgement among clinicians of the need to differentiate between an unspecific refusal to eat and primary anorexia nervosa. Loss of appetite is a common symptom of many conditions such as depression. However, throughout this chapter we will concern ourselves with primary anorexia nervosa, commonly further divided into two subtypes, namely 'restrictive anorectics' and 'bulimic anorectics'. The former drastically cut back on their food intake, while the latter alternate strict dieting with bingeing and purging.

The diagnostic criteria of anorexia (DSM-IV) are as follows:

1 The individual refuses to maintain a body weight over a minimum 'average expected body weight' (AEBW) calculated on the basis of age, sex and height.
2 There is a disturbance in the way in which the individual's body weight, size or shape is experienced; for instance, the person claiming to feel fat even when emaciated or believing that one area of the body is too fat even when clearly underweight.
3 The individual experiences an intense fear of gaining weight or becoming 'fat' even though s/he is actually underweight.
4 In women, the absence of at least three consecutive menstrual cycles when otherwise expected to occur.

Bulimia nervosa

Bulimia nervosa – 'bulimia' literally meaning 'ox hunger' – is a much more recent clinical concept than anorexia. Towards the end of the 1970s, there was an increasing recognition of the experiences of a group of people who fluctuated between periods of self-starvation and periods of uncontrolled eating. Although such individuals resembled those with anorexia in many ways, they were generally of normal weight. The patients Russell (1979) diagnosed as suffering from bulimia, for instance, all had powerful and intractable urges to over-eat, yet were morbidly afraid of becoming fat and sought to avoid the fattening effects of food by inducing vomiting and abusing laxatives. Most had experienced an episode of anorexia. DSM-IV gives the following diagnostic criteria for bulimia nervosa:

1 Recurrent episodes of binge eating (rapid consumption of food in a discrete period of time).
2 A feeling of lack of control over eating behaviour during the binges.
3 The person will also typically engage in regular self-induced vomiting, use of laxatives or diuretics, strict dieting or fasting or vigorous exercise in order to prevent weight gain.
4 A minimum average of two binge eating episodes a week for at least three months.
5 Persistent over-concern with body shape and weight.

On the whole, researchers have felt it important to distinguish bulimia from anorexia, thereby singling out the former as a 'disorder' in its own right with very specific dynamics. For instance, it has been argued that by defining the bulimic as a 'sort of anorexic' we fail to appreciate the specific dynamics that are symbolised by the bulimic symptomatology, whereby the taking in and then rejecting of food singles bulimia out as entirely different from anorexia (Dana and Lawrence, 1988) Others, however, have been more reluctant to differentiate between the two groups. The main difference they point to is the effectiveness with which the anorectic, as opposed to the bulimic, achieves weight loss (Welbourne and Purgold, 1984).

It is certainly the case that there do not appear to be any clear-cut differences in the thinking and the goals of anorectics and bulimics. When listening to the stories of individuals who have been diagnosed anorexic and bulimic respectively, it is the similarities rather than the differences between their experiences which are most striking. They both tend to make very similar statements about themselves and the world they inhabit. For both of them, food and weight control have become central preoccupations. Furthermore, about half of those with a diagnosis of anorexia alternate between episodes of dietary restraint and bulimic episodes.

While it is important to recognise the similarities between anorexia and bulimia, there is little doubt that the bulimic and the anorexic symptoms, respectively, are partly determined by an individual's personal history. In this respect the 'choice' of symptoms may be meaningful and worthy of exploration. For instance, research suggests that bulimic symptoms in particular are associated with a previous experience of sexual abuse (Waller, 1992b). There are also specific difficulties, both physical and psychological, that pertain to those individuals who binge and purge. Indeed, the distress experienced by such individuals has been exacerbated by society's negative attitude to the binge/purge cycle, as this means of controlling one's weight appears to be far less socially acceptable, and certainly less admirable, than the classic anorexic stance.

Unlike the anorectic who embodies our culture's concern with control, the bulimic is someone whose behaviour encapsulates our fear of being out of control. She eats in a frenzy whatever she can lay her hands on.[1] She may even start shoplifting, stealing food. Such behaviours elicit negative judgements. None the less people tend to be fascinated by her behaviour and as with the anorectic, can be voyeuristic about such excesses – after all we are often most fascinated by what we fear and what we cannot accept in ourselves. However, despite our curiosity we have no wish to be like the bulimic. The image of someone kneeling in front of the toilet and inducing vomiting is one from which we recoil. Such prevailing attitudes have undoubtedly contributed to the secrecy that often surrounds bulimic episodes and have thus prevented people from seeking help sooner.

Physical features and complications

Anorexia is typically accompanied by characteristic physiological changes. The prevailing medical opinion is that the anorectic's physical symptoms at low weight are those of a healthy person whose body is adjusting to the effects of persistent under-nutrition. There is therefore nothing mysterious about what we may observe happening to the anorectic's body: it is what would happen to us if we did not eat over an extended period of time. By the time the individual has fallen to 75 per cent of average expected body weight (AEBW),[2] the classic physical picture of anorexia begins to emerge. Overall the rate of their metabolism slows down. The individual will begin to look very obviously frail. The threshold where emaciation becomes physically dangerous is reached when a person's weight falls to 60–65 per cent of AEBW. The speed with which the weight has been lost will also make a difference. Someone who is losing weight very rapidly is more likely to be in immediate physical danger than someone who loses weight over an extended period of time, as the latter allows the body more time to adapt to the changes.

The literature on anorexia sways from those accounts which speak of anorexia as a purely psychological problem and pay very little attention to what is happening to the anorectic's body, to those books and articles which tend to focus on the physical aspects and which subscribe to the view that unless the anorectic's body has been restored to its normal weight no psychological help can be made use of by the individual. Such positions represent extremes which fail to take into account the actual bodily *and* psychological experiences of the anorectic. When working with an anorexic client it is encumbent on the therapist to remember that no matter how emaciated an individual is, she is always more than just a body and the help we offer her should be mindful of this fact.

There are several typical physiological consequences associated with prolonged starvation. It is important to be aware of these factors, particularly when working outside of a medical setting, since if weight loss has been extreme, hospitalisation may be required in order to save life. Anorexia has a fatal outcome in 5–10 per cent of diagnosed cases – a rate higher than that for any other psychiatric disorder. The physical complications associated with starvation include:

- amenorrhoea – cessation of menstruation
- bradycardia – slowing down of heart rate
- hypothermia – lowered body temperature

- hypertension – raised blood pressure
- gastrointestinal disturbance
- abdominal pains
- lanugo – appearance of fine body hair

If the sufferer binges, abuses laxatives and induces self-vomiting, further physical complications will arise (see Table 4). Such methods of weight control are more dangerous than self-starvation from a medical point of view and the individual may be in a precarious physical state due to electrolyte imbalance which, if extreme, can also lead to death. Metabolic disturbances, especially hypokalaemia (low potassium levels) are commonly associated with self-induced vomiting and purgative abuse and this can lead the individual to feel generally weak. Renal damage resulting from dehydration and electrolyte imbalance may also occur. In those cases where the electrolyte imbalance is very severe, the individual may also suffer from epileptic seizures. On the whole, the physical complications associated with bingeing and purging are all reversible. This is with the exception of dental enamel erosion due to the loss of calcium which is associated specifically with self-induced vomiting. The physical complications associated with bulimia are therefore:

Bingeing
- painless parotid gland enlargement
- acute dilation of stomach
- loss of stomach muscle tone
- menstrual disturbance

Vomiting/purging
- hypokalaemia (low serum potassium) – epileptic fits, weakness, muscle pains, renal damage, danger of heart arythmia
- constipation or diarrhoea
- gastric/oesophagus bleeding
- chronic hoarse voice
- dental erosion, caries and tooth loss

The anorectic's response to starvation

While it may be difficult for us to envisage how an individual who looks so frail and whose life seems to have become increasingly restricted could wish to continue on the path of self-starvation, we must not lose sight of the anorectic's reality. For any therapeutic work to take place, it is crucial that we meet the anorectic where she is at any given weight. We need to acknowledge what she says and, even if her statements may seem to us to be extreme, we should accept them none the less as accurate and real perceptions for her of her situation.

Her protruding bones may horrify us but they serve to remind the anorectic that she is in control, that this is the one thing no one can take away from her. It is when her weight is increased, if she is in a hospital, that she will begin to really feel 'bad' and may actually want to die. Suicide is the most common form of death among anorectics who die prematurely. Tragically at times, our perceived attempts to keep her alive may in some cases precipitate the individual in taking her own life as she may feel that that which was keeping her alive has now been removed from her sphere of control (Duker and Slade, 1988).

Psychological effects of starvation

Some researchers have postulated that many of the features of the anorectic's so-called 'psychopathology' could be a direct result of starvation (Garner et al., 1985). Thus, it is argued, that starvation leads to changes in the way people think. The way starvation is said to impair intellectual functioning is by progressively decreasing the individual's capacity for complex thought. Starving people are said to have fewer and fewer categories in which to place their experiences, and this hypothesis is invoked to explain the typically black-and-white, polarised thinking of the anorectic.

The ability to concentrate has also been found to decrease as weight falls. Indeed, it is not uncommon for anorectics to report that they experience difficulty in reading or studying for extended periods of time. While such difficulties may be the consequence of starvation, they can also be understood as a further manifestation of the anorectic's difficulty in taking in anything – from food to books.

Sexual feelings are also said to diminish when food intake is consistently reduced over long periods of time. The latter finding is frequently invoked to explain how, by reducing their sexual drive through starvation, the individual can temporarily resolve their sexual conflicts. Starvation also induces a state of euphoria. This experience is also known as the 'fasting high' with which some of us may be familiar if we have gone without eating for a period of time. This is quite a normal reaction and occurs when people consistently cut back on the amount of food they eat. Depending on an individual's weight and the extent to which she has reduced her intake of food, such a change can begin to take place quite rapidly, for instance within as little as 24–48 hours.

The idea that these commonly observed features of anorexia, as outlined above, are the consequences of starvation is based on an experimental study of starvation effects (Keys et al.,1950). Male volunteers underwent semi-starvation, losing about 23 per cent of body weight. As the weight loss progressed, the men began to think incessantly about food and were preoccupied with food-related activities, spending large amounts of time planning how and what to eat. They tended either to gulp their food or hoard it and eat it in small bites. Often they became asocial and quite reclusive. They reported significant impairments in their concentration as well as depressed mood.

Many of the experiences that the male volunteers underwent are also frequently reported by anorexic clients. However, while such research is of interest and it may prove useful to separate out the non-specific effects of starvation, we are not yet in a position to say with any certainty whether there is a causal link between such experiences and starvation. Moreover, it has not yet been satisfactorily demonstrated that such symptoms can be reversed by simply restoring body weight. Until such a time, we must proceed with caution and not explain away clients' experiences simply in terms of the effects of starvation.

Eating problems and sexual abuse

Eating problems have long been understood as arising in the context of a developmental process which has presented particular challenges to the individual with respect to their sexuality. Sexual development is an important aspect of maturation and problems in this area are not uncommon in those who develop eating problems. Indeed, the presence of sexual conflicts in many individuals with eating problems has been well documented. It has been claimed, for instance, that some feel sexually and otherwise inadequate and are frightened by sexual thoughts (Casper et al., 1981). Crisp (1980) saw the central psychopathology underlying 'weight phobia' as rooted in the biological and consequently experiential aspects of normal adult weight which include psychosexual maturity and its concomitant problems.

Psychoanalytic formulations of anorexia played an important role in establishing a link between sexual and eating problems. The theory was crystallised in the writings of Waller et al. (1940) who described the anorectic's disturbance as rooted in her inability to identify with her mother and the female role. They postulated unconscious guilt and anxiety about oral impregnation and suggested that such symptoms as amenorrhoea and constipation were respectively linked to an unconscious wish to be pregnant and to a wish to retain the baby. Anorectics began to be seen as essentially sexually repressed or puritanical figures. Allegedly, they feared that they could become pregnant from male sperm residue left on chairs or refused 'slimy' foods because they associated these with semen (Brumberg, 1988).

However, psychosexual dysfunction was by no means the whole story. Anorectics were also portrayed as hysterically exhibitionistic and seductive. Goiten (1942) suggested, in no uncertain terms, that the anorectic was a potential prostitute whose lack of appetite was an unconscious defence against promiscuity. Others claimed that the anorectic wanted to be force-fed because of fellatio fantasies. While such descriptions of the alleged fears and preoccupations of the anorectic make for some interesting reading, it is important to entertain the perhaps more likely possibility that such accounts instruct us more about the fantasies and preoccupations of the male professionals who reported them than those of the anorectic. More importantly, the emphasis on the fantasies of the anorectic conveniently diverted attention away from the more unpalatable possibility of actual past adverse sexual experiences in the lives of those individuals presenting with eating problems.

However, the reality of sexual trauma in the lives of individuals with eating problems is now beginning to be addressed. There is a growing body of literature which has documented instances of child sexual abuse, as well as rape incidents, in individuals with eating problems, particularly those with a diagnosis of bulimia. One such study reported that 30 per cent of patients referred to an eating problems clinic also had a history of sexual abuse (McLelland et al., 1991). Such figures are not uncommon with some studies reporting figures of up to 50 per cent (Hall et al., 1989; Waller, 1992a). The variation in the reported rates can be partly explained by the differences in the definitions of sexual abuse used by the researchers, a not uncommon problem in sexual abuse research. None the less, the association between a history of sexual abuse and eating problems is striking and suggests that for over a century we may have been ignoring a most important dynamic in our understanding of eating problems.

When we seriously entertain the potentially factual nature of the material that many of the early psychodynamic formulations presented as fantasies, certain aspects of eating problems become easier to comprehend. For instance, the difficulty in identifying with the mother pointed out by Waller et al. in the 1940s makes sense in the context of a relationship with a sexually rivalled mother or a mother who may have been experienced as collusive with a sexually abusive father. Similarly, the guilt and anxiety associated with impregnation is a quite understandable response if one has been sexually assaulted.

The research supporting an association between sexual abuse and eating problems is of therapeutic importance. If, as practitioners, we can allow ourselves to entertain the possibility of sexual abuse in our clients' lives, we may be able to help them to explore the symbolic associations that may exist for them between such experiences and subsequent eating problems. Frequently, the sexually abused individual experiences feelings of inferiority or disgust about her own femininity and sexuality. These may become entangled with concern about body weight, shape and size. The virtually phobic avoidance of normal weight, menstruation and secondary sexual characteristics commonly observed in clinical practice is well utilised by some clients as a form of denial by producing a shutdown of the physiological reminders of an unbearable and frequently guilt-ridden sexual past.

Andrea, who developed bulimic symptoms around the age of 22, revealed a history of sexual abuse. As a child she recalled being forced, over a period of years, to have oral intercourse with her father. This always took place in the toilet in the evenings while her mother was downstairs cooking the evening meal. As an adult, Andrea found it very difficult to take anything in. She experienced difficulties in her studies as she found it virtually impossible to retain any information, even though she was of average intelligence. This had in part contributed to her under-achievement and reinforced her low self-esteem.

Andrea felt constantly empty and this feeling elicited a great deal of anxiety for her. She eventually turned to food as a means of 'filling' herself up. However, she could not allow herself to keep the food in and she frequently resorted to making herself sick as a way of relieving the feelings of 'suffocation' which accompanied the ingestion of food. Her binges were characterised by a very violent quality and a pressing need to 'get it over and done with' – a sentence she also used to describe her recollections of oral sex with her father. Now, as she gorged herself, went to the toilet, locked the door and then put her fingers down her throat to bring up the food, she was poignantly replaying the traumatic experience of having her father's penis thrust in her mouth and then throwing up his semen. Now, however, she had become her own 'abuser' and to this extent she experienced a measure of control. Following a binge and having regurgitated the food, Andrea could find some temporary respite from her memories as she felt she had been able to rid herself of her 'badness' until the next time.

A history of sexual abuse – usually involving homosexual experiences – is also found in men with eating problems. However, as a history of child sexual abuse is less common in men than in women, this fact may also be seen to contribute a further explanation for the lower incidence of male eating problems. As with most psychological research, it is not possible to assert with any degree of certainty the meaning of an association between two variables. Not all sexually abused individuals develop an eating problem, and some individuals with eating problems have not been abused. Such facts suggest that sexual abuse is neither a necessary nor sufficient trigger for the emergence of an eating problem. While any causal role is likely to be partial and complex, those who have suffered such abuse may none the less present a particularly vulnerable population.

Epidemiology

Prevalence

Anorexia and bulimia are currently reported to be on the increase. It is most probably true that, as in the case of many 'disorders', the reported increase is to some extent due to heightened awareness of the classic signs and symptoms associated with eating problems, and increased reporting on the part of families and doctors. Indeed, Fombonne (1995) suggests, on the basis of his survey of the literature, that there is no evidence of an actual increase in true morbidity. The prevalence rate for anorexia is roughly one case per 500 girls and for bulimia approximately a rate of 1 per cent among adolescent and young adult women.

Age and gender

In general, most cases of primary anorexia nervosa occur after the onset of puberty and before the menopause. The modal age of onset is 16. One study reveals that around 70 per cent of adolescent girls in a sample of schoolgirls reported having dieted to lose weight (Hill and Oliver, 1992). However, there are exceptions to onset in adolescence. Although the incidence for younger, pre-pubertal children is not known, there is a suggestion that anorexia is increasing in this younger age group (Lask and Bryant Waugh, 1992). Equally, there are also reports of cases of anorexia with an onset in adulthood. Evidence suggests that both anorexia and bulimia are spreading beyond their original 14–25 year range (Attie and Brooks-Gunn, 1995). As therapists, it is important to be aware of such data as the stereotype of the young teenage anorectic is deeply ingrained and may prevent us from picking up concerns about weight and size in those who do not fit the stereotype. The age of bulimic clients at presentation tends to be older than those with anorexia, being mostly in their twenties, although, like anorexia, a wide age range is affected.

The vast majority of cases of anorexia and bulimia are female and this is an important social characteristic. The observed gender skew has attracted a great deal of attention and is the particular focus of sociocultural explanations of eating problems. However, this fact has perhaps led to an overemphasis on eating problems as 'female problems' and, as we will see later, this is not exclusively the case.

Social class

Anorexia has long been thought of as a disorder of the affluent – the 'rich girl' syndrome. Bruch (1973b and 1978), reported that many of her patients' families came from a higher socioeconomic background. Since then, others have confirmed Bruch's original findings. However, such a correlation needs to be interpreted with a degree of caution as it may simply reflect a bias of observation or in presentation to doctors. Those anorectics from a higher socioeconomic background may simply have easier access to health care and may come from families that would encourage them to seek help. The statistics may therefore not provide an accurate reflection of what is actually happening but rather serve to reinforce an unfortunate stereotype which may in practice deflect attention and resources from those who need them most. The social class distribution of clients with bulimia has not been systematically studied. However, there is a suggestion that it is broader than it has been believed to be for anorexia.

Cross-cultural factors

Until recently, eating problems – anorexia in particular – were regarded as exclusively a Western problem, more prevalent in cultures obsessed with slender figures. They were generally held to be largely confined to white women. However, recent evidence has challenged this prevailing assumption. Epidemiological research has shown that the incidence of anorexia in individuals of various ethnic origins is greater than it was originally believed to be. Eating problems have thus been documented in Japan (Azuma and Henmi, 1982), in blacks in the United States and in Britain (Holden and Robinson, 1988), and in Africa (Nwaefuna, 1981). Moreover, a recent sudy suggests that there are no significant differences between what in the study in question were referred to as 'white' and 'non-white' clients with respect to patterns of family relationships, social class and parental status (Soomro et al., 1995).

It is difficult to deny that there are Western cultural pressures to conform to a societal ideal of weight and shape. One study, for example, illustrated how attitudes to weight and shape may change with immigrant status in ethnic groups where plumpness is considered attractive and thinness is undesirable. Furnham and Alibhai (1983) used repertory grids to assess cross-cultural differences in the perception of female body shapes. Three groups of women – British Caucasian, Kenyan Asian and Kenyan Asian immigrants to Britain – were presented with a repertory grid in which the elements were figure silhouettes of varying degrees of fatness. They found that the Kenyan women rated the fatter figures more favourably and the smaller figures less favourably than the British women. However, the immigrant women were more extreme than the British women in their perceptions, reacting more positively to the thinner shapes.

While it appears that culturally determined attitudes to body shape play a significant role and may interact with psychological factors in the genesis of eating problems, what has been overlooked until recently is the experience of those individuals who have emigrated to the West and have thus been exposed to a different, and often conflicting, set of sociocultural norms and ideals. The confusion that is characteristic of adolescence – the most typical time when eating problems emerge – and which often centres around the individual's attempts to negotiate issues of autonomy, control and sexuality, may present particular challenges to those adolescents growing up in a situation involving a juxtaposition of two very different cultures. Research by Mumford et al. (1991) has shown that among a South Asian population of school-girls living in Britain, concerns around body shape and weight were associated with a more traditional cultural orientation and not, as might be expected, with greater 'Westernisation'. Thus De Nicola (1990) has proposed that anorexia may be viewed, for instance, as a 'culture change syndrome' whose onset may be triggered under conditions of sociocultural flux.

An estimation of the the true rate of eating problems in non-white groups is impossible without a large epidemiological survey. Our own ethnocentric assumptions concerning the likelihood of a non-white individual presenting with an eating problem may be a source of bias. Because of the presumed uncommon occurrence of such problems in ethnic minorities it may be that we sometimes fail to recognise eating problems in such groups. At present the research alerts us to a vulnerability to eating problems in individuals of varied ethnic origin.

Men and eating problems

As we have seen, eating problems are not just confined to white, middle-class adolescent girls. Rather, women and children of all ages may develop them irrespective of their social class and ethnic origin. They are now also no longer recognised as an exclusively female problem. However, the occurrence of anorexia and bulimia in males has been a sadly neglected area. Reports of such problems in men are rarely found in the early medical literature and the current literature on this topic is still relatively scarce in comparison to that devoted to women. None the less, many researchers now claim that up to 10 per cent of all cases are male. In younger samples, the proportion of boys with anorexia and bulimia appears to be somewhat higher, ranging from 20 to 30 per cent (Lask and Bryant-Waugh, 1992).

Many writers have drawn attention to the difficulty in diagnosing anorexia in the male highlighting how, even when the diagnosis is made, it tends to be made later in men than in women. There are several factors that may account for such results. Eating problems undoubtedly occur less frequently in males and this fact alone may incline us to be less likely to think of it as a potential male problem. Our openness to the possibility of an eating problem in a male client may be further constrained by three factors.

First, the language men tend to use to express their conflicts regarding their body shape and size may differ from those commonly used by women. For example, men rarely complain about how much they weigh or the size of the clothes they wear. Instead, they are more likely to express a desire to lose 'flab' and to achieve what our culture considers to be a more classical male definition of muscle groups.

Secondly, the reasons men give for dieting may, at least superficially, sound more medically plausible. In one study, some of the anorexic men reported having heard warnings directed towards a parent that they should lose weight in order to alleviate the symptoms of a medical condition such as heart disease. When accounting for their own weight loss, the anorexic men tended to explain it in terms of health concerns rather than dissatisfaction with their own body shape (Andersen, 1990). It is not clear why women who develop anorexia seldom begin to diet from fear of present or potential physical illness. This remains an interesting difference between male and female anorectics.

Thirdly, the methods men use to control their weight may attract less attention from others and may even be culturally valued activities. Many male anorectics use excessive exercise rather than self-imposed starvation to lose weight. The female anorectic's rejection of food is more likely to attract attention from those around her and to interfere more with her social life as so many of our social activities centre around food and eating. By contrast, the male anorectic's need to exercise fits in very well with an acceptable social activity; for instance, going to the gym with a friend. Thus the individual who self-starves will alert others more readily to the possibility of an eating problem in a way that the individual who compulsively exercises may not. In our fitness-conscious culture, the latter will not strike us as having a problem; rather, we will probably admire his stamina and determination and praise him for his efforts. The greater likelihood of men using exercise rather than fasting as a means of controlling their weight is perhaps understandable in terms of sex-role expectations. It may then be that for many men problems comparable to anorexia are often masked beneath a preoccupation with exercise and sports.

Increasingly, researchers have devoted attention to the role of exercise in eating problems. Although such research is still relatively new, an Australian study found that exercise, and not dieting, was the main behaviour that precipitated severe weight loss in nine out of 26 cases of anorexia (Beaumont et al., 1984). The connection between exercise and eating problems is particularly striking among young athletes. Surveys of college athletes (both male and female) reveal that a large number admit to fasting as well as the use of vomiting and laxatives to control their weight (e.g. Brooks-Gunn et al., 1988). In males, the incidence of eating problems is higher among wrestlers, jockeys, runners and swimmers. Wrestlers, in particular, often undergo dramatic fluctuations in their intake of food as they aim for a particular weight class.

As in the case of women, a great deal of attention has been focused on the male anorectic's and bulimic's sexuality. Some have suggested that anorexic men tend to exhibit 'gender dysphoria' (unhappiness with their sexuality) and are more likely to be homosexual than their female counterparts. Statistics tend to support the suggestion that homosexual men are over-represented in many samples of men with eating problems (Herzog et al., 1990). However, such findings are based on clinical as opposed to community samples. The former may actually under-represent heterosexual men who may be more reluctant than homosexual men to seek help for what is stereotypically considered to be a 'female problem'. One study reported that 69 per cent of the male homosexual clients attending an eating problems unit were self-referred, compared to only 29 per cent of the heterosexual men, thus lending support to the notion of a bias in referrals (Herzog et al., 1990).

The literature on eating problems in men suggests that there are no significant differences between male and female cases with regard to their clinical features, epidemiology and outcome (Scott, 1986). The similarities include social class background and age of onset. Both men and women have been found to express 'overvalued ideas' with regard to weight and shape, and panic at the prospect of weight gain. Methods of weight control also show some similarity, although women tend more to abuse laxatives while men are more likely to be involved in exercise.

While it may at first seem that many of the cultural explanations that have been invoked to account for the onset of eating problems in women could not apply to men, men may need help in coping with a different kind of cultural pressure and stereotype than that faced by women. While the societal pressures to be slim and svelte are exerted more strongly and consistently on women, frequently men also feel subtly or overtly under cultural pressure to achieve a classical male body shape. Homosexual men, in particular, may be at an increased risk of developing an eating problem because of cultural pressures within the homosexual community to be thin. Yager et al. (1988), for instance, found that male homosexual college students reported higher prevalences of bulimic behaviour and fears of weight gain than did a control group of heterosexual college men. Furthermore, men may be subjected to the demands of a 'macho' culture in which the display of emotion is taboo and where the valued activities and attitudes emphasise being strong and enjoying traditional male activities. Many men with eating problems are uncomfortable with this stereotyped role and are struggling to find a way to 'be' within such a world without feeling vulnerable to ridicule and rejection.

It appears, then, that a cultural pressure does exist for men also and this demands our acknowledgement. It cannot be dismissed as less important in the genesis of eating problems in men. When working with men with eating problems it will therefore be important to validate their experience of this pressure.

Theoretical approaches

The biomedical model

The possible contribution of physical factors to the aetiology of eating problems has focused mainly on anorexia. Since the 1970s, several different endocrinological and neurological abnormalities have been postulated as possible causes of anorexia: for example, hormonal imbalance, dysfunctioning in the satiety centre of the hypothalamus and lesions in the limbic system of the brain (Russell, 1979). Overall, the thrust of biomedical investigations suggests that if anorexia is associated with an organic abnormality, the hypothalamus is the most plausible sight for the origin of the dysfunction. Kaplan and Woodside (1987), in a review of the neurophysiological aspects of both anorexia and bulimia, outline the following: disturbances in the hypothalamic–pituitary axes which regulate gonodal, adrenal and thyroid functions; alterations in endogenous opioid activity; changes in carbohydrate metabolism and hyper- or hyposecretion of gastrointestinal hormones. However, taken together, the available evidence does not implicate a primary pathophysiology as most of the above-mentioned biological changes may be considered to be secondary to weight loss or binge/purge cycles.

The biomedical model presents some notable limitations in that it does not address important social characteristics. It fails to account for the common observations that it is mainly young women and not young men who become anorexic or bulimic and who are thus seemingly more susceptible to the particular biomedical disturbances that are highlighted by the proponents of this model of aetiology. Some writers have argued that the observed gender skew may be more readily understandable if we turn our attention to some simple physiological, as opposed to biochemical, facts. From a physiological point of view, puberty is a time when weight gain for girls is primarily in fat rather than muscle, particularly in the breasts and hips. Puberty in boys, however, entails the growth of muscles and growing larger is frequently a source of pleasure and power for boys (Nylander, 1971). Thus puberty, with its accompanying biological changes, takes girls further from our culture's prepubescent ideal body shape at a time when many girls come to believe that 'looks' are important. In other words, puberty, which may give the boy a sense of power, may be a time in the girl's life when she begins to feel powerless and dependent.

The sociocultural model

The sociocultural explanation of eating problems is very popular. It suggests that in a society seduced by the angular, slimness has now become the most important attribute of female beauty. Anorexia is seen to be caused by the relentless emphasis on dieting. We idealise the image of the 'woman' the media constantly sells to us in their advertisements for diet products: 'beauty' without effort. Indeed, we are surrounded by images, equating thinness and youth with glamour, fame and success. Women often compare themselves with such images and all too frequently feel themselves to be failures.

The pressure on women to diet and appear slim does, indeed, seem relentless. That such pressure may precipitate the development of anorexia seems to be supported by the finding that the condition is far more common in women who must rigorously control their size and shape, such as ballerinas and models (Garner and Garfinkel, 1980). Such observations underscore the possible importance of Western society's current value of thinness in women as a determinant in the increased prevalence of eating problems.

The most outspoken and influential proponents of this model of aetiology are feminists, often therapists, concerned with the full spectrum of eating problems. Within this conceptualisation, eating problems are understood as bearing witness to women's tortuous denial of need and dependency, as well as their persistent expressions of independence, so that women with anorexia appear to live out the contradictions of contemporary cultural dictates. While manifestly the anorexic or bulimic response is an attempt at a psychological solution, the point that many feminist writers are trying to make is that the solution that is sought, and the underlying psychology that makes such a response possible, are formed with reference to a particular set of social relationships which are inevitably bound up with the values inherent in Western culture (Orbach, 1986). As such, it is suggested, any treatment model that is generated to address the rise in anorexia needs to take into account the ways in which an individual's psychology absorbs and interprets cultural values.

The psychoanalytic model

The influence of the early psychoanalytic thinking on the study of anorexia gave rise to the search for a specific psychodynamic of the 'illness'. The observation that anorexia did not generally appear before puberty, that it was largely confined to girls and associated with amenorrhoea, led many workers in this field to suggest that it was causally related to sexual development.

In the 1930s and 1940s, case reports of the psychoanalytical treatment of anorexic women emerged. Some authors referred to the repression of sexual fantasies, doubts about sexual potency, the denial of adulthood and the exclusion of adult problems and sexual needs. However, the attempt to explain anorexia with a single psychodynamic formulation was rendered impossible by the complexity of anorexia. Indeed, since the early psychoanalytic formulations, the emphasis of psychodynamic writing has shifted. Ideas about the aetiology of anorexia have dealt more with so-called 'borderline pathology'.

Hilde Bruch's (1973b; 1978) writings have been particularly influential in the development of the psychoanalytic theory surrounding the aetiology of anorexia. She was the first to recognise the relentless pursuit of thinness as a central organising feature of anorexia, stressing the young girl's equation of thinness with her sense of identity and ownership of her body. According to Bruch, the difficulties experienced by the anorectic result from chronically disturbed mother–daughter interactions that leave the young girl with a pervasive feeling of limited autonomous control and an underdeveloped sense of self. The anorectic's characteristic striving for perfection and superior achievement are understood as one manifestation of her overcompliant or 'false self' adaptation (Winnicott, 1960).

Some psychoanalytic authors have viewed anorexia as a form of narcissistic pathology (Kohut, 1971), arising from a chronic disturbance of parental empathic responsiveness. The frequently observed absence in anorectics of internal self-regulating structures for self-soothing, for the management of anxiety and for the maintenance of a sense of well-being and security, are believed to be the outcome of persistent failures of parental empathy which, in 'good enough' circumstances would otherwise foster in the child the internalisation of such parental functions in their developing psychic structure.

Psychoanalytic formulations draw important attention to the way in which the individual's eating pattern symbolises her capacity to take in nurturing and her ability to nurture others (Dana and Lawrence, 1988).

In this sense, the anorexic feels that she has to deny that she has any needs at all whereby nothing can be taken in. The bulimic, on the other hand, who eats large amounts of food and then vomits, is using her symptom to express a different dynamic: while she is able to take things in, she cannot hold on to them, just as she cannot hold on to 'good' things in a much broader sense.

The cognitive-behavioural model

In the past decade, cognitive-behavioural approaches have been added to the conceptualisation and treatment of eating problems. The main thrust of the cognitive-behavioural conceptualisation is that the central disturbance in eating problems is the individual's 'overvalued ideas' about shape and weight. It argues that most of the other features of eating problems (for example, excessive exercising) are secondary to the individual's overvalued ideas.

The cognitive-behavioural therapist views the beliefs and values of the anorectic or bulimic as implicit rules which influence the way she evaluates and attributes meaning to her experience of herself and her world. Furthermore, the absolute nature of the beliefs and consensus held by the individual with regard to her shape and weight are said to reflect certain dysfunctional types of thinking. These include, among others, superstitious thinking and overgeneralisation. An example of the latter would be the belief that eating an extra slice of bread indicates the individual's total lack of self-control. Such a model, while elucidating some of the factors that may contribute to the maintenance of the eating problem, does not really throw much light on why the individual may have developed such particular beliefs in the first place. Indeed, within the cognitive approach to treatment, the 'why' of the behaviour is not considered to be very important.

The systemic model

Within the systemic model, the interpersonal aspects of eating problems are emphasised, viewing the latter, among other things, as a phenomenon of regulation between two people, for instance between an 'overprotective' parent and a developing adolescent struggling to assert her autonomy. Anorexia, for example, is thus defined not only by the behaviour of the anorectic but also by the inter-relationships of all family members.

According to Minuchin et al. (1978), who has been an influential proponent of this particular model, certain kinds of environment make it difficult for members to assert their individuality and encourage passive methods of defiance, for instance not eating. They describe the 'psychosomatic family' as controlling, perfectionistic and non-confrontational – adjectives which Minuchin equally applies to the anorectic. Minuchin has described what he calls the 'anorectic system' and identifies four factors which are typical of the anorexic family, namely enmeshment, over-protectiveness, rigidity and avoidance of conflict. Anorexia is thus understood as the only possible adaptation by a given individual to a given type of family functioning.

In the main, families of bulimic individuals have been thought to resemble those of anorectics with regard to enmeshment, over-protectiveness and rigidity. However, preliminary studies of family interaction suggest that overt conflict, miscommunication and indirect expressions of anger and hostility are more typical than closeness and over-involvement in families of bulimics (Humphrey, 1986, 1988).

Current interventions

While there are important differences between the treatment approaches that stem from the various theoretical orientations, they all have something in common, namely the difficulty of actually helping the client to change her behaviour. 'Therapeutic failures', reports of deaths and therapeutic pessimism are by no means uncommon in the literature on eating problems. Those individuals who become anorexic or bulimic have gained the reputation of being difficult to 'treat' or to 'help'. Indeed, a great deal of emphasis has been placed on the 'chronicity' of such problems, particularly in the case of anorexia. Many professionals find working with the anorectic difficult and wearing. The endless devices used to ensure that she does not put on any weight have earned the anorectic the reputation of being 'manipulative', 'devious' and 'deceitful'. The anorectic's apparent stubbornness in the face of impending death and pleas from all sides to eat can be experienced as frustrating as it seemingly blocks all attempts to help her. Her rejection of our attempts to help her can be very wounding and may arouse in us retaliatory feelings. Eating problems therefore appear to pose a great challenge to those who attempt to 'cure' them.

Compared with other clinical problems, what appears to render our attempts to help particularly difficult is that the anorexic system provides its own potent reinforcement. While, as outside observers, it may strike us that the anorectic is unhappy, it is important not to lose sight of the fact that weight loss may be her only source of pleasure and thus she has no wish to forego this single gratification. At a time when everything else in her life feels 'messy' and confused, here she may find a way of succeeding. Perhaps, more importantly, it is no longer just about being successful at something; rather, it has become her solution to 'being' as an end in itself. Success becomes measurable in terms of how many pounds have been shed and provides an immediate source of positive feedback. This may perhaps help to explain why the anorectic continues to lose weight even after she has reached her original target weight.

Outcome of eating problems

The outcome of treatment is not easy to assess. While, in the short term, weight restoration and a reduction in the frequency of vomiting and bingeing can be achieved by following particular regimes such as those that are imposed upon individuals as inpatients, more permanent changes have proved to be somewhat more elusive.

The reported recovery rates for anorexia vary considerably from study to study, depending on differing diagnostic criteria, patient selection, length and type of follow-up, and measures of outcome. The recovery rate is thus reported as lying anywhere between 23 and 86 per cent. More generally, while bearing in mind that comparisons between studies are difficult, the suggestion is that about 75 per cent of anorectics are better at follow-up than at initial presentation, at least in terms of body weight. However, outcome according to menstrual function is less satisfactory, and according to psychiatric status even less so. Social adjustment is also impoverished in a large proportion of cases. Poor outcome is frequently associated with the following:

- longer duration of the eating problem
- older age of onset and at presentation
- low weight during the illness and at presentation
- presence of symptoms such as vomiting
- poor parental relationships

Long-term outcome studies of people suffering from bulimia are few. Reports of treated groups suggest that between half and two-thirds of people sharply reduce or become free of their bulimic symptoms. A recent 10-year follow-up study of the outcome of bulimia in 50 patients found that, of 44 patients who were traced, 52 per cent had recovered fully; 39 per cent continued to experience some symptoms; and only 9 per cent showed no improvement (Collings and King, 1994). Significant predictors of favourable outcome were younger age at onset, higher social class and a family history of alcohol abuse. The authors explain the latter surprising finding in terms of the possibility that patients with such a family history suffer a form of bulimia more closely related to substance abuse than other eating problems and are more likely to recover. This is in line with suggestions that eating problems may be a variant of dependence disorders (Szmukler and Tantum, 1984).

Psychological treatments

Numerous management plans have been proposed for the treatment of anorexia. These have covered a broad range of therapeutic approaches. On the whole, treatment programmes tend to be multi-modal; that is, they may consist of individual, family and group approaches. The very nature of such approaches, however, has made it difficult to evaluate the respective contribution of each component to the final therapeutic outcome. In the case of bulimia, cognitive-behavioural interventions are favoured (Fairburn et al., 1986). However, studies which have looked at the effectiveness of such approaches suffer from methodological flaws which make it difficult to conclude that such approaches are indeed more effective than others. Generally speaking, although the outcome studies are few, other therapeutic approaches, including some psychoanalytically orientated therapies, have met with comparable rates of success (Roth and Fonagy, in press).

Family therapy is frequently the treatment of choice with younger clients (under 18 years of age). It is probably true that the younger clients are more amenable to family treatment. If one believes that it is important to intervene in the individual's context, the most immediate contextual field for the child is the family and, at a young age, this is likely to be accessible. In this respect one can see that it makes sense to treat the child as very much a part of a family.

However, the older the person the more resistant they are likely to be to such an approach. The findings of a study by Russell et al. (1987) are of particular relevance. They ran a study comparing family therapy with individual supportive psychotherapy in the treatment of anorexia and found that the former was more effective with individuals whose anorexia was not chronic and had begun before the age of 18. However, a more tentative, but interesting, finding was the greater value of individual supportive psychotherapy with older anorectics.

Those individuals with eating problems at the more severe end of the spectrum are often treated as inpatients. In such settings, treatment is aimed at weight restoration and the management of extreme methods of weight control. When weight restoration takes place in a hospital, the individual is gradually introduced to the consumption of regular meals and, by the end of two weeks, these are expected to be of normal quantity and composition, consisting of around 2,500 kcal a day. The latter amount does vary and may exceed 2,500 kcal. If such a pro-gramme fails, more strict 'operant' behavioural programmes may be introduced whereby 'privileges', such as watching TV or seeing visitors, are withdrawn until some weight has been gained. The effectiveness of such an approach for increasing weight cannot be doubted but upon discharge the relapse rates are high.

Practical considerations in assessment and management

The assessment session

On first meeting someone who presents with an eating problem, two questions seem pertinent: namely, what benefit does the person gain from continuing her attempts at weight control and what would she lose if she relinquished the symptoms? These questions are useful guides for the assessment.

While it is important to let the client lead the way, it is also helpful in the first session to get some information about the extent of the client's eating problem. The information you elicit will enable you to make a decision as to whether you feel able to help the client or whether a referral to another colleague would be more suitable. This, of course, applies to any problem we might encounter but is even more relevant when dealing with a condition which is accompanied by physical complications and which may require medical back-up.

At the initial meeting, it is helpful to gain an idea of the methods of weight control the client uses. It is also important to ascertain how much or how little food she consumes. For instance, if the person tells you that she binges, invite her to specify what a 'binge' consists of. Some will feel very ashamed to answer and it is important to be sensitive to this. However, in asking such questions you may also discover that the person has a very distorted perception of what constitutes a binge and this may alert you to some of the reference points by which she judges her own sense of self-worth. It is not so much the amount that is eaten that is important but whether it is experienced as excessive and uncontrolled.

Frequently, the anorectic's or bulimic's previous experience of discussing her eating habits and ways of controlling her weight will have been a negative one which has led to highly charged emotional exchanges with families, partners and other professionals. This will have contributed to her reluctance to share such information with others for fear that she will simply be told to eat. It is thus important that you communicate an attitude of acceptance to your client and acknowledge the desperation and courage which are both aspects of her attempt to find a way of being through self-starvation and other methods of weight control. However, a balance needs to be struck to avoid overwhelming the client with questions about her eating habits: asking too many questions may lead her to feel exposed too soon and this may then lead her to feel out of control of the situation, something she will be highly sensitive to. It is difficult, yet important, to find a balance as this will determine whether a working alliance can be established.

Developing a working alliance

Anorexia and bulimia in many ways represent attempts at self-sufficiency. Of the two, anorexia is the more extreme assertion that nothing or no one is needed. As a therapist, this will be one of the main obstacles to helping the client. First sessions often focus on the client's feelings about seeking help and the implications of acknowledging their needs for their self-perception. The acknowledgement of needs may feel very threatening and it frequently serves to confirm the person's sense that she is a 'mess' and not in control of her life after all. This may then lead her to assuage such anxieties by restricting her eating even further, thereby reasserting her tenuous hold on her life.

The client may have many fantasies about what you will think of her. Will you think she is a 'mess' or 'greedy' if she confesses that she has had two apples instead of one? It is important to explore such anxieties and gradually to work towards a reframing of the problem, not solely in terms of the difficulties around eating, but also in terms of the client's difficulty in letting someone help her, as this is frequently experienced as a surrender of control.

A strong working alliance is an important prerequisite for change. It does, however, take time to develop and your commitment may be put to severe test. Sessions may be missed with no explanation given. You may be accused of not understanding even if you feel that you have done your best to do so. Working with people with eating problems requires developing a very particular kind of attunement to the client's needs as a mother does with her developing baby: too many questions and interpretations and they may feel overfed; too little response and they may feel unable to reach out. Just as some parents find it very distressing when their child refuses the breast or their food, as therapists we may also feel rejected when the thoughtful interpretations we feed to our clients are dismissed or, indeed, actively rubbished by the client. This is a not uncommon dynamic that may evolve between clients with eating problems and their therapists.

The person's distress about her eating behaviour, weight and appearance should all be taken seriously. It is important that you accept the individual's beliefs about her shape and weight as genuine. With time, it will also be important to challenge her beliefs – but it is best to wait until you have established a good working alliance with your client before you do so. Reassuring the client, appealing to her will-power or concentrating on achieving an ideal weight are all likely to alienate her because these do not address the deeper problems to which eating problems are a solution.

A major obstacle to establishing a working alliance with an anorexic client is, as has been previously mentioned, the anorectic's resistance, resentment and defiance which may elicit very strong negative reactions in the therapist. These need to be carefully monitored and explored in supervision so as not to allow them to lead to retaliatory responses on our part.

One of the aims of therapeutic work with an anorexic or a bulimic client is 'more than anything else the task of translating the symptoms into the realities and details of everyday life' (Lawrence, 1984: 100). This involves understanding the myriad ways in which anorexia and bulimia enhance or interfere with the client's life: what can she do or feel now that she could not do or feel before or, conversely, what limitations are now imposed on her life?

Negotiating goals

The therapeutic work should proceed at the client's pace and not at the therapist's. It is important to acknowledge and communicate to the person that 'getting better' or being 'cured' is not just synonymous with achieving a given weight or with a reduction in the use of laxatives, even though these may be the initial signs of recovery. Rather, it is important to convey to the client that what matters is how they feel about themselves and their world and that improvement can only, in the final analysis, be measured against what they value.

In negotiating goals it is important to share with the person an understanding that the symptoms of eating problems have an adaptive function. It is best to adopt a deconstructive rather than a destructive approach to the client's symptoms thereby acknowledging their protective power while also pointing out the cost to her life and well-being. This will help the person to feel reassured that you are not going to force them to eat too much too soon.

The therapeutic frame

People with eating problems are particularly sensitive to the boundaries of the therapeutic relationship. In order to understand their experience, it is helpful to view the therapeutic hour as though it were a meal. For the anorectic, meals are highly structured events. She will probably spend several hours planning what she will eat, down to the last calorie. It is often important, if not imperative, that she prepares her own meal. If eating with others, it may at times be hard to sit through a whole meal. She may fear being asked to eat more or she may fear that *she* will want to eat more unless she physically removes herself from the table. The acknowledgement of her hunger is highly threatening to her as it will have become symbolically equated with the acknowledgement of her needs and these remind her that she is not in control.

If we transpose the above observations to the therapeutic relationship, we can gain some helpful insights. It will be important to the anorectic that she feels in control of the therapeutic relationship and of how much she can take in at any one time. She is thus likely to be highly sensitive to deviations from the therapeutic boundaries, such as extending the session even if only by a few minutes, as this may lead her to feel over-fed. Or she may herself establish her own boundaries which may require some adaptation on the part of the counsellor. Equally, the bulimic client may find it difficult to hold on to the insights gained in a session as this may have become equated with the taking in of food. Once taken in, it cannot be kept in. Sessions may then be rubbished as if they were like a bad feed or they may be missed so as to purge herself of what had been taken in.

Sue, a 28-year-old anorexic client, finished her session each week a few minutes before I would say that it was time. As she got up to leave I would simply remind her that she had some time left. It was important to acknowledge that I was clear about the boundaries of our relationship even though it was Sue's prerogative to leave when she wanted. It was only several months later that Sue remarked on this particular pattern herself. By leaving the session early before I called time, Sue was attempting to retain some control in a situation which she experienced as very threatening. Just as she had described her fear at the dinner table with her parents who would insist that she should eat more, she feared that if she stayed till the end of the session I might also try to force-feed her. With time, Sue became able to stay till the end of her sessions.

Ethical considerations and dilemmas

There is little doubt that working with someone with an eating problem, particularly if she is severely emaciated or is purging very frequently, raises a number of ethical dilemmas for the therapist. By their very nature, eating problems have great power to disturb those who attempt to work in this field. This power stems from two sources: namely, the potentially life-threatening nature of anorexia and bulimia and the challenge it can pose to the therapist's personal beliefs about the importance of being thin.

It is not easy to watch someone wasting away before our very eyes. However, our own anxieties, which may lead us to act in ways that are not always necessarily 'therapeutic', may arise because we may be feeling unclear about the extent of our responsibility in relation to the individual who self-starves. Even if we appreciate the anorectic's anxieties surrounding weight gain and want to support her in overcoming these, as therapists it is also important that we clarify our own position in relation to the physical safety of the client.

Therapists vary with regard to the extent of a client's weight loss that they are prepared to work with. This may be less of an issue for those already working within a medical setting where it is likely that such decisions will be taken by a medical doctor. If working privately and the client is at or below 65–60 per cent of average expected body weight (AEBW), this represents a medical emergency. At a weight level of 50 per cent of AEBW the individual will die unless she eats. However, it is medically safe to work with someone who is at 75 per cent of AEBW, even though the medical consensus is that an individual is not 'cured' if her weight is restored only up to this level.

Our own anxieties may be alleviated if we carefully think through the limits of our responsibility as therapists. For instance, is it our responsibility if our client dies because we have not sought medical assistance? Conversely, what 'right' do we have to breach the confidentiality of the counselling relationship and contact the client's GP even against her wishes? Bearing in mind that many counsellors will not be faced with such extremes of behaviour, we need none the less to consider such ethical dilemmas. A way in which we may practically translate what we feel responsible for in relation to the individual who self-starves is in terms of the weight level below which we would not be prepared to work without also organising medical support.

More often than not the anorexic individual will not perceive her self-starvation as problematic. Rather, what is experienced as problematic are other people's attempts to interfere with the individual's dieting. This raises the difficult question of whether the anorectic's mental state is such that her self-starvation may be considered to be rational and self-directed. The prevailing view is that the anorectic's actions are actually out of control and irrational. It is on the basis of such views that the anorectic's compulsory admission to hospital is sanctioned under the Mental Health Act 1983 when there is a possible threat to the individual's life. Once admitted to hospital, the anorectic may be force-fed (intravenously) and may be subjected to a variety of treatment programmes to restore her to a 'normal' weight.

This course of action may at first appear to be justified in order to save a life. However, it also raises important ethical issues which arise whenever compulsory admission to hospital is enforced. Such issues are thus not specifically related to anorexia or bulimia and there are no simple solutions to questions of such philosophical and therapeutic importance. It may feel difficult and punitive having to tell a client that if she falls below a certain weight or if she continues to abuse laxatives you can only continue to work with her if she also seeks medical assistance. However, this is not necessarily a punitive stance. We are not asking the client to restore her weight to her AEBW, something which many anorectics would find extremely difficult. We are merely acknowledging that if she falls below a certain weight and does not receive medical help she might die.

Often the client may express anger at your setting of limits and may initially feel that you do not understand her and thereby feel rejected. However, she may also feel contained in knowing that you are clear about how far you are prepared to accompany her along the path of self-starvation. Duker and Slade (1988) have described the anorectic as being caught in a 'whirlpool of starvation' whereby she may have no sense that she can stop. By offering her clear boundaries, you may be providing her with a space within which she may not necessarily be forced to resume her AEBW but where she will know that she is not going to die.

If in the course of your work, your client shows signs of continuing to lose weight, this fact needs to be addressed. While some therapists may feel uneasy about sharing their own anxieties about a client's weight loss, we need not necessarily be reluctant to do so, as long as our anxiety is well grounded and informed and as long as we are consistent and not overwhelmed with panic. Indeed, it is not appropriate for therapists to remain unconcerned where their client's weight is at or below 65 per cent of AEBW and she is still cutting back on food. In such a situation it would be appropriate for them to share their anxiety as a fact relating directly to the client's deteriorating condition. This is a fact that needs to be communicated to the client in a straightforward manner that shows awareness of her feelings. For instance, you may tell your client that, while you know that she has been feeling good about her weight loss, you are concerned because she has continued to lose weight and you wonder whether there are times when she also feels concerned, but is finding it difficult to eat. It is important to own your anxieties while also opening up the possibility for the client to acknowledge her anxieties about her well-being and safety.

The dilemmas that result from the potentially life-threatening nature of anorexia and bulimia are not the only challenge that they pose to the therapist. By their very nature, eating problems also challenge the therapist's personal beliefs as the ordinary values that many people cherish play an important part in creating a potentially life-threatening condition. Female therapists, in particular, are likely to find that they share some, if not all, of the individual's values and aspirations regarding food regulation and self-control. It is not infrequent to hear female professionals in this field saying in passing 'I could do with a bit of anorexia myself.' Such comments are frequently laughed off but perhaps they warrant closer examination as they suggest a remarkable – and perhaps uncomfortable – similarity between those actions valued by our clients and those many of us also value. Recognising the similarities between ourselves and our clients is not easy. It can be disconcerting to realise the extent to which the client's extreme actions grow out of 'ordinary' values that we tend to take for granted.

Notes

1. The feminine pronoun is used to reflect the greater prevalence of eating problems in women.

2. This is calculated on the basis of a person's age, sex and height.

9

Psychosis

The nature of the problem

A few weeks ago I obtained final confirmation that I am Jesus. I wasn't sure up until then but when I saw the crucifixion and Mary spoke to me and I could feel the nails going through my hands, I knew. . . . Everything makes sense now. I feel calm, contented. I know what I have to do and once the whole world will know this I can get on with my work. I'm not sure when this will be but I'm not in a hurry anyway. I just feel it's important that I can explain to the world why there is so much unhappiness, you know, but I feel accepting now.
(Tony, age 32, diagnosed 'schizophrenic')

Tony is a small, thin man with a childlike face which one could describe as almost 'angelic'. The experiences he relates are not felt by him to be disturbing in any way. On the contrary, they appear to have lent meaning to his life. Yet he is considered to represent a risk to others. This is because Tony also believes that as Jesus Christ it is acceptable for him to have sexual relationships with young children. Tony cannot understand why people are worried about this. As far as he is concerned he loves the children and does not wish to harm them in any way. He is in fact condemnatory of those who are motivated by 'lust' as he considers this to be the work of the devil. He has not had any sexual relationships with either men or women but feels that now that he is sure that he is Jesus Christ he can legitimately have such relationships with young children.

Tony is described by his relatives as having always been a rather 'strange' child. He was an only child born to a somewhat older couple. He was very withdrawn as a baby and found it difficult interacting with peers when at school. His parents separated when he was nine but he has no recollection of these events and reports no feelings about it. He talks about his past in a flat, monotonous voice. Although he clearly experienced difficulties in interacting with others, he was quite successful academically and obtained a place at a good university. Tony had his first psychotic breakdown when he was in his first year at university. He experienced auditory hallucinations of people telling him he was Jesus Christ, could no longer concentrate on his work and became increasingly withdrawn and self-neglecting. He left university and managed to hold down a job for a few months but his psychotic symptoms worsened. He eventually stopped going to work altogether and was hospitalised several times. Although he expressed his belief that he was Jesus Christ at the time, he was not himself altogether convinced about this. It was only on his fourth admission to hospital – prompted by his attempts to meet young children which alarmed their parents – that he revealed the strength of his conviction in his belief that he was Jesus Christ.

Tony displays a number of *psychotic* symptoms which are typically associated with a diagnosis of schizophrenia, namely his delusional belief that he is Jesus Christ and his reports of auditory, visual and tactile hallucinations consisting respectively of voices speaking about him in the third person, his visions of the crucifixion and his sensations of the nails going through his hands. Schizophrenia is the psychiatric label given to a heterogeneous pattern of behaviours and modes of thinking primarily characterised by disordered thought and delusions. Because of the heterogeneity of the experiences and symptoms subsumed under the diagnosis of schizophrenia, the latter is the subject of continued controversy. In view of this we will focus here largely on describing and attempting to understand the nature and function of psychotic symptoms, while also concisely reviewing the problems and research findings associated with schizophrenia as a diagnostic entity.

Definitions and clinical features

Neurosis v. psychosis

At the simplest level, most of us can see the distinction between neurosis and psychosis in terms of our greater difficulty indentifying with the psychotic experience and our greater capacity to identify with the neurotic experience which we see in terms of exaggerated reactions to life circumstances. Psychosis, on the other hand, relates to experiences which feel to many to be qualitatively different. Although we may well in fantasy entertain the idea of being someone other than who we really are, in the main we are unlikely to assume this alternative identity completely and to behave accordingly. The psychotic individual, however, as in Tony's case, is more likely to identify himself totally with another figure and may come to believe that he is in fact that very person. Although it has been part of received wisdom that psychotic people rarely act on their delusions, more recent research suggests that this is in fact far more commonly the case, especially in response to persecutory delusions (Wessely et al., 1993).

From a more formal perspective, the distinction between neurosis and psychosis has traditionally focused on the question of the contact, or otherwise, with so-called reality. The varied uses of the term 'psychosis' have contributed to its imprecise and vague meaning. Broadly speaking, 'psychosis' refers to a state of being in which the person is unable to distinguish reality from his own thoughts, ideas, perceptions and imaginings. Here the term is used to refer to a spectrum of cognitive, behavioural and emotional experiences characterised by a marked impairment in the individual's capacity to remain in contact with reality and in his psychosocial functioning whereby his ability to interact with his environment is adversely affected. The psychotic state is taken here to refer to a heterogeneous set of experiences and to be on a continuum with so-called normal mental states resulting from a number of potentially interacting causes. While in a psychotic state, the individual may feel very confused and may display disorders of thought and expression, most typically manifested in delusional beliefs and hallucinatory experiences as in Tony's case, all of which are understood to represent the person's attempts to make sense of themselves and the world.

What is schizophrenia?

Before the end of the nineteenth century, there was some confusion about the different types of psychotic manifestation. Various German psychiatrists described different syndromes, namely hebephrenia and catatonia, but these were not distinguished from manic-depressive psychosis until Kraeplin made a distinction between what he called 'dementia praecox' (meaning premature mental deterioration) which later came to be called schizophrenia, and manic-depressive psychosis. This was on the grounds that the former condition normally began in adolescence and that it involved an irreversible mental deterioration, whereas manic-depressive conditions were characterised by relapses and remissions. By contrast, Eugen Bleuler, a Swiss psychiatrist, coined the term 'schizophrenia' (from the Greek *schizen* meaning 'to split' and *phren* meaning 'mind'). Because of its association with splitting, the term is often taken by the layperson to mean a split personality. Bleuler was, however, referring not to a splitting of the personality but rather to a split within or between different psychic functions within the individual. He believed that in the mind of the schizophrenic, emotions, ideas and perceptions no longer operated as an integrated whole. One set of ideas might dominate the personality, while other thoughts or drives were split off and became impotent. Emotions might also be split off from perceptions and thus seem very inappropriate in a given situation. To use Bleuler's words, 'the personality loses its unity' (1950 edn: 9). While Bleuler was most sensitive to the frightening and debilitating experiences of his psychotic patients, unlike Kraeplin, he remained more optimistic about the chances of recovery.

Presently, schizophrenia is diagnosed when the following criteria are met (DSM-IV):

1 Two or more of the following, if present during a one-month period for a significant portion of the time:
   • delusions
   • hallucinations
   • disorganised speech (for example, incoherence)
   • grossly disorganised or catatonic behaviour
   • negative symptoms (for example, apathy)
2 For a significant portion of the time the person is impaired by contrast to the level achieved prior to onset in one or more areas of functioning such as work, self-care and interpersonal relationships.
3 Continuous signs of disturbance persisting for at least six months.
4 The disturbance is not due to the effects of a substance (for example, drugs).

Schizophrenia is a controversial diagnosis as it is by no means clear what schizophrenia is and what it is not as the diagnosis has varied cross-culturally, although there now appears to be considerable agreement over it in European countries and in the developing world. This should not, however, be taken as undisputable evidence that there exists such a thing as schizophrenia as agreement over its diagnosis may simply reflect increases in the reliability with which the diagnosis is now made. Reliability in diagnosis in no way implies, however, that schizophrenia is a valid construct. Approaching the subject from the standpoint of the philosophy of science, Boyle (1990, 1994) has argued that there is no convincing evidence that schizophrenia is a valid diagnostic entity or that there exists a recognisable pattern of abnormal phenomena which can be unamibiguously shown to be symptomatic of brain dysfunction. Although the controversy over the validity of the concept of schizophrenia continues, it is now held by many to be a stress-related biological disorder, that is, stress can trigger a psychotic breakdown in a vulnerable individual. This vulnerabiity is conceptualised differently by the various theoretical schools (see below).

Psychotic symptomatology

The actual experience of being in the grip of a psychotic episode has been likened to the experience of dreaming. In dreams our minds are flooded by thoughts and sensations whose logical connections and meaning may elude us. We may feel persecuted and frightened by bizarre occurrences or alternatively feel ourselves to be all powerful. Our emotions might strike as wholly inappropriate in our waking state. In dreams the chaotic and the fantastical are real to us just as the experiences of the psychotic may feel intensely real to the individual experiencing them. Psychotic symptoms manifest themselves as disturbances in thought content, speech, perception and mood.

Thought content Abnormalities of thought content typically make themselves apparent in the form of *delusions* which are frequently of a paranoid nature. *Delusions of reference* refer to the belief that one is being abnormally attended to, such as the belief that one is being spied upon or talked about on television. In *thought alienation*, the person believes that his thoughts are under the influence of some external force which controls his thinking. *Passivity experiences* include the belief that one's actions, emotions or sensations are being constructed and controlled outside of the self by an alien force, at times against the person's will. This may include *thought withdrawal* where the individual experiences his thoughts as being taken out of his mind, and *thought insertion*, where thoughts which are not recognised as originating from oneself are reported to have been inserted into the person's mind. Such phenomena are examples of what is termed 'ego boundary disturbance'; that is, the person is no longer able to delineate where his own internal world of thoughts, feelings and intentions ends and the external world begins. *Thought disorder* is also observed in some people and includes a rather heterogeneous group of difficulties in the form, as opposed to the content, of thought. It is typically characterised by loosening of association in which shifts in topic are only very loosely connected so that speech tends to be incoherent.[1] This is different to 'flight of ideas' where, notwithstanding extremely rapid speech and thought, the rapidly changing topics usually have understandable points of connection. In extreme cases of thought disorder there may be a jumble of unrelated words also referred to as 'word salad'.

Delusions deserve more detailed consideration as they have long been considered to be the basic characteristic of madness (Jaspers, 1963). They are defined in DSM-IV as 'erroneous beliefs that usually involve a misinterpretation of perceptions or experiences'. Although some recurrent themes have emerged from attempts to define a delusional belief, a concise and universally accepted definition has not been forthcoming. Definitions have included such criteria as the belief being held with absolute conviction, being unmodifiable and lacking in cultural determinants. However, it is clear from recent work that conviction in delusions is not always total nor unchanging (Kingdon et al., 1994) and that delusions are open to modification (Garety, 1991; Tarrier, 1994). Delusions are held with different degrees of intensity and last for varying lengths of time. Moreover, it has been suggested that the cognitive processes whereby delusions are formed differ in no important respects from those by which non-delusional beliefs are formed (Maher, 1988).

Theories of delusion formation have proliferated. Psychoanalysts were foremost in seeing delusions as meaningful and as expressions of individuals' premorbid desires or fantasies. Delusional beliefs may serve to bind anxiety, justify particular actions or give support to defensive concerns (Lansky, 1977). The fixity or incorrigibility traditionally ascribed to delusional beliefs are probably characteristic of any challenged belief, delusional or not, if that belief enhances or actually supports self-esteem. Indeed, that which frequently distinguishes delusional beliefs from other beliefs is the sense of specialness, for instance as in grandiose delusions, that the delusion confers on its holder but that is not based in any way on the person's actual circumstances. By conferring a sense of specialness, the delusion may be understood as being restitutive of self-esteem. This was poignantly highlighted in study by Roberts (1991). He looked at a group of chronically deluded patients compared to a group of previously deluded patients now in remission and two non-patient groups. He found that the chronically deluded patients scored more highly on a measure of perceived purpose and meaning in life and reported lower levels of depression and suicidal ideation in contrast to the goup of patients in remission. This strongly suggested that for some deluded people there may be satisfaction in psychosis as the delusion serves an adaptive function helping them to overcome past hurts and disappointments.

Maher (1988) conceptualises psychotic phenomena generally as the result of an entirely understandable attempt to account for abnormal perceptual experiences. He suggests, for example, that the individual who hears voices searches for an explanation for this puzzling experience. Because the experience itself is so 'strange', this leads to an abnormal explanation such as the voice is being transmitted from an alien spaceship. The explanation, albeit odd, brings about relief and this serves to maintain the delusional belief. Others have understood delusions as resulting from abnormal brain states such as organic brain damage (Cutting, 1985); others still as the result of a reasoning bias whereby deluded people are seemingly more influenced by stimuli immediately present in the environment and make less use of previously acquired information, resulting in a type of 'jumping to conclusions' response style (Garety, 1991). In addition, a cognitive bias has also been identified in the maintenance of paranoid delusions resulting from selective attention to threat as well as a tendency to make external attributions for negative events and internal attributions for valued outcomes – the converse of depression where we observe more typically the tendency to make internal attributions for negative events (Bentall, 1992).

Some delusional beliefs, though often bizarre, at times may none the less have a culturally acceptable equivalence in beliefs which are more widespread, such as the belief that thoughts are being put into someone's mind, which finds its more acceptable equivalent in telepathy. Delusions of control by external forces also resemble beliefs in the supernatural. Although such beliefs are scientifically disputable, they are none the less widespread in Western culture and held by people we would not regard as psychotic (Cox and Cowling, 1989). Relating such culturally acceptable beliefs to psychotic phenomena could assist us in destigmatising them to clients and laying them open for exploration of their personal meaning to the individual. Fleeting, grandiose or paranoid ideas are by no means uncommon experiences for many of us, but at times of stress the search for meaning might lead to more ready acceptance of such beliefs, all the more so where the individual might be isolated (Johnson, 1988).

It is important, therefore, to be mindful of the degree to which the definition of a delusion or a hallucination is culturally relative. It is evidently the case that the accepted beliefs of some cultures (witchcraft, the existence of God) could be regarded as delusional in others. In practice, this means that therapists working in this field must always consider the delusional status of a person's beliefs in terms of their being inconsistent not only with the available evidence but also with the prevailing beliefs in the social and cultural group the person identifies with.

Perceptual abnormalities The most dramatic type of perceptual disorder is the *hallucination*, a sensory perception which is said to occur in the absence of any appropriate external stimulus. Freud (1900) affirmed the ubiquity of hallucination in our mental life by suggesting that the baby hallucinates the breast when it has a need for it. Studies of the 'normal' population suggest that between 10 and 50 per cent of people have experienced auditory or visual hallucinations (Bentall and Slade, 1985). Across cultures we can observe marked differences in attitude to the experience of hallucinations where we find that some cultures do not respond to them as signs of pathology (Al-Issa, 1995).

Hallucinations, particularly of the auditory type, are very common in psychosis. They usually take the form of a voice or voices referring to the individual in the third person ('he' or 'him') and which comment, argue about or direct the individual. At times the voices may be obscene or highly critical. Visual, olfactory, gustatory and tactile hallucinations also occur but are less common.

While many people who are psychotic are able to recognise that the voices they hear are only in their heads, many others are unsure whether their hallucinations are real or imagined and a smaller proportion are in fact convinced that their hallucinations are perceptions of objectively real events. Some authors have argued that voices are not auditory hallucinations at all but reflect disturbances in the person's self-consciousness instead of perceptual disturbances (Stephen and Graham, 1994). The voices that people report are said to be the person's own voice, reflecting their thoughts or inner speech but the person has the impression that the voice and the speech acts it expresses are those of another. As with any overt behaviour, whether individuals regard an episode of their inner speech as something they wilfully cause to happen depends on whether they find its occurrence explicable in terms of their own theory of their intentional state. Along similar lines, Bentall et al. (1994) have hypothesised that hallucinatory experiences occur when there is a failure to attribute internal, mental events to the self, leading to misattribution to a public source.

Research suggests that the distress occasioned by voices is linked not simply to the fact or content of the auditory hallucination but to the beliefs that the person holds about them. While all voices are appraised as being powerful, some are interpreted as benevolent, others as malevolent. Those who believe the latter are distressed when they hear the voices (Chadwick and Birchwood, 1994) and are consequently more motivated to comply with the various psychological and medical treatments offered to them.

Speech The disturbances in thinking present in psychosis can give rise to disturbances in speech whereby the person's speech may reveal unusual logic or the idiosyncratic use of words or made-up words, known as *neologisms*. Words and phrases may also be combined into what appears to be a completely disorganised fashion, producing what is referred to as *word salad*.

Mood Disturbances in mood are not uncommon and manifest themselves as *incongruous affect* whereby the person's emotional responses are not in keeping with the situation, such as inappropriate laughing when given bad news. However, such incongruous responses may also reflect the individual's psychotic experiences such as being on the receiving end of threatening auditory hallucinations. In addition, *flatness of affect* – a kind of emotional blunting – is frequently observed.

Secondary depression in schizophrenia is also often described. In a review of 29 studies, Siris (1991) reports varying figures ranging from 20 per cent during the year following an acute episode to 45 per cent concurrent with an acute episode. Suicide in people with a diagnosis of schizophrenia, which may affect up to 10 per cent of people, is associated with a history of depression (Drake and Cotton, 1986). The association between depression and schizophrenia has been variously explained as a consequence of neuroleptic medication, as an intrinsic part of the psychotic process itself and as a psychological response to an apparently uncontrollable life event (that is, schizophrenia as an illness). The latter suggestion receives frequent clinical confirmation as many people who experience a psychotic breakdown report major changes in their lives, including family and work disruption, stigma, loss and rejection, all of which contribute to a state of depression. In such circumstances, depression can be understood as a not unsurprising response to circumstances which are experienced as beyond the person's control and which challenge the person's very sense of their own identity.

'Negative' symptoms   The experience of psychosis is frequently accompanied by other symptoms such as apathy, social withdrawal, motivational problems, lack of responsiveness and underactivity. These are particularly associated with a diagnosis of schizophrenia and are referred to as 'negative symptoms' by contrast to the 'positive symptoms' we have just reviewed. Unlike positive symptoms, negative symptoms are not usually responsive to medication but tend to improve with the help of psychosocial interventions. Although the medication may be partly responsible for some negative symptoms, such as apathy and underactivity, historical evidence suggests that such symptoms were observed even before the introduction of neuroleptic medication. The presence of negative symptoms at discharge is an important predictor of poor outcome. One study found that those patients who were still displaying negative symptoms at discharge were more impaired in their social functioning at one- and two-year follow-ups (Hwu et al., 1995).

Epidemiology

Prevalence and incidence

Prevalence studies of schizophrenia have produced different rates, largely as a consequence of differences in the diagnostic criteria used by researchers. Notwithstanding such problems, it is generally reported that 1 per cent of adults is diagnosed as schizophrenic at some time during their lives. The annual incidence (the number of new cases per year) is roughly 15–20 per 100,000 in the UK.

Age and gender

The peak incidence of schizophrenia occurs between 25 and 30 years of age and onset prior to adolescence is rare. There are no significant gender differences in the rate of occurrence of schizophrenia in the industrial world. However, this apparent similarity masks the fact that there appear to be wide differences between the sexes in the incidence of schizophrenia at specific ages (Warner, 1994). The incidence is roughly twice as great for men aged 15–24 years than for women of the same age. Warner accounts for this discrepancy with respect to labour market stress. He argues that this peak for men may actually reflect the career and work-related stress placed upon men at that stage of life as their participation in the labour market is substantially greater than women at all ages. It is when we look at the 25–34 age range that the incidence of schizophrenia in women rises. This may reflect the life stresses which present themselves more typically to women in this age range, such as childbearing and childrearing, both of which require women to make substantial and often stressful role adjustments.

Gender differences have also been noted with respect to outcome. Women who receive a diagnosis of schizophrenia appear on the whole to fare better than men. One follow-up study of schizophrenic patients who had been hospitalised in Finland showed that women were more likely than men to be symptom-free, working and functioning independently (Salokanges, 1983). This is understood by Warner (1994) to be a function of labour force dynamics, whereby women are more likely than men to have a valued social role when not earning a wage which may facilitate their reintegration into their communities following hospitalisation and decrease the likelihood of stigma and devaluation.

Social class

Higher rates of schizophrenia are reported in the lower social classes and in inner-city areas. Such findings have been interpreted quite differently. Some have argued that this social class skew results from the consequences of schizophrenia and the handicaps associated with it which lead individuals with the diagnosis to drift into lower status occupations and low income inner-city areas. This is known as the 'social drift hypothesis' (Turner and Wagenfeld, 1967). Other authors understand the predominance of working-class people as a result of the greater stresses on this group which render them more vulnerable to developing schizophrenia. In rural areas the social class gradient is absent. This may reflect the drifting away from rural areas of people with a diagnosis of schizophrenia. Alternatively, as Warner (1994) suggests, it may be a function of the difference in the level and nature of the stresses of rural and urban working-class life.

Cross-cultural perspectives

The prevalence of schizophrenia is significantly lower in the developing world. This is most probably due to the general finding that people with a diagnosis of schizophrenia in the developing world are not only more likely to recover quickly, as we shall see later, but also to die young by comparison with the industrial world. The incidence of schizophrenia is, however, roughly similar in both the developing and industrial worlds (WHO, 1973).

One of the most interesting findings to emerge from cross-cultural research is that the outcome for individuals experiencing a psychotic breakdown is better in the developing world even though psychiatric care is low on their list of priorities (Jablensky et al., 1992). In an engaging discussion of the role of social and economic factors in the course and outcome of schizophrenia, Warner (1994) puts forward a number of explanations for this finding. First, he argues that if we accept that the work role is important in giving individuals a sense of purpose, belonging, status and value within their community, then it may well be that the high productivity demands and competitive performance requirements in the West are particularly unsuitable for someone recovering from a psychotic episode, preventing their re-entry into his or her community.

The importance of social expectations geared around a psychotic episode cannot be overstated. The social consensus for recovery and the willingness and the capacity of a community to reintegrate the psychotic individual are influenced, Warner suggests, by whether the individual can serve a useful social role. This is more likely to be possible in the developing world as it benefits from traditional community life. In this sense it is of interest to note that in the developing world the outcome of schizophrenia is worse in the well educated – a finding which can be accounted for by the greater labour market stresses affecting those with a higher degree of education.

Secondly, Warner draws our attention to the value of the so-called 'folk diagnosis' of schizophrenia typically found in the developing world whereby the features of psychosis can actually lead to an elevation in status. The sociologists Rogler and Hollingshead (1965), for instance, found that Puerto Ricans who displayed the symptoms of schizophrenia and who consulted a spiritualist were not only more likely to recover than those who went to a psychiatric hospital, but were also so successful in their social reintegration that their wives found them more acceptable as husbands that did the wives of non-schizophrenic men!

Finally, Warner suggests that the extended family structure found in the developing world allows for a diffusion of emotional over-involvement and interdependence among family members which benefits recovery. This is in keeping with one of Wing's (1978) criteria for a successful outcome in schizophrenia, namely freedom for the individual from emotional demands or criticisms within the family.

Cross-cultural research, as we saw in Chapter 1, has also alerted us to the tendency of professionals to overdiagnose schizophrenia in people from ethnic minorities in comparison to their indigenous counterparts. Taken together, the evidence from cross-cultural research serves as an important reminder that even if it could be proved beyond doubt that schizophrenia is a biological disorder, the part played by sociocultural factors – including the economic forces in a given culture – in its onset, course and outcome cannot be ignored. Counselling or psychotherapy are thus best viewed as adjuncts to other socio-environmental interventions.

Theoretical approaches

Schizophrenia as one of the functional, as opposed to the organic, psychoses has generated a vast amount of literature regarding its aeti-ology, perhaps reflecting our own need to understand and encapsulate an experience which threatens us. It is now generally thought to be a stress-related biological disorder and various models have been proposed to account for it. The question of aetiological heterogeneity has been raised (Murray et al., 1992).

Genetic theories

All experts are agreed that if anything is inherited in schizophrenia it is a predisposition to it rather than a certainty of developing it. Genetic models are supported by the general finding that, whereas the lifetime risk for schizophrenia in the general population is approximately 1 per cent, the risk for an individual who has a sibling or parent who is schizophrenic is about 12 per cent, and for the child with two parents with schizophrenia it is approximately 40 per cent. For narrowly defined schizophrenia (as for bipolar affective disorder), the lifetime risk of developing schizophrenia in first-degree relatives is 5–20 times higher than that of general population controls (Tsuang and Faraone, 1990). The concordance rates for dizygotic twins have also been found to be roughly that of normal siblings, whereas the concordance rates for monozygotic twins lies in the range of 40–60 per cent even when the twins have been reared apart. Studies of people adopted in infancy lend further support to a genetic model of aetiology for they suggest that the children of schizophrenic parents share a similar increased prevalence of schizophrenia whether they are raised by their biological or their adoptive parents (Kety et al., 1976).

On the face of it, the evidence from both twin and adoption studies is compelling. However, as Boyle (1990) has thoroughly documented, such studies are replete with both methodological and conceptual problems which cast significant doubt on their validity, such as how the samples were selected and how zygosity was determined, not to mention the way in which schizophrenia itself was diagnosed in the various studies. In addition, it is clear that even if one uncritically accepts the findings from such studies they do not in themselves provide sufficient evidence for a genetic basis to schizophrenia. This is because, even though identical twins share the same genetic make-up, the risk of both twins developing schizophrenia is only in the order of 40–60 per cent. Moreover nearly two-thirds of people with a diagnosis of schizophrenia have no relative at all with a similar diagnosis (Gottesman, 1991). Generally speaking, the more controlled the studies, the lower the concordance rates. The variability in outcome even in cases where there is a family history of schizophrenia strongly suggests that environmental factors are implicated in its aetiology.

Biochemical theories

It is the case that changes in mood, for example, have a biochemical basis and it is therefore unsurprising to find that the symptoms of schizophrenia are also correlated with certain changes in the brain's biochemistry. Biochemical models which strive to account for the emergence of psychotic symptoms have focused on abnormalities in the action of chemical neurotransmitters. The 'dopamine hypothesis' has received the most widespread support. It suggests that an overactivity in the tracts of neurones in which the neurotransmitter is dopamine is the underlying biochemical deficit in schizophrenia. In situations of acute stress the dopamine turnover increases and this, in turn, may precipitate a psychotic episode in a vulnerable individual (Meltzer and Stahl, 1976). The evidence for the dopamine hypothesis comes from two sources, namely that antipsychotic drugs work by reducing the activity in dopaminergic tracts and that amphetamine, which is known to increase the release of dopamine in the brain, will produce an acute psychosis if it is taken in sufficient amounts.

While the dopamine hypothesis is seductive, it has not gone un-criticised. For example, Jackson (1990) in a review of the literature highlights that no consistent differences in dopamine levels have been found between drug-free schizophrenics and normal subjects. Research on other neurochemical substances has also failed to produce any consistent findings.

Structural theories

Structural abnormalities in the brain have also been implicated but the evidence for such abnormalities has been slow to accumulate. Post-mortem studies of the brains of people diagnosed as schizophrenic have failed to produce general agreement on any neuroanatomical changes specific to schizophrenia. However, some evidence for anatomical changes in the brain has resulted from computed tomographic (CT) scans which have revealed mild cerebral atrophy in a proportion of people with schizophrenia (van Horn and McManus, 1992). The cause of such atrophy is not known but it is believed possibly to reflect earlier non-specific brain injury from intrauterine drug effects, birth trauma, viral infections and influenza (Takei et al., 1994). For example, a study carried out in the UK suggests that maternal influenza between the third and seventh month of pregnancy is associated with an increased risk of schizophrenia to the child in adult life (Sham et al., 1992). Other studies suggest that people with schizophrenia show complex alterations in regional patterns of brain activity rather than any single deficit in brain function (China and McKenna, 1995).

Work on the brain functioning of people with schizophrenia has highlighted that most people with schizophrenia, as well as their close relatives, show an abnormal response to environmental stimuli, that is, they appear to be overly responsive to sensory information (sights, sounds) and experience difficulty in blotting out irrelevant material. The capacity to discriminate stimuli and to focus attention – tasks which we take for granted – may be disrupted in people with schizophrenia. If this is so, given sufficient stress, the individual could become overwhelmed, leading to an increase in arousal. The response of withdrawal typically observed in schizophrenia may be understood as an adaptation by the person to their excessive vigilance towards irrelevant stimuli. Such a formulation is still speculative.

In conclusion, both structural and biochemical models of schizophrenia have received mixed support. This is unsurprising given that the term schizophrenia itself covers an heterogeneous set of experiences with most probably varying aetiology, course and outcome (Bentall, 1990).

Social theories

Frequently reported in the literature is an association between life events and schizophrenia even though the results of research in this area have been largely ambiguous. There is, however, considerable evidence that changes in a person's social environment or too much pressure on clients in rehabilitation programmes can lead to the emergence or re-emergence of psychotic symptoms in vulnerable individuals. A comparatively recent review of the literature on this association concludes that while there does appear to be a relationship between life events and psychotic symptoms over time in those who are vulnerable to schizophrenia, there is less convincing evidence that people diagnosed as schizophrenic have experienced higher levels of life-event stressors than those people with other diagnoses (Norman and Malla, 1993).

Psychological theories

Psychological models have proliferated over the past 30 years. They have focused on cognitive and perceptual abnormalities, on the patterns of communication within families, as well as the aetiological importance of early experience as postulated by psychoanalytic theory. Let us briefly review these.

Cognitive and perceptual abnormalities   Researchers have postulated a primary attentional deficit in schizophrenia, leading to a decrease in the selective and inhibitory functions of attention thereby flooding the individual with stimuli (McGhie and Chapman, 1961). Broadbent (1971) extended this model and proposed a specific deficit in what he termed 'pigeon holing', that is, a filter mechanism which screens irrelevant stimuli from a limited capacity decision channel. This deficit would account for the difficulty people with schizophrenia are reported to have in screening out irrelevant information. However, Hemsley (1988) suggests that the evidence for this is as yet inconsistent.

People with schizophrenia have also been said to show a deficit in information processing which manifests itself as generalised slowness when performing a variety of tasks, such as choice reaction time experiments. What appears to be most difficult is for the individual to respond in situations where there is greater response uncertainty. This is compatible with Broadbent's 'pigeon holing' deficit.

Finally, Frith (1979) has postulated a deficit in the mechanism that controls and limits the contents of consciousness. He accounts for psychotic symptoms in terms of a specific cognitive impairment. Within this system delusions, for example, are conceptualised as attempts to explain and understand the misperceptions resulting from this basic impairment. While this is an interesting proposition, this model fails to account for the fact that psychotic people sometimes show no such impairment and are able to function without their psychotic symptoms. Psychological approaches which have focused on the reasoning styles of people with schizophrenia have stressed another possible deficit in information processing which suggests that people with delusional beliefs are unable to weigh up new evidence and so modify their beliefs.

The role of the family   Family dynamics have long been held to play a part in the aetiology of schizophrenia. Such a view was crystallised in the writings of the psychoanalyst Frieda Fromm-Reichmann (1948), who suggested that some mothers, described as cold and distant, fostered schizophrenia in their children. The anthropologist Bateson et al. (1956) put forward his 'double bind hypothesis' which postulated that a pathogenic parent presented paradoxical communication to the child which contained contradictory messages (that is, contradiction between the content of a verbal message and the tone of voice). Taking further the theme of communication problems in the family, Laing and Esterson (1970) viewed schizophrenia as a valid and understandable response to confusing patterns of communication. Such theories became very popular and led to the widespread assumption that schizophrenia is somehow caused by the family, but recent research does not confirm this causal hypothesis. Nevertheless, abnormalities in patterns of communication have been observed in the families of people with schizophrenia that are not evident in families without a schizophrenic member.

Family factors are now believed to play an important part in influencing relapse. Attempts to measure the possible mediating factors in relapse led to the development of a semi-structured interview – the Camberwell Family Interview – which measures the emotional atmosphere in the home. Frequency ratings are made from an audio-taped interview of critical comments and positive remarks; overall ratings are made of warmth, hostility and emotional over-involvement. This results in an overall rating of expressed emotion (EE) in the family. Studies using the EE measure have consistently found that a measure of high EE in the family (where there is a high level of criticism, hostility and emotional over-involvement) predicts relapse in follow-up studies (Bebbington and Kuipers, 1994). However, such research does not elucidate whether the observed communication problems are the cause or the effect of the psychogical problems in the psychotic family member. In addition, such research has been criticised on the grounds that relapse is often defined in terms of the presence of psychotic symptoms, without paying attention to general social func-tioning. It is debatable how truly representative of family functioning one audiotaped session of family interaction can really be. It has also been suggested that the phenomenon of EE is largely limited to Western cultures (e.g. Leff et al., 1987; Jenkins, 1991). For example, lower levels of EE have been found in families of the Mexican Americans in California who tend to maintain traditional extended family ties and who explicitly recognise interdependence within the family, by contrast to counterpart Anglo-American families.

Psychodynamic theories

Several psychodynamic theories of causation have been proposed. Freud originally understood schizophrenia as a withdrawing of the libido into the self so that the outside world became meaningless and was replaced by a more meaningful inner world of fantasy. By directing the libido inwards, the individual is more likely to feel estranged and depersonalised. Essentially, psychotic conditions were seen to represent a regression to more primitive modes of thinking, i.e. to primary process thinking which has little regard for logic or reality testing. Melanie Klein understood psychotic conditions as being characterised by a domination of primitive defense mechanisms such as splitting and projective identification. The psychotic person was thought to be prey to his inner world of phantasy which led to a distortion in his perception of reality.

Although there is no unanimity, many psychoanalytically orientated therapists, while not necessarily denying the role of constitutional and biological factors, understand schizophrenia as a developmental problem resulting from negative interpersonal experiences early in life. There is certainly no paucity of literature documenting emotional and physical deprivation in the lives of those who later receive a diagnosis of schizophrenia (Strean, 1989). Such literature highlights the difficulties the individual experiences in relating to others, describing those who have either lost or never achieved a sense of trust with others and therefore fall back on a predominantly paranoid orientation to the world.

Current interventions

Course and outcome

When schizophrenia was originally described it was thought to have an inevitably deteriorating course. Longitudinal studies, however, suggest that schizophrenia can be more episodic in nature (Harding et al., 1987). Nevertheless, the outcome for schizophrenia is generally worse than for any other diagnosis. It is associated with a high risk of mortality through suicide and physical illness usually caused by self-neglect.

Generally speaking, following a first psychotic episode, 15–25 per cent return to premorbid levels of functioning; 30–35 per cent make a partial recovery and are vulnerable to further relapses; 40 per cent relapse chronically; and 10 per cent present a chronically disabled picture and are likely to remain hospitalised over long periods of time. This variable outcome is in part predictable from the following factors:

- age – early onset carries a less favourable prognosis
- sex – men fare worse than women
- marital status – single people have a worse outcome
- gradual onset without a clear precipitating cause
- family history of schizophrenia
- poor previous work record
- high expressed emotion in the home environment

Medication

Any psychological approach to schizophrenia needs to be considered alongside the widespread prescription of neuroleptics (anti-psychotic medication) (Hemsley, 1994). Such drugs may be taken orally or by injection, referred to as 'depot antipsychotic'. The effects of the injection last for several weeks thus circumventing the problems encountered when people forget to take their medication. The most common neuroleptics are follows:

chlopromazine (Largactil)	promazine
thioridazine	trifluoperazine
flupenthixol	fluphenazine
pimozide	haloperidol
zuclopenthixol	clozapine

All these drugs are essentially similar but their efficacy varies from individual to individual. Indeed, although such drugs help some people by suppressing or attenuating psychotic symptoms, they do not work for everyone. Very little is actually known about how the drugs work except that most neuroleptics have a sedating effect and that most block dopamine receptors in the brain. Many people are prescribed neuroleptic medication alongside antidepressants. This is not only because some psychotic people are also depressed but also so as to counteract the depressive side-effects of some neuroleptics.

After initial enthusiam in the 1950s, when neuroleptics were first introduced, their inadequacies have now become apparent. Many people fail to adhere to their medication regimes (Buchanan, 1992) and, of those who do take the medication, 30–50 per cent will relapse in the first year (Hogarty et al., 1979). Others continue to experience psychotic symptoms despite medication. Importantly, many people experience unpleasant and sometimes irreversible side-effects. The commonest side-effects are the ones affecting the neuromuscular system leading to stiffness, restlessness and shakiness, otherwise referred to as 'extra-pyramidal effects' because of the effects on the extra-pyramidal system in the brain. Some people experience symptoms closely resembling Parkinson's disease, with difficulty in controlling the movements of the eyes and tongue, walking or shuffling with short steps and shaking of the hands. Another adverse effect which can be extremely uncomfortable is neuromuscular restlessness known as 'akathisia', which manifests itself in an inability to sit still and the irresistible urge to move – all of which can render sitting in a room with a therapist extremely difficult. The drugs can also affect the blood and bodily hormones, resulting in changes in menstruation, impotence and enlargement of the breasts. They also make the skin more sensitive to sunlight.

A very serious side-effect called 'tardive dyskinesia' (TD) can also develop as a result of damage to the extra-pyramidal system in the brain. It is a disorder of the central nervous system in which abnormal and uncontrollable muscular movements occur (for example, pursing and smacking of the lips, muscle tics and spasms). These can be experienced as very embarrassing by the afflicted individual. TD is unlikely if the medication has been taken for less than six months but is more common in people who have been on moderate to high doses for longer periods. If identified early, TD may disappear if the drugs are stopped. However, for the majority of people these side-effects are irreversible.

Psychological interventions

The psychological approaches to psychosis are now largely dominated by cognitive-behavioural and family interventions. *Cognitive-behavioural approaches* have proliferated and the results of preliminary studies are very encouraging (Garety et al., 1994). Such approaches make the problem of managing psychotic symptoms akin to the problem of managing a condition such as diabetes where the aim is to help the person to take responsibility for managing his or her own condition. When questioned, people who experience psychotic symptoms usually report having developed some self-styled strategies for coping with the symptoms, such as listening to a walkman to deal with auditory hallucinations or distracting themselves in other ways. Cognitive-behavioural approaches capitalise on such strategies by encouraging the individual to use them more systematically and to develop ever more adaptive coping strategies. In addition, emphasis is placed on challenging the evidence sustaining delusional beliefs with the aim of modifying such beliefs (Fowler et al., 1995).

Family interventions have been supported by the research on expressed emotion (EE) (see above). There exists considerable evidence now suggesting that it is possible to provide effective support for families and that this can significantly reduce the risk of relapse (Leff et al., 1990; Tarrier et al., 1989). Such interventions consist of a number of elements: a psycho-educational component (for instance, helping the family to understand that the lack of motivation and withdrawal are symptoms and not wilful behaviours on the part of the individual); problem-solving skills, and non-specific emotional support (Barraclough and Tarrier, 1992).

The efficacy of psychodynamic psychotherapy remains questionable, largely due to the paucity of well-controlled research with sufficiently big samples. On the basis of single case studies it seems, however, that some people derive benefits from such an approach. It is important to note that where such an approach has been used and has proved helpful, it has been within the context of considerable medical/psychiatric back-up in inpatient settings (Jackson and Williams, 1994). Even though it could be argued that anyone could benefit from a 'psychoanalytic attitude', as Jackson (1995) suggests, the selection of those people displaying psychotic symptoms who are suitable for psychoanalytically orientated psychotherapy is a very complex and highly specialised area. For a significant number of clients, therapies of a more supportive, as opposed to expressive, 'insight-orientated', nature appear to be more helpful (Gunderson et al., 1984).

Practical considerations in assessment and management

As we have just seen, a variety of therapeutic approaches has been applied to the alleviation of psychotic symptoms with some methods, such as cognitive-behavioural interventions, claiming an encouraging rate of success. Although psychodynamic approaches are, for many clients, not appropriate, the insights of those psychoanalysts who have attempted work with such clients are none the less very enlightening and can assist us in the management of psychotic clients (Ellwood, 1995). Counselling as an intervention has not itself been formally evaluated, but it is clear that underscoring all psychological approaches to psychosis there is an appreciation of the importance of listening to the individual's experiences and helping them to make some sense out of seeming psychic chaos.

Assessment

When encountering someone who reports delusions or hallucinations, the therapist needs to convey a genuine interest that is not collusive in understanding how such beliefs or experiences have developed and place them in a historical context which may highlight the meaning and function of these experiences to the individual. As Jackson and Williams (1994) remind us, simply listening to a person's delusional experiences and taking them seriously is helpful as this breaks the isolation often inflicted by psychosis. The aim is to give the person an experience of being listened to by someone who demonstrates in their approach a belief that the person's bizarre and frightening experiences may be understood in a less confusing way. Placatory answers tend to impair rapport, undermining the person's belief that she is taken seriously. The aim is to understand why the person needs a delusional explanation for her distress – many psychotic symptoms reveal meaningful content if care is taken to collect a careful personal history. At the assessment stage, it will therefore be important to devote time, not only to how the client explains her symptoms, but also to her developmental history as the following example highlights.

Mary, a 66-year-old woman, was admitted to hospital following a psychotic breakdown characterised by paranoid delusions that the council was after her, stealing her belongings and threatening to kill her, as well as visual hallucinations of war planes which were shining their lights on her. Her paranoid delusions made her very fearful of others, while her hallucinations appeared to bring about a measure of relief as she felt the war planes were 'keeping an eye' on her at a time when she definitely felt herself to be at war with the world.

Mary related her history to me conveying a sense of intrigue. She felt members of her family had plotted against her and that this was now continuing with the council – they all knew each other she told me. The intensity of her belief in her delusion indicated her need to hold fast to an important dimension of her history. As a child Mary had been left in the care of a mother who was herself quite disturbed. Mary left home when she was 14 years old and fell pregnant. Because of the times and the illegitimate status of her child, she was placed by her family in a mental institution, labelled 'mentally defective' and, once born, her baby was taken away from her. Her family refused to see her from that point onwards as she was told that she had shamed the family.

Mary felt deeply betrayed by her family and over the years developed a rather elaborate conspiracy theory, which while delusional on one level, clearly stemmed from her very real experience of having been abandoned and then totally rejected by her family as well as being separated from her own child without consultation about any of these

decisions. She recalled that while she was in the institution as a young woman she used to hear the war planes above her and dream of being whisked away by a soldier. These fantasies developed over the years into visual hallucinations which brought her relief when she felt lonely. The war planes were there to ensure her safety. As there was no one in the real external world that cared for Mary she herself created her own comforters – she had created a world where she was never alone.

Where the person reports hearing voices telling them to harm or kill themselves or others, or if they express delusional ideas (especially of a paranoid nature) which lead them to plan an attack, for example, on someone they believe to be following them, this should be taken very seriously and a referral for a psychiatric assessment should be made. If in any doubt as to whether the person is likely to act on what the voices are saying, a referral to a hospital casualty department is advised. This would be the case, for instance, if a mother who has recently given birth reports hearing voices telling her to kill her baby. This is not uncommon in cases of puerperal psychosis which affects a very small minority of women after childbirth.

Interpretative v. supportive work

Throughout the therapeutic literature the importance of a supportive, containing, relationship in work with psychotic individuals has been stressed. An episode of psychosis is frequently preceded and followed by a variety of psychosocial stresses which have implications for the day-to-day functioning of the person. People may lose their families, their jobs, their homes while contending with their inner experiences of psychic disintegration. Many feel hopeless in the face of an uncertain future and the fear of relapse, making the transition back to their everyday life an immensely challenging task. The opportunity to discuss their fears and anxieties with a supportive person who can bear to hear the distress can be very containing. This needs to take place in the context of a relationship where it is possible to destigmatise confusing and frightening experiences, while not losing sight of the fact that the extent of the person's difficulties may be such that he requires more than just a therapeutic relationship to manage his life (Kingdon and Turkington, 1991; 1994). The therapist can help the person to consider alternative explanations of such experiences by challenging the evidence for them rather than the belief itself. It is not the case that the therapist's version of events is necessarily the correct one but rather that some constructions of reality are more adaptive than others. For some people, however, their delusional beliefs bring comfort and relief in a life which would otherwise lack meaning (Roberts, 1991). In such cases, it is arguable whether an attempt should be made to challenge their beliefs even if they are judged by the therapist to be delusional in nature. However, delusions of a persecutory nature are very distressing and it is therefore helpful to facilitate an exploration of the delusional belief so as to help the person regain some control over his experiences and so not be dominated by his delusions.

Paranoid clients have a tendency to attribute negative events to external, global and stable causes (the reverse is often observed in depressed clients who are more likely to blame themselves when something goes wrong). In other words, they utilise projection to manage what they experience as 'bad' within themselves and for which they may fear retribution; one consequence of this is that the world may become a very frightening place. Delusions of persecution have been found to be closely related to a person's self-concept and, more specifically, the discrepancy between how the person perceives himself and how he would like to be (the ideal self) (Kinderman, 1994).

Although containment and support of the client is necessary, it is not always sufficient (Steiner, 1994). One danger is that the client comes to rely so much on the therapist to contain all the projected emotions that she fails to develop her own separate identity – a task which can only be achieved if the person is able to own again her painful and frightening mental contents. This suggests that there is a place for interpretative work with psychotic individuals helping them to understand their need to split off feelings and thoughts and project them into the outside world. Interpretations relate what may be frightening and alienating psychotic experiences to the person's past and present life, thereby stimulating an organisation of psychotic fragments into a unifying frame which lends meaning and decreases the sense of inner chaos.

The dangers of interpretative work are, however, well known (Benedetti, 1987; Mueser and Berenbaum, 1990). The psychotic individual presents with a very weak ego, that is, he does not necessarily have the capacity to stand back and observe himself, so that uncovering work of a psychodynamic nature may be too overwhelming. Indeed, as Steiner (1994) aptly points out, meaning is often dreaded by the psychotic person whose priority is to gain relief from mental pain. So while we as therapists may feel that the person needs to understand himself, and believe that his delusions are meaningful, we must be sensitive to the person's wish not to understand or to think about his experiences.

Although interpretative work should never be undertaken lightly and without the back-up of a supportive network, whether in the community or a hospital to manage those individuals who may need medical input, it remains encumbent on us to question any reluctance to engage in interpretative work with the psychotic individual. By remaining purely supportive in our role, we may be expressing our own unconscious need to inhibit in advance the person's aggressiveness towards us or our unconscious fear of facing the psychotic parts of our personality and, in so doing, deprive the person of an opportunity to face her experiences and discover her own inner strength (Searles, 1965).

Interpretative work is mostly only done by very experienced therapists. One of the reasons for this is because of the difficulty the psychotic person has with boundaries. In psychosis the question of where the psychotic self ends and the other person's self begins is of paramount importance and is a central feature of any kind of therapeutic work. In our everyday life a certain degree of blurring of boundaries between self and other is taken for granted. However, in psychosis the problematic nature of boundaries becomes explicit: 'For the psychotic the natural interweaving of self and other may turn into a terrifying sense of dissolution or invasion' (Eigen, 1986: 33). This carries a number of implications for therapeutic work whether of a supportive or interpretative nature.

First, while a more interactive approach is indicated with many psychotic individuals with less emphasis on fostering a transference relationship, increased activity on behalf of the therapist may be experienced as an 'implosion' that is, as intrusive, (Laing, 1959) in those whose ego boundaries have begun to disintegrate. Secondly, while some therapists work far more actively with the transference relationship, such work should be embarked upon extremely cautiously and only under supervision as it may be very difficult for the psychotic person to appreciate the 'as if' quality of the transference relationship because of the person's own precarious boundaries. In short-term therapeutic work, such interpretations are contraindicated as this may precipitate a further psychotic episode by intensifying the person's sense of unreality. It is often more helpful to the person to give unambiguous messages if the therapist is in some way incorporated into the person's psychotic experiences so as to draw the boundaries between client and therapist clearly. For example, if a psychotic client tells the therapist that he believes him to be the devil, it is important to acknowledge to the client how frightening it is to be in the room with someone he thinks is the devil, but also to remind him of the therapist's real identity and the purpose of their meeting (that is, to make sense together of such frightening experiences). This does not, of course, preclude the possibility of exploring why this happens.

The therapeutic alliance

A valuable contribution from psychoanalytic theory has been the notion of a psychotic part of the personality, with an autonomous existence which works against the development of rational thinking as this might give rise to intolerable psychic pain. This part of the personality will work against any therapeutic endeavour. In view of this, Rosenfeld (1965; 1987), a psychoanalytic practitioner with considerable experience in the field of psychosis, advocated the importance of creating a therapeutic alliance with the healthy side of the ego which may be able to hear and to bear psychological insights.

While the dangers of a very interactive style were outlined above, one of the most common problems when working with psychotic people is to engage them in the therapeutic work. This can be helped if the therapist is willing to establish contact with the person's real existence and to engage in a 'real' relationship with him, not only one which is a symbolic mirror of earlier realities. The therapist can act as a mirror to the saner part of the personality which has been destroyed or denied by the psychosis (Benedetti, 1987).

Countertransference issues

Working with people who are psychotic represents one of the most challenging areas of clinical work. This is largely because such work places the therapist under considerable emotional pressure. The therapist's own primitive modes of experience and interpersonal relationships are subject to being revived in the course of the work (Searles, 1979). The pressure is partly in response to the many projections, often quite violent, that the client makes onto the therapist and which the therapist has to manage. Failure to do so may confirm the client's fears that their projections have damaged the therapist. In order to manage the client's projections, the therapist needs to understand and contain his or her own hidden psychotic areas and the associated anxieties of psychic disintegration. As Rosenfeld put it: 'The most frequent but often unconscious anxiety is the fear of being driven mad by the patient' (1987: 18). Because of the internal pressures the therapist may be put under, it is essential when undertaking such work that the therapist is well supported by peers and in his or her own therapy if that is available.

Note

1. Often only the incoherence in speech which typifies thought disorder is apparent. If one knows the person and their history and takes into account the context in which the interaction takes place it may be possible to identify meaningful links (see, e.g., Laing (1959)). This view is not however held by all mental health practitioners.

10
Personality Disorders

What is personality?

Personality disorder is one of the most controversial categories in psychopathology. The concept first appeared in the psychiatric literature in the nineteenth century where it was used to denote alterations in consciousness and included states such as hysterical dissociation (Berrios, 1993). What was then referred to variously as 'character', 'temperament' or 'constitution' is essentially what we now view as 'personality'. The very notion of personality itself is, however, problematic. As Allport (1937: 27) incisively put it, 'Personality is one of the most abstract words in our language and like an abstract word suffering from excessive use its connotative significance is very broad, its denotative significance negligible. Scarcely any word is more versatile'.

Even though the word, as Allport suggests, has become so versatile as to be perhaps meaningless, the notion of personality is part of our psychological language. The critical question is whether there exists such an entity as a 'personality' or do we only possess a series of behavioural dispositions that are activated depending on internal stimuli (for example, fantasies, feelings) and external stimuli. It would none the less be fair to say that most people recognise particular traits in themselves which are experienced as representative or in some way characteristic of their person. Some, for example, feel themselves to be shy and reserved, while others are more extroverted or easily excitable.

Although temperamental proclivities may be more or less obvious depending on the situations in which people find themselves, personality traits are believed, by some theorists, to retain some stability over time and across situations (Millon, 1995). Indeed, a common distinction in the literature has been drawn between personality traits and states, the former referring to characteristics which are fairly constant, while the latter refers to more situation-specific responses. Personality traits are defined in DSM-IV as 'enduring patterns of perceiving, relating to and thinking about the environment and oneself that are exhibited in a wide range of social and personal contexts' (APA, 1994).

Personality traits can thus be said to refer to prominent features of a person's behavioural repertoire.

Some authors have placed particular emphasis on the interaction between the person and the environment as the major determinant of an individual's responses rather than on assumed stable personality. While such an interactional approach should underscore any attempt to understand how and why an individual responds to a given situation or event in a particular manner, clinically we encounter people who, with respect to a number of socially relevant variables, show substantial stability over time and across settings. It is, of course, the case that certain situations or events may be more likely to trigger off or exacerbate particular responses for some people which would otherwise not be as salient, while other situations may be more containing for the individual and attenuate certain responses. Thus to propose a notion of personality with the implicit assumption of stable traits does not imply a unidirectional causality from the person to behaviour (Blackburn, 1988).

Normal *v.* disordered personality

Working on the assumption that we can speak of personality, researchers and clinicians (particularly those of a psychoanalytic persuasion) turned their attention to 'disorders' of the personality. The concept of personality disorder implicitly assumes that we know what a normal personality is even though this is very difficult to define. In DSM-IV it is 'only when personality traits are inflexible and maladaptive and cause significant functional impairment or subjective distress' (APA, 1994) that a personality disorder is diagnosed. A personality disorder is defined as 'an enduring pattern of inner experience and behaviour that deviates markedly from the expectations of the individual's culture, is pervasive and inflexible, has an onset in adolescence or early adulthood, is stable over time and leads to distress or impairment' (APA, 1994). Personality disorders are grouped in DSM-IV into three clusters:

Cluster A: Paranoid, schizoid and schizotypal
               (typically characterised by 'eccentric' behaviour)
Cluster B: Antisocial, borderline, histrionic and narcissistic
               (typically characterised by impulsive and dramatic
               behaviour)
Cluster C: Avoidant, dependent and obsessive-compulsive
               (typically characterised by anxiety and fear)

While these three clusters and the diagnoses suggest clear demarcations, in practice there exists considerable overlap between the various diagnoses of personality disorder. Some studies have found up to an average number of 2.8 diagnoses of personality disorder per client (Zanarini et al., 1987). Also, Tyrer et al.'s (1993) large-scale study concluded that categories of personality disorder did not have any predictive value with respect to response to treatment thereby querying their utility.

DSM-IV differentiates diagnoses on Axis 1 (clinical syndromes such as depression and schizophrenia) and Axis 2 (personality disorders). This differentation does not, however, imply any causal independence as a diagnosis of a psychiatric problem may be understood as an extension of coping strategies which characterise particular personality disorders (Derksen, 1995). Indeed, this is a view expressed by psychoanalytic practitioners who have tended to understand symptomatic disturbance essentially as secondary manifestations of an underlying and more enduring personality disorder. In practice, nevertheless, most psychoanalysts working within the field of psychiatry would acknowledge that the clinical syndromes and their assumed personality roots are by no means so clearly linked, as, for example, in the case of conversion hysteria and the histrionic personality disorder (usually referred to as the hysterical personality or the 'hysteric'). Zetzel (1968) points out that only a small number of hysterical personalities are prone to develop conversion hysterical symptoms.

The term 'personality disorder' is really a misnomer, as it is clearly not an 'illness' not even in the sense that some might argue schizophrenia is. As Millon and Davis (1995: 633) put it, 'Personality disorders are not disorders in the medical sense. Rather they are reified constructs employed to represent varied styles or patterns in which the personality system functions *maladaptively* in relation to its environment.' This, however, still leaves open the question of how we might define 'maladaptive' as some of the traits characteristic of some of the personality disorders have functional value such as the obsessional style with its emphasis on orderliness and punctuality. Indeed, the notion of personality disorders contains an inherent cultural bias: for example, a well-adjusted employee in Japan might be regarded as having an obsessive-compulsive personality from the perspective of a European. The criteria for diagnosing personality disorder will inevitably reflect the individual and cultural biases of the diagnostician as they are typically attributes which require a subjective decision on their presence or absence; they refer to tangible behaviours (such as self-harm) but also to what is inferred by the behaviour.

In some contexts even, people with a personality disorder may flourish: take as an example the stereotypical narcissistic personality who may be very talented and make a significant contribution to the arts so that the environment tolerates him in spite of his 'difficult' personality. This is an important point as an element of social judgement pervades the very notion of personality disorder. Since the time of Schneider, there has been a tendency to judge personality disorders by their effects on others (Tyrer et al., 1993). Some people with a diagnosis of personality disorder see the world rather than themselves as being in some way 'at fault'. This allegedly characteristic 'lack of insight' has lent to this client group the label of being 'difficult' (Vaillant, 1987). Some regard personality disorder as the 'diagnosis of despair' (Tyrer et al., 1993). Indeed, its treatment is believed by many clinicians to be long and arduous, if ever successful. Although personality disorders are believed to be especially challenging because they are thought to be ego-syntonic, this is not always the case as many people are acutely distressed by their behaviour and relationship difficulties and seek help to relieve these. It is interesting to note, however, how few paranoid, narcissistic and antisocial personalities come forward for help of their own accord by comparison with other personality disorders.

In an attempt to distill differentiating criteria into the normality–abnormality distinction with respect to personality, Millon and Davis (1995) point to three features which they consider to be characteristic of 'maladaptation':

1　The individual is said to have acquired few strategies for relating and is indiscriminate in their application. The approach to relationships and to the environment is characterised by *adaptive inflexibility*.
2　A tendency for the person's needs, perceptions and behaviour to foster *vicious circles* which perpetuate unhelpful patterns and provoke reactions from others which maintain the problem.
3　The person's adaptation is characterised by *tenuous stability* which reflects fragility or lack of resilience when faced with subjective stress.

These features, taken together, lead us to a view of personality disorder as reflecting relatively stable and rigid interpersonal styles and behavioural repertoires which essentially fail to engender desirable outcomes for the person. Most people develop an habitual style of relating to others which reflects their beliefs and expectancies about self, others and the world. These lead the person to behave in particular ways which frequently elicit complementary behaviours from others.

Constitutional *v.* environmental factors

The aetiology of individual differences in personality is likely to encompass both biogenic and psychogenic influences in a dynamic interplay.

Maladaptive patterns of behaviour are generally assumed to develop at an early age through the internalisation of explicit and implicit messages conveyed in families about how people talk, fear, love, solve problems, relate and communicate with others. Particular behaviours may also reflect the child's attempt to cope with specific stresses which undermine feelings of security or to pre-empt further painful rebuffs from critical, hostile or less-responsive parents. For example, children who display a so-called 'ambivalent attachment pattern', when reunited with a parent following a brief separation, refuse to be comforted and display anger or passivity. The angry behaviour which is often observed has been interpreted as a strategy of exaggerating attachment behaviours so as to elicit a response from less-responsive parents. When observed at home it has been reported that mothers of 'ambivalently attached' children tend to be more disengaged and less responsive to infant crying than mothers of securely or avoidantly attached children (Lyons-Ruth et al., 1987).

Although it is generally held that childhood experiences exert a powerful determining influence on the development of the personality, more recent evidence also lends support to the role played by constitutional factors (McGuffin and Thapar, 1992). Every child is endowed with a very distinctive pattern of dispositions and sensitivities. Anyone who has had or worked with babies will know that they differ in the regularity of their biological functions including, for example, sensory alertness to stimuli, characteristic moods, intensities of response and distractability and persistence. Some researchers have now also begun to investigate the behaviour of foetuses, identifying quite clear tendencies and patterns within the womb which appear to correlate with the baby's behaviour after birth (Piontelli, 1992). In practice, this means that each person's nervous system, with its distinctive biological characteristics, to an extent determines how the world is responded to. Biogenic dysfunctions may result in problems of adaptation and contribute to a person's deviation from so-called normal development, but even so psychological and social determinants almost invariably shape the form of its expression. A person's genetic disposition is thus open to modification by environmental factors. If we extend this to the question of personality traits, then we might say that the inherited qualities, while predisposing people to certain traits, are none the less influenced by people's experiences in their environment. A child's temperament may evoke particular responses from others that may then confirm or accentuate initial temperamental dispositions. The converse is also true, however, namely that temperamental dispositions may be reversed by environmental influences.

As we saw in Chapter 2, development consists of a sequence of dynamic interactions between person and environment. Capsi and Elder (1988) speak of 'cumulative continuity' of personality traits to describe the way in which a person's disposition leads her to select or construct environments which will, in turn, reinforce and sustain such dispositions. Millon and Davis (1995) argue that an important variable in determining whether a child's temperament will eventually result in a pathological adaptation is the parents' acceptance or otherwise of the child's individuality. Personality may be understood, then, as a compromise between temperament and psychosocial environment, reflecting a series of life choices in response to important life experiences which are likely to impact differently depending on the individual's developmental stage.

Clinical relevance of the concept of 'personality disorder'

In a review of epidemiological studies, Weissman (1993) reports a prevalence rate of between 10 and 13 per cent of diagnosed personality disorders. The prevalence rates for each of the personality disorders are low, the highest being for the schizotypal and borderline personality disorders. Although few individuals receive the diagnosis, those who do present a considerable challenge to therapists and place a great demand on resources because their problems are often acute and chronic. In addition, the research literature suggests that the diagnosis of a personality disorder along with other psychiatric problems, such as depression and anxiety, is associated with a poorer prognosis with respect to what may be achieved through psychotherapeutic as well as medical interventions (Shea et al., 1992).

It would be fair to say that there is some reticence among clinicians to diagnose personality disorders, reflecting the lack of agreement that exists about this diagnostic category. While DSM-IV may have sharpened its operational criteria and thus increased the reliability with which diagnoses are made, this does not imply that such diagnoses are valid ones. In view of these difficulties, it is more helpful to view personality problems or traits as dimensional rather than categorical, that is, there are graded steps between a so-called normal personality and a personality disorder; we all display certain traits to a greater or lesser extent (Goldberg et al., 1994). A dimensional appproach also avoids the problem of overlapping categories referred to earlier. More importantly, no person with a label of personality disorder is only made up of the negative attributes of the label. Indeed, it is the hallmark of good therapeutic practice that the therapist is always striving to identify with and work with the more healthy and functioning parts of the personality. Rather than pigeon-holing clients into particular categories, it is therefore more useful to describe which traits give a more accurate reflection of people and their habitual ways of relating, always bearing in mind that such traits as 'dependent' or 'avoidant' or 'borderline' refer to *parts* of a person and do not define them in their entirety. In addition, as with any client, the emphasis should be on identifying the areas of functioning where clients experience some difficulty as well as those areas where they show strengths.

Many of the clients who seek therapy or are referred for therapy present with interpersonal conflicts which reflect deeply ingrained and long-standing patterns of feeling, behaving and relating. The majority of the criteria in DSM-IV for personality disorders refer to inter-personal behaviour. For example, one of the criteria for 'avoidant personality disorder' is that the person is unwilling to get involved with people unless he feels confident that he will be liked. For 'dependent personality disorder' one of the criteria is that the person needs others to take responsibility for major areas of her life. Given this emphasis it might be more helpful, as Derksen (1995) suggests, to speak of 'inter-personal style' or 'disturbed relationships' as opposed to a disorder of the personality. Essentially this is very much the model that psycho-analysis proposes.

Notwithstanding all the difficulties which are encountered when we speak of 'personality', and more specifically of a disordered personality, the notion of personality can serve as a useful dynamic background from which therapists can better grasp the meaning and significance of their client's more florid or transient difficulties. It can also help the therapist to understand and manage how and why a person is likely to respond in a particular way under certain circumstances. For example, a person whom we might typify as a 'paranoid personality' may be more prone to misinterpret what the therapist says as well as being more hostile to any help offered. With respect to a person's social functioning, personality difficulties, as reflected in interpersonal prob-lems, are likely to exert a significant influence on, as well as represent-ing a risk factor for, psychopathology as a consequence of the difficulties they promote in the person's life (Quinton et al., 1995).

Let us now look at the various personality types referred to in DSM-IV with illustrative case examples.

Paranoid personality

The paranoid personality is one that is particularly mistrustful and suspicious of others leading to frequent misinterpretation of their experiences in relation to other people. The person is often very pre-occupied with questions of loyalty and trust. They may also be heavily involved in litigation which may include taking legal action against their carers. They are especially sensitive to rebuffs from others. Their anticipation of other people's malevolency towards them provokes anger and hostility which is not always based in reality. Their subjective experience is frequently one of persecution.

Frances is an articulate 35-year-old woman. As a child she was not told of the identity of her mother, only for this to be disclosed to her on the day of her mother's death. She had been a rather suspicious person since that time, preoccupied in her thoughts with how others viewed her. She invariably ascribed to them hostile attitudes towards her which appeared to have little basis in reality (even though her paranoid stance towards the world was readily understandable given her early experience of having critical information about her mother withheld from her). Yet Frances would expend considerable energy on her 'counter-attacks', firmly believing that her perceptions were accurate. This, in turn, alienated friends and family as they felt unjustly accused of misdemeanours and they then tended to respond in a more hostile, rejecting manner which simply served to confirm Frances' original beliefs about herself and the world.

Frances arrived for one of her therapy sessions in a very angry manner. I had gone to collect her from the waiting room one minute late she said and this was in fact accurate. I acknowledged this fact and invited Frances to tell me more about how she felt. She accused me of being irresponsible and wanted to submit a complaint to my managers regarding this matter. Frances felt I had preferred to be on the 'phone to one of my friends and that I was laughing at her, knowing she had been waiting there for me but that I simply did not care.

Schizoid personality

The schizoid pattern was first described by Bleuler (1911) who used it to denote an inwardly directed tendency, a retreat from the outside world with an accompanying lack of emotional expressivity. The schizoid personality is characterised by an overall detachment which manifests itself in a withdrawal from social and interpersonal contacts. Such people typically have few friends and appear more engrossed in their own fantasy life. Their interactions with others are marked by emotional coldness and unresponsiveness. All emotions appear blunted. This affective unresponsiveness renders such people rather unattractive to others and they tend to be avoided as interactions with them can feel very unrewarding if not altogether rejecting. This type of response from the environment merely reinforces the person's withdrawal and state of detachment. The term 'schizoid' has also been used by psychoanalysts (for example, Fairbairn, Winnicott and Khan) to refer to far more socially adapted personalities who nevertheless are also very inwardly directed. This has created some confusion in the literature.

Mark is 28. His early and middle childhood were characterised by a lack of warmth and affection. His family appeared to relate in a somewhat remote manner. He felt always misunderstood by his mother in particular whom he felt cared little for him. As a young child he recalled spending hours on his own with few toys even to stimulate his interest. The parenting he had received seemed to have been carried out in a rather perfunctory way.

As an adult Mark was very detached. He had no intimate relationships and actively avoided people. When he spoke to me in therapy about his relationships, I was invariably struck by his difficulty in interpreting other people's communications and his attendant difficulty in responding meaningfully. Lacking such skills, Mark came across as unresponsive and cold. In the context of therapy, Mark frequently missed sessions without giving any reason and found it quite normal not to give any explanation for his absence. He had so few expectations of others that he himself struggled to imagine that someone might be waiting or thinking about him. However Mark appeared not to care about this, responding to my attempts at empathic intervention in a very detached manner. He appeared indifferent to anything I said and I experienced him as impenetrable. Such were his difficulties in interaction that he broke off the therapeutic relationship a few months later. This is not atypical in people who share similar characteristics to Mark.

The schizotypal personality

This personality is one that comes closest to schizophrenia but is by no means synonymous with it. It is, however, believed to be based on a genetic relationship with chronic schizophrenia. Its name reflects the emphasis on the presence of psychotic-like phenomena in the personality, such as suspiciousness and paranoid ideation as well as behaviour and appearance that is odd and eccentric. Like the schizoid personality, the schizotypal personality experiences considerable difficulty in relationships, marked by acute discomfort with personal affection and closeness. As a result such people turn increasingly to solitary thought where, unchecked by logic, their ideas and beliefs may acquire a delusional quality. This may well reflect an attempt to create illusions that enable them to feel central and important rather than peripheral figures. The primary distinguishing features between the schizoid and schizotypal personality are the cognitive eccentricities present in the latter.

Andy is 26. He is an articulate and in many respects a sensitive man. He has lived alone for six years after leaving his rural home town to live in an inner city. As a child, Andy recalls being painfully shy. He was bullied at school and felt a terrible sense of shame. He has always been reticent about discussing his family and I know very little about his early life as a consequence. However, he portrays a family in which there was little communication. In fact, when he took a severe overdose at the age of 15 his parents were not even seen by the hospital staff. Since his move from his home town, he has had scant contact with them.

Andy is now unemployed and has no friends or acquaintances. He spends most of his time in his flat. When he goes out he has to wear heavy layers of clothes, no matter what the weather as he otherwise feels exposed. His coat has to hang in a very particular fashion and he has even adjusted his posture to adapt to the flow of his coat. He expresses considerable paranoid fears, describing intricate plots of people who are tormenting him. These appear to have some basis in reality but his elaboration of these facts has a delusional quality. He feels himself to be the focus of attention and, while this distresses him on one level, it also clearly helps him to feel that at least he receives *some* attention.

The antisocial personality

This type of personality, also referred to as the 'psychopathic personality', has attracted considerable interest and has been most comprehensively studied as people who receive the diagnosis of 'antisocial personality disorder' (ASPD) tend to be those who present a significant challenge and risk to others. Prison settings show a high prevalence of ASPD, between 39 and 76 per cent of inmates (Cote and Hodgkins, 1990). The essential features of the antisocial personality are patterns of irresponsible conduct and antisocial behaviour, including, for example, failure to conform to social norms with respect to lawful behaviour, recklessness, impulsivity, lack of remorse, instability, aggression and inability to sustain consistent work behaviour. The diagnosis is only made in someone aged 18 or over and where there is evidence of conduct disorder in childhood as indicated by the presence of, for example, truancy, fights, cruelty to animals and to people, fire setting, lying and stealing. ASPD represents the only personality category that has been derived from empirical research (Coid, 1993).

Sam is 22. She comes from a large family where she was the eldest. Her parents were violent with each other as well as towards her. They separated when she was 12 and Sam's mother died of a drug overdose when Sam was 14. She reports a long-standing history of aggressive and violent behaviour from the age of 11. She was expelled from several schools because of truanting, drug-taking and violence to peers. Since then she has abused a variety of drugs including heroin and on meeting her she is usually very high, having taken a cocktail of drugs the night before. In one of early sessions, she told me of numerous incidents with peers where she had been verbally and physically aggressive, including cutting a friend's face with a knife because she felt she was not being taken seriously by her. When asked how she felt about the incident, she said 'nothing, she deserved it.' Then, almost in the same breath, she told me she could not understand why this person was no longer speaking to her. She then shared with me her fantasy of wanting to strangle someone as she imagines this could feel very exciting. Sam recalled having tried to suffocate her baby sister when she was herself only 12 years old because she wanted to see what would happen to her face.

Borderline personality

The notion of a borderline personality originates from the psychiatric interest in states of schizophrenia, which were variously described as 'ambulatory' and 'pseudo-neurotic', in which there were transient psychotic states, as well as by psychoanalysts such as Helene Deutsch, who described the 'as if' personality. Psychoanalysts in America, in particular Kohut (1971) and Kernberg (1975, 1984), have written extensively on this topic.

'Borderline' refers essentially to a personality structure. Kernberg (1975, 1984) proposed three structural organisations, namely the neurotic, borderline and psychotic, which are in part distinguished by the modes of defence operative within the individual. The neurotic personality organisation uses repression and other so-called advanced defences, while both the borderline and psychotic organisations show a predominance of more primitive defences centred on splitting, such as idealisation, projection, omnipotence, devaluation and denial, all of which serve to protect the individual from intrapsychic conflict. In both the neurotic and the borderline client, reality testing is not impaired but in the psychotic it is severely impaired. The borderline organisation can be further differentiated from a neurotic one in respect of the difficulty in tolerating anxiety, very poor impulse control and very limited capacity for sublimation accompanied by other manifestations of ego-weakness.

Research has highlighted a characteristic set of features of the borderline personality organisation which largely echo those outlined by Kernberg, namely unstable personal relationships, idealisation and denigration of others, impulsive and unpredictable feelings and self-destructive behaviour (Berelowitz and Tarnopolsky, 1993). The aetiological factors presumed to be related to borderline personality disorder include a childhood environment characterised by neglect, instability, marital discord, physical and sexual abuse and where there is no 'good' figure which can act as a buffer against these difficult circumstances. Unlike most of the other personality disorders, there is now considerable evidence to support the significance of such childhood antecedents to the later development of a borderline organisation, affecting in particular the individual's identity and the risk of self-destructive behaviour. Such traumatic histories are more common in those who function at a borderline level than for most of the other personality disorders (Millon and Davis, 1995).

Such clients often present for help as their functioning is adversely affected by their behaviour and they are frequently in crisis. They can present as very angry and pessimistic, leading to violence or recriminations against the world. The anger may also be turned against themselves and is manifested in impulsive, self-damaging behaviour. They may slide easily from impulsive actions to frankly psychotic behaviour, which is nevertheless usually short-lived and subsides following the reduction of stress. They often also present as depressed. The depression is not so much characterised by hopelessness or guilt but rather by a pervasive sense of emptiness or loneliness. Relationships with other people tend to reveal the neediness of the person, who may be very clingy or demanding with a tendency towards devaluing the other person, who is also desperately needed and at times even idealised.

Sarah is a 35-year-old woman who frequently presents in the casualty department of her local hospital with deep lacerations to her arms and/ or overdoses. This pattern of behaviour is long-standing and has led to multiple admissions to hospital and secure units over the years. Such behaviour appears to be in response to acute stress, usually in her interpersonal relationships.

Sarah hates herself. She thinks she is 'ugly' and unworthy of any love – these were messages that were conveyed to her as a child from a mother who was herself quite disturbed, spending much of her time in and out of hospital, and a father who sexually abused her over a period of years. Sarah is prone to paranoid ideation and this was a feature of her relationship with me around the time of a break when she typically accused me of not caring, of speaking ill of her in her absence and of plotting with the doctors to have her admitted. Although there was a basis in reality for some of her anxieties about my liaison with the doctors and the hospital, such anxieties gave rise to violent verbal attacks which belied her tendency to denigrate me when she feared my abandonment. Her denigration alternated with an idealisation of me which was never, however, sustained for long. This was a re-enactment of her repeated disappointments with her mother who would at times show Sarah some love, lulling her into a false sense of security, only then to brutally snatch it away from her.

Histrionic personality

This personality has long been described in the psychoanalytic literature as the hysterical character. Freud elaborated two forms of hysterical syndrome: conversion hysteria (e.g. hysterical paralysis) and anxiety hysteria. He argued that the hysterical personality underlay the syndrome of conversion hysteria (see above). The hallmark of histrionic personality is the dramatic manner in which such individuals express their need for attention. This may manifest itself in inappropriate sexual behaviour where they may behave in a very provocative and seductive manner. The relationships they establish are often shallow. Even though they may approach others in dramatic and intense ways, these attachments tend to be short-lived. Displays of emotion (for example, crying inconsolably or angry tantrums) can be very easily aroused and just as easily overcome. In practice, it may be very difficult to make the distinction between the histrionic and the borderline personality.

Angelina was a strikingly attractive 'image consultant' aged 30. She was referred from the abortion clinic where she had had her fifth termination of pregnancy. In the letter from the male consultant who referred her, he commented on her inappropriate flirtatiousness. When I received the medical notes from the psychiatric unit to which she had been admitted ten years ago after an overdose, I noted that she had had an affair with one of the junior doctors. She came across in the initial assessment with me as charming and articulate but also very easily tearful and her manner of speaking was childlike. She complained of frequently feeling depressed and told me of the many disappointments in her relationships with men, although she also described a tendency to reject and even humiliate men. She was very guarded about committing herself to any therapy and told me that she planned to go on holiday to a beauty and health clinic which would surely improve her mood. She was also suspicious of my ability to help her and somewhat competitive in her manner. Her main concern it seemed was to know whether I agreed with her idea that she should have reconstructive surgery to enlarge her breasts.

In her background it turned out that Angelina was the daughter of a very beautiful fashion model who had had little time for her or for that matter Angelina's father, with whom Angelina had a close relationship which was marred by his death when she was 13 years old. It was at this point that her mother moved back to live with her own mother and began a series of love affairs. The grandmother was cruel and rejecting to Angelina but her holidays with her doting paternal grandparents formed a small but significant compensation for this lack of love.

Narcissistic personality

The narcissistic personality is widely recognised in clinical practice and has received particular attention from psychoanalytic theorists. The central problem for the narcissistic person is one of self-esteem. The person may exhibit feelings of grandiosity and come across as haughty and arrogant, a presentation which usually belies considerable anxiety about not being 'good enough' or being unlovable. The person demands admiration from others and can feel very easily slighted if the devotion expected is not forthcoming. Their need for admiration leads them to use others in a rather exploitative manner. Relationships are sought which will enhance the person's self-esteem but there is little tolerance on the part of the narcissistic person for the other's shortcomings.

Annie is a 27-year-old woman who presents as very assertive. She described her work as an author in glowing terms even though she is actually unemployed and has had difficulty getting enough work. She feels that most authors she reads write 'rubbish' and that her own work is of far superior quality. She in fact begrudges the success of other authors, feeling that her own work is far more deserving of admiration. Annie has always sought relationships which she feels can in some way advance her career. She speaks of her relationships in a rather cold and calculated manner. As she describes her friends and relatives, she reveals her difficulty in recognising the desires, feelings and subjective experiences of others. However, she herself expects dedication from others and is quite intolerant of people who put their needs before hers. She surrounds herself with people whom she then treats as 'puppets on a string'. When they no longer let her pull the strings she becomes very angry, at times even quite sadistic, such is her response to any experience of rejection (real or construed as such) which she finds very painful to tolerate.

Avoidant personality

This personality is characterised by a pervasive feeling of inadequacy and hypersensitivity to rejection, both of which seriously interfere with the person's confidence to engage in relationships with other people. Hence such individuals tend to withdraw. However, their conflict lies precisely in their need for affection, along with their mistrust and fear of humiliation. They differ from the schizoid and schizotypal personalities in that they actually desire relationships but dare not initiate them. They are not indifferent to relationships as the schizoid is and therefore may be overtly anxious in their interaction with others. They view the world as hostile and dangerous. Their detached and mistrustful behaviours create distance between them and others and evoke complementary responses of rejection from the environment.

James is a 38-year-old unemployed man. He comes across as very tense and restrained in his manner. He finds it hard to speak and, when asked what makes it so difficult, he replies that he fears I shall find him boring and stupid and that I will most probably laugh at his inadequacies. He describes finding it 'impossible' to find a job and, although this distresses him, he is also relieved at not having to mix with other people at work. When he was working he recalls dreading going into work as he found it very stressful. What he found most stressful were his relationships with colleagues. He says he also found it difficult to initiate any conversation as he feared he would make a fool of himself and that others would ridicule him. He was also overly preoccupied with his appearance, feeling inferior to others in all manner of ways. He is very self-deprecating and anticipates criticism and rejection from others. Although he said he feels lonely he seems unable to reach out to others, feeling himself to be painfully shy. He recalled always being left out at school at breaktime when he would sit in a corner of the playground watching his peers enjoying themselves. He had envied their spontaneity and spoke of more recent acquaintances in a similar way.

Dependent personality

This personality reveals a pervasive and excessive need to be taken care of which is accompanied by clinging behaviour and separation anxiety. Such people find it hard to make decisions for themselves (even about quite trivial matters) because they lack confidence as opposed to motivation. This leads to reassurance seeking. Responsibility for themselves is handed over to other people. This over-reliance on others intensifies fears of abandonment. This fear may lead individuals to agree with others even if they really disagree and to remain in quite damaging relationships where they may be actually mistreated as this is a more appealing alternative to being left alone. They experience difficulty in expressing aggression, a quota of which is necessary to make separation possible.

Patricia was a rather childish looking 35-year-old who arrived for her assessment accompanied by her rather sullen partner. She complained of getting increasingly frequent panic attacks which occurred when her partner went abroad on business trips. She insisted on him coming into the room with her and only after the second session would she allow me to see her on her own. She was a friendly person who wanted to know early on what I thought was the matter with her and she was often seeking my reassurance and advice. The whole therapy was in fact marked by her very clinging behaviour towards me which included long letters written during holiday breaks and occasionally between sessions.

Her life seemed divided between looking after her partner and spending time with her invalid and very critical mother who lived in the flat above hers. In her past history, Patricia had a period of behaviour therapy for school phobia when the family had moved from a small village by the sea to a big industrial town where she was sent to a convent school. At around this time her mother had developed rheumatoid arthritis and had become wheelchair bound. The school phobia had resolved but unfortunately her father died of a heart attack just when she was planning to leave home and have a more independent life, training to be a secretary in another town. When she was 20 she fell in love with an old family friend who worked in her father's firm as an electrician. He himself suffered from diabetes and was somewhat moody. There had never been a very active sexual relationship and neither partner had wanted a child.

Obsessive-compulsive personality

This personality is characterised by extreme feelings of personal insecurity, doubt and caution. The obsessive personality is fundamentally a wary and suspecting person who needs to create structures (as in compulsive rituals) which serve to bind anxiety. They do not cope well when faced with novel situations which challenge their attempts to create a stable and orderly world around them where things are predictable. The tendencies towards preciseness, orderliness and the insistence upon maintaining rigid control of oneself means that feelings are seldom given expression. The need for perfection and control may lead these individuals to impose upon others their way of doing things. Rigidity and excessive doubt may be present. Work with such people is sometimes marked by the boring quality of their story in which every event of their life has to be described in the most minute detail. Any interruption by the therapist in the hope of speeding things up can be expected to be met either with irritation or with more detail about the particular episode in the story.

Arnold, an acountant aged 45, came to his first consultation largely at the request of his wife who was becoming increasingly frustrated by aspects of their relationship. He was very tense and had been waiting in the waiting room for at least half an hour before the time of our appointment. It was a hot summer's day and he was dressed in a suit, looking very formal. His face had little expression to it and his manner was, if anything, somewhat querulous. He wanted to know how long the assessment would take and what its purpose was because he was very concerned that he might be late for his next appointment. He said to me that, although he had come at his wife's insistence because she found him increasingly withdrawn and cold, he had noticed himself becoming depressed and finding that he was unable to keep up with all the demands at work where new computers had been installed. He found himself getting irritated with colleagues and clients for no obvious reason.

When I asked him to describe his day to me he explained how he had to get up extremely early at 5 am so as to get ready to leave the house by 6.30 am to catch the local suburban train for the City. Getting ready to go out involved making sure that he put on freshly pressed clothing with matching tie and socks. Lately his wife, who had been upset about their son's failure to get into university, had forgotten on various occasions to put out the right items of clothing. This had upset and irritated him considerably. At work he had taken on a new assistant whose manners he found casual and everybody had been shocked at the way Arnold had torn a strip off this seemingly in-experienced youth when he had been found to make a minor mistake in the accounts of a client. He had been particularly upset at the fact that this young man had not followed his way of doing things.

Current interventions

Course and outcome

Generally speaking, people with a diagnosis of personality disorder require long-term if not continuous input from mental health services. This reflects the seemingly intractable and chronic nature of some of their difficulties, as well as the rather acute presentation of their symptoms (for example, repeated, and in some cases, very severe self-harm). The response to any kind of psychotherapeutic treatment is relatively poor (Roth and Fonagy, in press). One of the difficulties of assessing the effectiveness of any particular intervention for this group of clients is that, as was pointed out earlier, the results are confounded by the frequent co-morbidity of one personality disorder with another personality disorder and psychiatric problems.

Psychological and medical interventions

Those who receive a diagnosis of personality disorder have been offered a range of treatments including pharmacotherapy, cognitive-behavioural therapy and psychoanalytic psychotherapy. The use of medication in the treatment of personality disorder has received mixed results. It would seem that some people with a diagnosis of schizotypal and borderline personality disorders respond positively to neuroleptic medications which are aimed primarily at the more psychotic-like symptoms and impulse control, though in some instances depression and anxiety are also ameliorated. However, as yet there is no specific medication which has been shown to be especially effective in the treatment of any one of the personality disorders (Roth and Fonagy, in press).

Psychotherapeutic work with this client group tends to be of a long-term nature. Work in this field represents one of the main areas where psychoanalytic approaches appear to have the most to offer. This partly reflects the nature of the main presenting problems of people with a diagnosis of personality disorder, namely their relationship difficulties. Given the emphasis in psychoanalytically orientated approaches on working through the therapeutic relationship, both in terms of transference and countertransference, such approaches focus in considerable depth on the client's most significant area of difficulty. Although controlled studies are few and the sample sizes too small for clear conclusions to be drawn from them, psychodynamic and interpersonal approaches appear to be the most helpful (Roth and Fonagy, in press). Dialectical behaviour therapy, which is an approach integrating elements of cognitive-behavioural and supportive psychotherapies, has been shown to be especially effective in the treatment of borderline personality disorder (Linehan et al., 1993).

Practical considerations in assessment and management

It is beyond the scope of this chapter to enter into a detailed discussion of the assessment and management implications for each of the personality types described above. Instead, this section will concentrate on some broad guidelines especially pertinent to the assessment stage. It is also not in the spirit in which this chapter has been written to approach the interpersonal difficulties which are so characteristic of this group of clients from the standpoint of 'treatment'. Rather, it is hoped that the various descriptions will be useful in alerting the therapist to the possible dynamics that may transpire between them and a given 'type' of client and that this understanding will assist the therapist in helping clients manage their relationships in a more satisfactory way. An important aim of work with people with a personality disorder, who more often than not present as chronically disabled by their interpersonal difficulties, is to begin to help them develop coping strategies. The emphasis of the work is not on 'curing' or 'treating' people of their personality but rather helping them to manage in spite of their vulnerabilities.

It is often very difficult to make an accurate assessment of a dominant personality trait. Indeed, some clinicians would argue that the diagnosis is often not established until the end of a psychotherapy. A client may appear charming, well motivated and even a little insightful, but may turn out also to be highly destructive and demanding and prone to rapid deterioration when rejected in a relationship. These less appealing signs of a deeper vulnerability may be the first indication that you are working with a more borderline than a neurotic personality. A great deal has been written about the borderline personality and, generally speaking, such clients can be extremely challenging to work with and this is reflected in the literature. It is always helpful to pay attention to the experiences of other clinicians with these clients even though this should not prejudice one's own concern to help a given person. The greatest difficulty, and the hardest thing to gauge, will be the client's capacity to form not only a trusting relationship but also one in which she is prepared to make changes in her life based on the insights gained from the therapy. The more disturbed the client is the more realistic the therapist needs to be about the limitations of any therapeutic endeavour. It may be helpful not to set out with a rigid plan or goal but, in the course of the therapy with a very disturbed client, to begin to think about whether (a) the work is likely to remain purely supportive in its nature and (b) how much of oneself needs to be given to be of any meaningful use to the client. This involves thinking carefully about the intensity and frequency of sessions as well as giving careful consideration to the duration of a therapy.

On the whole, therapists are very wary of embarking on deep, insight-orientated therapies with very paranoid, narcissistic, schizoid and schizotypal clients where the capacity in the client for basic trust can be very limited. In the case of a borderline personality, a lot of good psychoanalytic work had been done but clearly these are people who are best handled by experienced therapists in a safe setting so that, for example, episodes of self-harm can be anticipated and managed with minimal disruption to the therapy. With the antisocial personality, there may be many hazards, not least the person's capacity to act out in criminal and destructive ways, but also quite often their low motivation and commitment to therapy and the real possibility that it may be very difficult for the person to be honest with the therapist.

With the dependent personality, change may be limited by the particular network of relationships that sustains and promotes the degree of emotional immaturity in the person. For this reason, family and marital strategies may be more effective in the first instance.

Some of these types of client (especially the borderline, antisocial, dependent and obsessive-compulsive personalities) may have formed over-dependent relationships with their GPs and other medical specialists who will have resorted, in exasperation at times, to over-prescription of medication or to over-referral to other specialists or at worst to hospitalisation which only fosters greater dependency in the client and more frustration and sense of helplessness in the carers (Main, 1957). The therapist, in forming a long-term, stable relationship, may then also consider as one of his or her goals trying to help the client to wean herself off so much alternative support, especially the unnecessary use of psychotropic medication.

Short-term work with this group of clients is unlikely to be helpful. However, a useful role may exist in the case of crisis intervention where an understanding of the personality givens may help the therapist to focus more accurately his or her shorter-term therapeutic interventions. Sometimes, even though these clients experience difficulty in establishing a therapeutic alliance, following a good assessment they may none the less return months later for a few further sessions and may make sporadic use of the therapist as a containing agent in times of crisis. The value of such supportive work should not be under-estimated.

11
Conclusion

The antipsychiatry movement: its challenges and limitations

I would like to conclude this book on a more personal note. This is because writing on psychopathology for the purposes of a textbook of this kind encourages a somewhat detached, empirical approach to a subject matter which is subjective and emotive. A book on psychopathology is about human beings and is therefore so much about *us* and our own experiences that it is difficult to remain objective. As Podvall put it 'madness is everyone's concern; if you have a mind it can go mad' (1990: 317). It is in this spirit, albeit one that creates some necessary tension, that I hope this book will have been read. Such a book, structured around diagnostic categories and using psychiatric labels, may have jarred with some therapists committed to deconstructing the notion of mental illness and to moving as far away as possible from the medical model of psychopathology. So I would like to say a little about my position which has inevitably influenced my approach to the subject matter.

The antipsychiatry movement, so popular in the 1960s, introduced an important new approach which questioned the assumptions underlying the medical model and its proposed treatments for psychopathology. The social historians who then penetrated the privileged preserves of psychiatric history deserve credit for drawing our attention to the possibility of science and medicine's unwitting subservience to self-interest, and inequitable political, legal and socioeconomic trends (Sedgwick, 1973; Starr, 1982). However, as Wallace (1994) has pointed out, these new historians were overzealous in explaining virtually all medical and psychiatric developments by reference to sociocultural forces and professional motives for prestige and power. Not surprisingly, they joined forces with likeminded social philosophers and scientists (Goffman, 1961; Ingleby, 1980). These scholars, also influenced by the French philosopher Michel Foucault (1962; 1965), viewed psychiatry as legitimising the imprisonment of the socially and economically deviant.

The antipsychiatry perspective has been helpful in offering us a much needed balance against so-called, 'scientific' psychiatry. It is certainly correct to assert that external (including political) and not merely scientific and clinical factors played a part in determining the original inclusion in DSM-II, for example, of homosexuality as a psychiatric diagnosis, which now no longer exists as a diagnostic entity (Wallace, 1994). In addition, the important arguments put forward by the antipsychiatry movement, for instance about psychiatric labelling and its sociopolitical implications, should not be ignored. The stigma attached to psychiatric labels has serious repercussions on people's lives in terms of their own and other people's expectations. Nevertheless, when carried to extremes and ignoring or negating other determinants, such perspectives reveal their limitations. We should also ask to what extent the arguments of the antipsychiatry movement did actually benefit those who were and still are the carriers of psychiatric labels. The problems of those who are in emotional distress are not addressed simply by refusing to label them as 'mentally ill' (van Deurzen-Smith, 1992). To question the effects of labelling is merely a starting point, but all too often it has appeared as the end point in the debate on the so-called mentally ill that has left those in distress still in the depths of their misery, without any label to pin on that misery.

At times, those supporting an antipsychiatry stance in rejecting the medical model also seemingly rejected the scientific method *per se* and, unfortunately, along with it, rational argument of any kind. The critics of mainstream psychiatry often argued contradictory positions and did so with little evident concern for the requirement to support their arguments with evidence as opposed to rhetoric. While there are undoubtedly problems inherent in the scientific method for investigating the nature of emotional distress and what can help to alleviate it, there are also contexts where scientific findings are useful. This is not to suggest that a scientific approach more than any other would provide us with the answer but, as Ussher (1991) suggests, its rejection is as limited as that which uncritically accepts scientific findings as more meaningful. It is unhelpful to be prescriptive about the nature of the therapeutic endeavour itself or the nature of the distress we seek to alleviate. However, it is equally unhelpful to ignore the vast experience of clinicians and researchers in the fields of psychopathology, psychotherapy and counselling, which is now available to us. Their perspectives and their research findings can enhance our understanding of our clients and inform our practice by alerting us to some of the difficulties we may encounter in our work with particular types of client or problem and therefore assist us in our assessment and the ensuing decisions we need to make regarding appropriate intervention. The very notion of 'types of clients' may alienate some therapists who feel it important to approach the client as an individual and not as a labelled caricature. However, to categorise does allow us to organise our clinical experience and plan our interventions. The danger lies in forgetting how subjective this endeavour can be and so be lulled into a false sense of security. Then we may fall into the trap of believing we know what the client is feeling without really listening to their story.

The notions of treatment and cure

These two notions carry medical connotations and are not considered by everyone to have a place in a dialogue on mental health problems. Indeed, the actual ways in which people in emotional distress are helped arouses considerable debate. Broadly speaking, the debate has centred around the question of how and where people with psychiatric problems should be helped. This, in turn, reflects varied assumptions about the very nature of psychopathology. It is certainly the case that some people at least approach their mental health problems as they would any other physical condition, seeking relief from their distress. The idea that they are receiving 'treatment' for an 'illness' and that they are viewed as 'patients' is not necessarily experienced as demeaning or alienating by them. On the contrary, it may be experienced as containing and reassuring. It is essential, however, that treatment, be it pharmacotherapy or psychotherapy, is not conceptualised merely as the administration of a particular drug or technique, but that it rests on an appreciation of the dynamics of the process of any intervention and, more specifically, on the quality of the client–therapist relationship.

If we are to speak of treatments for psychopathology, it is clear that these are to be *aimed at a person* living in a particular sociocultural context and not aimed at curing a disorder. Indeed, the notion of cure has little place in the context of psychopathology which cannot really be understood or alleviated unless we take into account its psychological as well as sociocultural aspects. Many of the psychiatric problems we have reviewed in this book can be conceptualised as understandable, even if on some level 'maladaptive', responses to life events which may give rise, for example, to considerable anxiety and depression. To say that we are 'treating' the person who presents with such difficulties suggests that their distress can in some way be removed. It is often more meaningful to speak of helping people to manage their lives more successfully or finding alternative ways of 'being-in-the-world' – to borrow a phrase from the existential philosophical literature – which are more adaptive for a given person. Speaking of the plasticity of the brain, Sacks makes the interesting observation that 'it may be necessary to redefine the very concepts of "health" and "disease", to see these in terms of the ability of the organism to create a new organisation and order, one that fits its special altered disposition and needs, rather than in terms of a rigidly fixed "norm"' (1995: xiv).

People hold particular beliefs about the nature of their distress and what may have caused it. Such beliefs lend structure and meaning to the person's experiences. Any psychological or medical intervention will need to be sensitive to this. In addition, because the causes of a person's psychopathology are often varied and interact with each other in highly complex ways, these interventions need to be aimed at the different areas of a person's experience (for example, social, psychological, physical) and the context in which the person lives. 'Treatment' for mental health problems is therefore at its best a multi-disciplinary activity. Even where there may be more or less recognised organic causes for the psychological disturbance and associated emotional distress, medical interventions should always be accompanied by an opportunity for people to make sense out of their experience. Organic processes are always also personal. The mind and the body are interdependent and our interventions need to reflect this; reductionist models, whatever their emphasis, simply fail to do justice to our complexity.

It is too easy and all too tempting to criticise biomedical interventions when we realise just how haphazard the prescription of medication can be and so dismiss it outright. At times, such approaches are used defensively both to keep the disturbing client quiet and to protect the therapist or doctor from the client's distress. Solely to prescribe medication, for example, to people who are depressed is unlikely to resolve all their difficulties: the environment they live in may also need to change or the person may be facing some very real stresses which medication simply cannot remove. However, the prescription of medication is not used exclusively in the service of defence. Even though our understanding of why certain medications help some clients and not others remains unclear, it is certainly the case that some people at least appear to benefit from medication. Biomedical and psychosocial interventions at times complement each other and reflect the complexity of the problem they are ostensibly addressing. The experience of emotional distress cannot be reduced to an underlying biochemical process in the brain as it undoubtedly reflects very real problems in living. However, to deny our biology altogether is to ignore a fundamental feature of human being.

In our therapeutic work we each approach our task quite differently, depending on our underlying philosophies with respect to the very notions of what psychopathology, psychotherapy or counselling are, as well as our role and responsibilities as therapists in relation to people who are in some way distressed or feel alienated from themselves, other people or just life itself. Even if our inclination is to view the problems which have been addressed in this book as simply 'problems in living'

(Szasz, 1960; 1961), it remains important none the less to be cognisant of the research findings which have been presented here and not to ignore these merely on the basis of personal prejudice. Our primary aim in therapeutic work is to offer the best possible service to those who seek our help. Any therapeutic intervention we make therefore needs to be carefully considered in light of who the person is, what is congenial to him, the information available to the therapist regarding the problem in question and the interventions which appear to be the most effective. This should not deter us from being innovative and from challenging received wisdom, but we should always remain committed to attempting to assess critically why we do what we do. Although all this may appear to emphasise an altogether too empirical approach to therapeutic intervention, I still consider it important in therapeutic work to meet, as far as it is possible, each client and even each session with an open attitude, or as one psychoanalyst put it without memory, desire or understanding (Bion, 1967). This minimises the temptation, when faced with a very distressed client, to slot the person quickly into a recognisable category which offers some suggestions for how to intervene and so contains our anxiety.

Institutional *v.* community care

The question of the settings in which people are best helped has traditionally found a focus in the debate over institutional versus community care. The emphasis originally placed on community care by the anti-psychiatry movement was very important as this is by far the most effective way of helping the majority of people with psychiatric problems. It is clear that the environments of the old style psychiatric hospitals and the care provided in them were not conducive to helping people resolve their difficulties. In many instances, the presenting problems were exacerbated and the person left hospital with added 'disabilities', which can be understood to be the iatrogenic effects of the restrictive environments and practices of certain institutions.

Care in the community became a live concern after the Second World War when the therapeutic community movement emerged side by side with new understandings about psychiatric rehabilitation. A number of factors precipitated an interest in alternatives to hospital care. Clearly the introduction of some more effective medications (for example, antipsychotic drugs and antidepressants) contributed to the move towards care in the community. However, it was not only practical considerations or medical advances that turned attention towards community care but also a change in social attitudes towards mental illness. Thus in 1961 at a MIND conference in Britain a decision was made to reduce the number of beds in psychiatric hospitals by 50 per cent. The main reduction has been in the long-stay beds but acute admissions have largely remained the same.

Following the early enthusiasm and ideals of those who understood the damaging consequences of institutional care, we are now faced with the results not so much of a movement guided by a particular philosophy but of a movement which is now largely driven by financial and political considerations. We are now confronted with the reality of community care which in many respects has 'lost its innocence' (Turner, 1988). Discussions about the benefits of care in the community are all too often based on the implicit assumption that institutional care should be avoided at all costs as it is damaging *per se*. I think this is a mistaken view. The argument that it is preferable to help people in the community is important as admission to hospital can be very disruptive. However, this ignores the fact that hospitals are part of a community and are an essential element of an integrated approach to community care. The environment of a hospital may be experienced by some people as very containing of their distress and may even be essential in instances where people's behaviour is so disturbed that it places themselves or others at risk. For other people, such as those suffering from an organically based condition such as dementia, which gives rise to very disabling psychological problems, care in a hospital may also be required.

To this day, the environment of some psychiatric institutional settings is simply not 'good enough' and we should be fighting for improvements in the standards of care offered to the more vulnerable members of our society. The poor standards are, however, not an intrinsic quality of institutional care but are an indictment of a system which has been extensively run down through lack of adequate resources as a result of misguided governmental policies. Not only are the physical environments run down but they often only manage to attract staff who are either not very committed to the work in the first place or, even if they are caring individuals, they soon become disenchanted with the pressure of the work and the heavy emotional demands placed on them along with meagre financial rewards. Moreover, the pressure on hospital beds is such that those who need to be admitted do not always manage to receive the care they need or they may be discharged prematurely without adequate follow-up or they may even be moved around from hospital to hospital with little continuity of care. The problem is therefore not so much whether psychiatric hospitals should be closed down and replaced by alternative structures in the community, but rather how we can best provide the degree of containment and 24-hour care needed by a minority of people. This care needs to be provided in environments which are congenial and supportive to the individual, respectful of them and which offer them some choice with respect to treatment. As well we need to develop better alternatives for the vast majority of people who require professional help but do not need inpatient care.

As therapists, in our pursuit of political correctness or as a consequence of a genuine belief in the essentially existential nature of what I have termed in this book 'psychopathology', we often shy away from an acknowledgement that, for whatever reason, some people are very disturbed and disturbing and require a degree of containment and/or medical care that is not always possible in community settings.[1] I have often been struck by how some of the most fervent supporters of community care undergo a change of mind when one of the recipients of community care becomes their next door neighbour and keeps everyone awake at night because they are on a manic high or frightens their children through their bizarre behaviour. Polemic and reality are not comfortable bedfellows.

The extent to which some people's behaviour can be disturbed may be hard to imagine for the therapist who has had no, or little, exposure to acute psychiatric settings. This is a serious shortcoming of much psychotherapy and counselling training. Any informed argument on the nature and management of psychopathology must rest on practical experience with people who present in very chaotic, disturbed and highly distressed states and who make up the vast majority of the population found in acute psychiatric settings. This experience is sobering and can be very distressing but it is invaluable and no textbook can replace it.

The limitations of a textbook on psychopathology

If in reading this book you had hoped to find an endorsement of a theory which explained emotional distress in its many guises, you will by now be disappointed as you will not have found such an answer here. Both the critics and the supporters of the notion of mental illness will also disappoint you because they provide only partial explanations for psychopathology. The uncertainty to which this points is unsettling but this may be all we can hope for given the inherent difficulties in such an enterprise. There can be at present no simple answer to what is psychopathology but we need to keep on asking questions and investigating them as thoroughly as possible. We may choose to view 'mental illness' as a construction used to control those that threaten us in some way or perhaps we may choose to see it truly as an illness with clear organic causes. Perhaps, as Ussher (1991) suggests, it is both or neither or it may simply depend on the problem in question. What is certain, however, is that given the present state of our knowledge, psychopathology cannot be accounted for within any one explanatory system. We are therefore left with our doubts and anxieties and with the burden of responsibility for keeping our questions open and alive without succumbing to the temptation of pledging allegience to one particular explanatory model to the exclusion of all others. In the end, each of our individual lifetime's experience of dealing with our own distress and conflicts and those of our clients should form the basis for an understanding of psychopathology that is deeper, more meaningful and more varied than any textbook can ever hope to account for.

Note

1. Most community services operate on a 9–5 basis and are not able to offer support out of hours, over weekends or on public holidays.

References

Abraham, K. (1911) 'Notes on psychoanalytic investigation and treatment of manic depressive insanity and allied conditions', in M. Bryan and A. Trachey (trs), *Selected Papers of Karl Abraham*. London: Hogarth Press.

Abramson, L., Seligman, M. and Teasdale, J. (1978) 'Learned helplessness in humans: critique and reformulation', *Journal of Abnormal Psychology*, 87: 49–74.

Al-Issa, I. (1995) 'The illusion of reality or the reality of illusion', *British Journal of Psychiatry*, 166: 368–73.

Allgood-Merten, B., Lewinsohn, P. and Hops, H. (1990) 'Sex differences and adolescent depression', *Journal of Abnormal Psychology*, 99: 55–63.

Allport, G. (1937) *Personality: a Psychological Interpretation*. New York: Holt.

Altschul, S. and Pollock, G. (eds) (1988) *Childhood Bereavement and its Aftermath*. New York: International University Press.

American Psychiatric Association (1994) *Diagnostic and Statistical Manual of Mental Disorders*, 4th edn. Washington: APA.

Andersen, A. (1990) 'Diagnostic treatment of males with eating disorders', in A. Andersen (ed.), *Males with Eating Disorders*. New York: Brunner/Mazel.

Angst, J. (1992) 'Epidemiology of depression', *Psychopharmacology*, 106: 571–4.

Arkowitz, H., Hinton, R., Perl, J. and Hiwadi, W. (1978) 'Treatment strategies for dating anxiety in college men based on real life practice', *Counselling Psychologist*, 7: 41–6.

Ashurst, P. and Hall, Z. (1989) *Understanding Women in Distress*. London: Routledge.

Attie, I. and Brooks-Gunn, J. (1995) 'The development of eating regulation across the life span', in D. Cicchetti and D. Cohen (eds), *Developmental Psychopathology*, vol. 2. New York: Wiley.

Austin, C., Lydiard, R., Fossey, M. et al. (1990) 'Panic and phobic disorders in patients with obsessive-compulsive disorder', *Journal of Clinical Psychiatry*, 51: 456–8.

Azuma, Y. and Henmi, M. (1982) 'A study on the incidence of anorexia nervosa in schoolgirls', *Annual Report of Research Group in Eating Disorders*, pp. 30–4.

Bandura, A. (1977) 'Self-efficacy: towards a unifying theory of behaviour change', *Psychological Review*, 84: 191–215.

Barkham, M., Rees, A., Shapiro, D., Agnew, R., Halstead, J. and Culverwell, A. (1994) 'Effects of treatment method and duration of severity of depression on the effectiveness of psychotherapy: extending the second Sheffield Psychotherapy Project to NHS Settings', Sheffield University SAPU Memo 1480.

Barlow, D. and Wolfe, B. (1981) 'Behavioural approaches to anxiety disorders', *Journal of Consulting and Clinical Psychology*, 40: 448–54.

Barraclough, C. and Tarrier, N. (1992) *Families of Schizophrenic Patients: Cognitive-Behavioural Intervention*. London: Chapman Hall.

Bass, C. (1992) 'Chronic somatization', in K. Hawton and P. Cowen (eds) *Practical Problems in Clinical Psychiatry*. Oxford: Oxford University Press.

Bateson, G., Jackson, D. and Haley, J. (1956) 'Towards a theory of schizophrenia', *Behavioural Science*, 1: 251–64.

Beardslee, W., Bemporad, J., Keller, M. and Klerman, G. (1993) 'Children of parents with major affective disorder: a review', *American Journal of Psychiatry*, 140: 825–32.

Beaumont, P., Touyz, S. and Hook, S. (1984) 'Exercise and anorexia nervosa'. Paper presented at the 3rd International Conference on Anorexia Nervosa and Related Disorders, Swansea, Wales, September 1984.

Bebbington, P. and Kuipers, L. (1994) 'The predictive utility of expressed emotion in schizophrenia: an aggregate analysis', *Psychological Medicine*, 24: 707–10.

Bebbington, P. and McGuffin, P. (1989) 'Interactive models of depression', in K. Herbst and E. Paykel (eds), *Depression: an Integrative Approach*. London: Heinemann.

Bebbington, P., Wilkins, J., Jones, P., Forester, A., Murray, R., Toone, B. and Lewis, S. (1983) 'Life events and psychosis', *British Journal of Psychiatry*, 162: 72–9.

Beck, A., Brown, G. and Steer, R. (1989) 'Prediction of eventual suicide in psychiatric inpatients by clinical ratings of hopelessness', *Journal of Consulting Clinical Psychology*, 57: 309–10.

Beck, A., Emery, G. and Greenberg, R. (1985a) *Anxiety Disorders and Phobias: a Cognitive Perspective*. New York: Basic Books.

Beck, A., Rush, A., Shaw, F. and Emery, G. (1979) *Cognitive Therapy of Depression*. New York: Guildford Press.

Beck, A., Steer, R., Kovacs, M. and Garrison, B. (1985b) 'Hopelessness and eventual suicide: a ten year prospective study of patients hospitalised for suicidal ideation', *American Journal of Psychiatry*, 142: 559–66.

Beck, A., Ward, C., Medelson, M. et al. (1962) 'Reliability of psychiatric diagnosis: a study of consistency of clinical judgements and ratings', *American Journal of Psychiatry*, 19: 351–7.

Beliappa, J. (1991) *Illness or Distress? Alternative Models of Mental Health*. London: Confederation of Indian Organisations.

Benedetti, G. (1987) *Psychotherapy of Schizophrenia*. New York: New York University Press.

Bentall, R. (ed.) (1990) *Reconstructing Schizophrenia*. London: Routledge.

Bentall, R. (1992) 'Reconstructing psychopathology', *The Psychologist*, 5: 61–6.

Bentall, R., Haddock, G. and Slade, P. (1994) 'Cognitive behaviour therapy for persistent auditory hallucinations: from theory to therapy', *Behaviour Therapy*, 25: 51–66.

Bentall, R. and Slade, P. (1985) 'Reliability of a scale measuring disposition towards hallucination: a brief report', *Personality and Individual Differences*, 6: 527–9.

Berelowitz, M. and Tarnopolsky, A. (1993) 'The validity of borderline personality disorder: an updated review of recent research', in P. Tyrer and G. Stein (eds), *Personality Disorder Reviewed*. London: Gaskell.

Berg, M. (1992) 'The construction of medical disposals: medical sociology and medical problem solving in clinical practice', *Sociology of Health and Illness*, 4: 151–80.

Berman, A. (1991) 'Child and adolescent suicide: from the homothetic to the idiographic', in A. Leemans (ed.), *Lifespan Perspectives of Suicide: Time-lines in the Suicide Process*. New York: Plenum.

Berrios, G. (1993) 'Personality disorders: a conceptual history', in P. Tyrer and G. Stein (eds), *Personality Disorder Reviewed*. London: Gaskell.

Bhatt, A., Tomenson, B. and Benjamin, S. (1989) 'Transcultural patterns of somatisation in primary care: a preliminary report', *Journal of Psychosomatic Research*, 33: 671–80.

Bion, W. (1967) *Second Thoughts*. New York: Aronson.

Blackburn, R. (1988) 'Psychopathy and personality disorder', in E. Miller and P.J. Cooper (eds), *Adult Abnormal Psychology*. London: Churchill Livingstone.

Bleuler, E. (1911) *Dementia Praecox: the Group of Schizophrenias*, trans. J. Ziukiu (1950). New York: International Universities Press.

Bleuler, M. (1984) 'What is schizophrenia?', *Schizophrenia Bulletin*, 10: 8.

Bowlby, J. (1981) *Attachment and Loss*, vol. 3: Loss: sadness and depression. Harmondsworth: Penguin.

Boyd, J., Rae, D., Thompson, J. et al. (1990) 'Phobia: prevalence and risk factors', in *Social Psychiatry and Psychiatric Epidemiology*, 225: 314–23.

Boyle, M. (1990) *Schizophrenia: a Scientific Delusion?* London: Routledge.

Boyle, M. (1994) 'Schizophrenia and the art of the soluble', *The Psychologist*, 7(9): 399–404.

Bradley, V. and Power B. (1988) 'Aspects of the relationship between cognitive theories and therapies of depression', *British Journal of Medical Psychology*, 61: 328–38.

Brewin, C. (1988) *Cognitive Foundations of Clinical Psychology*. London: Erlbaum.

Broadbent, D. (1971) *Decision and Stress*. London: Academic Press.

Brockington, I., Kendell, R. and Leff, J. (1978) 'Definitions of schizophrenia: concordance and prediction of outcome' , *Psychological Medicine*, 8: 399–412.

Brooks-Gunn, J., Burrow, C. and Warren, M. (1988). 'Attitudes towards eating and body weight in different groups of female adolescent athletes', *International Journal of Eating Disorders*, 7: 749–57.

Broverman, I., Broverman, D., Clarkson, F. et al. (1970) 'Sex role stereotypes and clinical judgements of mental health', *Journal of Consulting Clinical Psychology*, 34(1): 1–7.

Broverman, I., Vogel, S., Broverman, D. et al. (1972) 'Sex role stereotypes: a current appraisal', *Journal of Social Issues*, 228: 59–78.

Brown, G. (1989) 'Depression: a radical social perspective', in K. Herbst and E. Paykel (eds), *Depression: an integrative approach*. Oxford: Heinemann.

Brown, G. and Harris, T. (1978) *Social Origins of Depression: a Study of Psychiatric Disorder in Women*. New York: Free Press.

Bruch, H. (1973a) 'Anorexia nervosa: therapy and theory', *American Journal of Psychology*, 139: 1531–8.

Bruch, H. (1973b) *Eating and Disorders: Obesity, Anorexia Nervosa and the Person Within*. New York: Basic Books.

Bruch, H. (1978) *The Golden Cage*. New York: Vintage Books.

Brumberg, J. (1988) *Fasting Girls*. Cambridge, Mass.: Harvard University Press.

Buchanan, A. (1992) 'A two year prospective study of treatment compliance in patients with schizophrenia', *Psychological Medicine*, 22: 787–97.

Budd, S. (1994) 'Transference revisited', in S. Budd and U. Sharma (eds), *The Healing Bond*. London: Routledge.

Burke, K., Burke, J., Rae, D. and Refier, D. (1991) 'Comparing age at onset of major depression and other psychiatric disorders by birth cohorts in a US community population', *Archives of General Psychiatry*, 48: 781–95.

Burnham, J. (1986) *Family Therapy*. London: Routledge.

Campbell, D. and Hale, R. (1991) 'Suicidal acts', in J. Holmes (ed.), *Textbook of Psychotherapy in Psychiatric Practice*, London: Churchill Livingstone.

Campling, P. (1989) 'Race, culture and psychotherapy', *Psychiatric Bulletin*, 13: 550–1.

Camus, A. (1955) *The Myth of Sisyphus*. Harmondsworth: Penguin.

Canetto, S. (1994) 'Gender issues in the treatment of suicidal individuals', in A. Leenaars, J. Maltsberger and R. Neimeyer (eds), *Treatment of Suicidal People*. Washington: Taylor and Francis.

Capsi, A. and Elder, G. (1988) 'Emergent family patterns: the intergenerational construction of problem behaviour and relationships', in R. Hinde and J. Stevenson-Hinde (eds), *Relationships within Families: Mutual Influences*. Oxford: Clarendon Press.

Casper, R., Offer, D. and Osrov, E. (1981) 'The self image of adolescents with acute anorexia nervosa', *Journal of Paediatrics*, 98(4): 655–61.

Chadwick, P. and Birchwood, M. (1994) 'Challenging the omnipotence of voices: a cognitive approach to auditory hallucinations', *British Journal of Psychiatry*, 164: 190–201.

Chess, S. and Thomas, A. (1989) 'Issues in the clinical application of temperament', in G. Kohustamm, J. Bates and M. Rothbart (eds), *Temperament in Childhood*. New York: Wiley.

Chessler, P. (1972) *Women and Madness*. New York: Harcourt Brace Jovanovich.

China, S. and McKenna, P. (1995) 'Schizophrenia: a brain disease? A critical review of structural and functional cerebral abnormalities', *British Journal of Psychiatry*, 166: 563–82.

Cicchetti, D. and Garmezy, N. (1993) 'Prospects and promises in the study of resilience', *Developmental Psychopathology*, 5: 497–502.

Cicchetti, D. and Toth, S. (1995) 'Developmental psychopathology and disorders of affect', in D. Cicchetti and D. Cohen (eds), *Developmental Psychopathology*, vol. 2. New York: Wiley.

Clark, A.M. and Clark, A.D. (1976) *Early Experience: Myth and Evidence*. London: Open Books.

Clark, D. (1986) 'A cognitive approach to panic', *Behaviour Research and Therapy*, 4: 461–70.

Clark, D. (1988) 'A cognitive model of panic attacks', in S. Rachman and J. Mason (eds), *Panic: Psychological Perspectives*. Hillsdale, NJ: Erlbaum.

Clark, D. and Horton-Deutsch, S. (1992) 'Assessment in absentia: the values of the psychological autopsy method for studying antecedents of suicide and predicting future suicides', in R. Maris, A. Berman, J. Maltsberger and R. Yuft (eds), *Assessment and Prediction of Suicide*. New York: Guildford Press.

Clarke, J. (1990) *On Being Mad or Merely Angry*. Princeton, NJ: Princeton University Press.

Cohen, L., Whichel, R. and Stanley, M. (1988) 'Biochemical markers of suicide risk and adolescent suicide', *Clinical Neuropharmacology*, 2: 423–35.

Cohler, B. (1987) 'Adversity, resilience and the study of lives', in E. Anthony and B. Cohler (eds), *The Invulnerable Child*. New York: Guildford Press.

Cohler, B., Stott, F. and Musick, J. (1995) 'Adversity, vulnerability and resilience: cultural and developmental perspectives', in D. Cicchetti and D. Cohen (eds), *Developmental Psychopathology*, vol. 2. New York: Wiley.

Coid, J. (1993) 'Current concepts and classifications of psychopathic disorder', in P. Tyrer and G. Stein (eds), *Personality Disorder Reviewed*. London: Gaskell.

Collings, S. and King, M. (1994) 'Ten year follow up of 50 patients with bulimia nervosa', *British Journal of Psychiatry*, 164: 80–7.

Coltart, N. (1993) *How to Survive as a Psychotherapist*. London: Sheldon Press.

Cote, G. and Hodgkins, S. (1990) 'Co-occurring mental disorders among criminal offenders', *Bulletin of the American Academy of Psychiatry and Law*, 18: 271–81.

Cox, D. and Cowling, P. (1989) *Are You Normal?* London: Tower Press.

Coyne, J. (1976) 'Towards an interactional description of depression', *Psychiatry*, 39: 28–40.

Crisp, A. (1980) *Anorexia: Let Me Be*. London: Academic Press.

Cullen, E. and Fernando, S. (1989) Unpublished Report of Ethnic Minority Monitoring Survey by Interest Group in Race and Culture, Chase Farm Hospital, Enfield, England.

Cureton, S. and Newnes, C. (1995) 'A survey of practice of psychological therapies in an NHS Trust', *Clinical Psychology Forum*, 76: 6–10.

Cutting, J. (1985) *The Psychology of Schizophrenia*. Edinburgh: Churchill Livingstone.

Dalgard, P.S., Bjork, S. and Tambs, K. (1995) 'Social support, negative life events and mental health', *British Journal of Psychiatry*, 166: 28–34.

Dana, M. and Lawrence, M. (1988) *Women's Secret Disorder: a New Understanding of Bulimia*. London: Grafton.

Davis, H. and Fallowfield, L. (eds) (1991) *Counselling and Communication in Health Care*. London: Wiley.

Dersken, J. (1995) *Personality Disorder: Clinical and Social Perspectives*. London: Wiley.

van Deurzen-Smith, E. (1992) 'Dialogue as therapy', *Journal of the Society for Existential Analysis*, 3: 15–23.

Derksen, R. (1989) 'Suicide and attempted suicide: an international perspective', *Acta Psychiatrica Scandanavica*, Suppl. 345: 1–24.

Di Nicola, U. (1990) 'Anorexia multiforme: self-starvation in historical and cultural context', *Transcultural Psychiatric Research Review*, 27(4).

Downey, G. and Coyne, J. (1990) 'Children of depressed parents: an integrative review', *Psychological Bulletin*, 108: 50–76.

Drake, R. and Cotton, P. (1986) 'Depression, hopelessness and suicide in chronic schizophrenia', *British Journal of Psychiatry*, 148: 554–9.

Duker, M. and Slade, R. (1988) *Anorexia Nervosa and Bulimia: How to help*. Milton Keynes: Open University Press.

Edelmann, R. (1990) *Coping with Blushing*. London: Sheldon Press.

Edelmann, R. (1992) *Anxiety: Theory, Research and Intervention in Clinical and Health Psychology*. London: Wiley.

Egeland, J., Gerhard, D., Pauls, D., Sussex, J., Kidd, K., Allen, C., Hostetter, A. and Housman, D. (1987) 'Bipolar affective disorders linked to DNA markers on chromosome 11', *Nature*, 325: 783–7.

Eigen, M. (1986) *The Psychotic Core*. New Jersey: Jason Aronson.

Elk, B. (1971) *The Sacred Pipe*. Baltimore: Penguin.

Ellwood, J. (ed.) (1995) *Psychosis: Understanding and Treatment*. London: Jessica Kingsley Publications.

Emmelkamp, P. (1987) 'Obsessive and compulsive disorder', in G. Michelson and L. Ascher (eds), *Anxiety and Stress Disorders: Cognitive-behavioural Assessment and Treatment*. New York: Guildford Press.

Emmelkamp, P. (1988) 'Phobic disorders', in C.G. Last and H. Hersen (eds), *Handbook of Anxiety Disorders*. New York: Guildford Press.

Emmelkamp, P., Bouman, T. and Scholing, A. (1989) *Anxiety Disorders. A Practitioner's Guide*. London: Wiley.

Everitt, B., Goular, A. and Kendell, R. (1971) 'An attempt at validation of traditional psychiatric syndromes by cluster analysis', *British Journal of Psychiatry*, 19: 388–412.

Eysenck, H. (1967) *The Biological Basis of Personality*. Springfield: Charles C. Thomas.

Fairbairn, G. (1987) 'Responsibility, respect for persons and change', in S. Fairbairn and G. Fairbairn (eds), *Psychology, Ethics and Change*. London: Routledge and Kegan Paul.

Fairburn, G. and Cooper, P. (1988) 'Eating disorders', in K. Hawton, P. Salkowskis, J. Kirk and D. Clark (eds), *Cognitive Behaviour Therapy for Psychiatric Problems*. Oxford: Oxford Medical Publication.

Fairburn, G., Kirk, J., O'Connor, M. and Cooper, P. (1986) 'A comparison of two psychological treatments for bulimia nervosa', *Behaviour Research Therapy*, 24: 629–43.

Favazza, A. (1989) 'Why patients mutilate themselves', *Hospital and Community Psychiatry*, 40: 137–45.

Feldman, M. (1988) 'The challenge of self-mutilation: a review', *Comprehensive Psychiatry*, 229: 252–69.

Fenton, S. and Sadiq, A. (1990) 'South Asian women in UK and depression'. Paper presented at the Conference of the British Sociological Association, Edinburgh.

Fernando, S. (1991) 'Theoretical issues in the mental health of the ethnic communities', in *Concepts of Mental Health in the Asian Community*. London: Confederation of Indian Organisations.

Fidell, L. (1982) 'Gender and drug use and abuse', in I. Al-Issa (ed.), *Gender and Psychopathology*. San Diego: Academic Press.

Fombonne, E. (1995) 'Anorexia nervosa: no evidence of an increase', *British Journal of Psychiatry*, 166: 462–71.

Fonagy, P. (1992) 'The theory and practice of resilience'. Paper presented at the 1992 Conference of the Association of Child Psychology and Psychiatry, York, England.

Foucault, M. (1962) *Mental Illness and Psychology*, Berkeley, Calif.: University of California Press.

Foucault, M. (1965) *Madness and Civilization*. New York: Vintage Books.

Fowler, D., Garety, P. and Kuipers, E. (1995) *Cognitive Behaviour Therapy for Psychosis*. London: Wiley.

Frances, A. (1994) Foreword, in J. Sadler, O. Wiggins and M. Schwartz (eds), *Philosophical Perspectives on Psychiatric Diagnostic Classification*, Baltimore: The Johns Hopkins University Press.

Frankish, C. (1994) 'Crisis centres and their role in treatment', in A. Leemans, J. Maltsberger and R. Neimeyer (eds), *Treatment of Suicidal People*. Washington: Taylor and Francis.

Freud, S. (1894) 'On the justification for detaching a particular syndrome from neurasthenia under the description of "anxiety neurosis"', in J. Strachey (ed.), *Standard Edition of the Complete Works of Sigmund Freud*, vol. xx. London: Hogarth.

Freud, S. (1900) *The Interpretation of Dreams*, vol. 4. London: Penguin.

Freud, S. (1917) *Mourning and Melancholia*. vol. 11. London: Penguin.

Freud, S. (1926) *Inhibitions, Symptoms and Anxiety*, vol. 10. London: Penguin.

Frith, C. (1979) 'Consciousness, information processing and schizophrenia', *British Journal of Psychiatry*, 134: 225–35.

Fromm-Reichmann, F. (1948) 'Notes on the development of treatment of schizophrenia by psychoanalytic psychotherapy', *Psychiatry*, 11: 263–73.

Fulford, K., Smirnov, A. and Snow, E. (1993) 'Concepts of disease and the abuse of psychiatry in the USSR', *British Journal of Psychiatry*, 168: 801–10.

Furnham, A. and Alibhai, N. (1983) 'Cross cultural differences in the perception of female body shapes', *Psychological Medicine*, 13: 829–37.

Garety, P. (1991) 'Reasoning and delusions', *British Journal of Psychiatry*, 159: 14–18.

Garety, P., Kuipers, L., Fowler, D. et al. (1994) 'Cognitive behavioural therapy for drug resistant psychosis', *British Journal of Psychiatry*, 67: 259–71.

Garner, D. and Garfinkel, P. (1980) 'Sociocultural factors in the development of anorexia nervosa', *Psychological Medicine*, 10: 647–56.

Garner, D., Rockert, W., Olmsted, M., Johnson, C. and Coscina, D. (1985) 'Psychoeducational principles in the treatment of bulimia and anorexia nervosa', in D. Garner and P. Garfinkel (eds), *Handbook of Psychotherapy for Anorexia and Bulimia*. New York: Guildford Press.

Gelder, M. and Marks, I. (1966) 'Severe agoraphobia: a controlled prospective trial of behaviour therapy', *British Journal of Psychiatry*, 112: 309–19.

Gilman, S. (1988) *Disease and Representation: Images and Illness from Madness to AIDS*. New York: Cornell University Press.

Goffman, E. (1961) *Asylums*. New York: Doubleday.

Goiten, P. (1942) 'The potential prostitute: the role of anorexia in the defence against prostitution desires', *Journal of Criminal Psychopathology*, 2: 359–67.

Goldberg, D., Benjamin, S. and Creed, F. (1994) *Psychiatry in Medical Practice.* London: Routledge.

Goldstein, A. and Chambless, D. (1978) 'A re-analysis of agoraphobia', *Behaviour Therapy*, 9: 47–59.

Goodyear, I. (1990) *Life Experience, Development and Childhood Psychopathology.* Chichester: Wiley.

Gotlib, I. and Hammen, C. (1992) *Psychological Aspects of Depression: Towards a Cognitive-Interpersonal Integration.* Chichester: Wiley.

Gottesman, I. (1991) *Schizophrenia Genesis: the Origins of Madness.* New York: W.H. Freeman.

Gunderson, J., Frank, A. and Ronningstam, E. (1984) 'Effects of psychotherapy in schizophrenia', *Schizophrenia Bulletin*, 10: 564–98.

Graham, P. and Stevenson, J. (1985) 'A twin study of genetic influences on behavioural deviance', *Journal of the American Academy of Child and Adolescent Psychiatry*, 24: 33–41.

Grossman, K. and Grossman, K. (1991) 'Attachment quality as an organiser of emotional and behavioural responses in a longitudinal perspective', in C. Murray-Parks, J. Stevenson-Hinde and P. Harris (eds), *Attachment across the Lifecycle.* London: Routledge.

Hall, R., Tice, L., Beresford, T. et al. (1989) 'Sexual abuse in patients with anorexia nervosa and bulimia', *Psychosomatics*, 30: 73–9.

Halpern, R. (1993) 'Poverty and infant development', in C. Zeanah Jr (ed.), *Handbook of Infant Mental Health.* London: Guildford Press.

Harding, C., Brooks, G., Asrinkaga, T., Strauss, J. and Breier, A. (1987) 'The Vermont longitudinal study of persons with severe mental illness', *American Journal of Psychiatry*, 144: 727–35.

Harkness, S. and Super, C. (1990) 'Culture and psychopathology', in M. Lewis and S. Miller (eds), *Handbook of Developmental Psychopathology.* New York: Plenum Press.

Harper D. (1994) 'The professional construction of "paranoia" and the discursive use of diagnostic criteria', *British Journal of Medical Psychology*, 67: 131–43.

Harré, R. (1972) *The Philosophies of Science.* London: Oxford University Press.

Harris, T. and Bifulco, A. (1991) 'Loss of parent in childhood, attachment style and depression in adulthood', in C. Murray-Parks, J. Stevenson-Hinde and P. Harris (eds), *Attachment across the Lifecycle.* London: Routledge.

Hawton, K. (1987) 'Assessment of suicide risk', *British Journal of Psychiatry*, 150: 145–53.

Hawton, K. and Fagg, J. (1988) 'Suicide and other causes of death following attempted suicide', *British Journal of Psychiatry*, 152: 359–66.

Heisenberg, W. (1962) *Physics and Philosophy: The Revolution in Modern Science.* New York: Helvetica Physica Acte.

Helzer, J., Robins, L. and McEvoy, L. (1987) 'Post-traumatic stress disorder in the general population', *New England Journal of Medicine*, 317: 160–164.

Hemsley, D. (1988) 'Psychological models of schizophrenia', in Miller, E. and Cooper, A. (eds), *Adult Abnormal Psychology.* London: Churchill Livingstone.

Hemsley, D. (1994) 'Schizophrenia treatment', in S. Lindsay and G. Powell (eds), *The Handbook of Clinical Adult Psychology.* London: Routledge.

Herzog, D., Bradburn, I. and Newman, K. (1990) 'Sexuality in males with eating problems', in A. Andersen (ed.), *Males with Eating Disorders.* New York: Brunner/Mazel.

Herzog, D., Franko, D. and Brotman, A. (1989) 'Integrating Treatments for Bulimia Nervosa', in J. Bemporad and D. Herzog (eds), *Psychoanalysis and Eating Disorders.* New York: Guildford Press.

Hetherington, E. (1989) 'Coping with family transitions: winners, losers and survivors', *Child Development*, 60: 1–14.

Hill, A. and Oliver, S. (1992) 'Eating in the adult world the rise of dieting in childhood and adolescence', *British Journal of Clinical Psychology*, 31(1): 95–104.

Hillman, J. (1965) *Suicide and the Soul*. New York: Spring Publications.

Hirsch, F., Walsh, C. and Draper, R. (1982) 'Parasuicide: a review of treatment interventions', *Journal of Affective Disorders*, 4: 299–311.

Hirshberg, L.M. (1989) 'Remembering: Reproduction or Construction?', *Psychoanalysis and Contemporary Thought*, 12: 343–81.

Hirshberg, L.M. (1993) 'Clinical Interview with Infants and their Families', in C. Zeanah (ed.), *Handbook of Infant Mental Health*. New York: Guildford Press.

Hirschfeld, R. and Davidson, L. (1988) 'Risk factors for suicide', in A. Francis and R. Hales (eds), *Review in Psychiatry*. Washington DC: American Psychiatric Press.

Hoekstra, R., Visser, S. and Emmelkamp, P. (1989) 'A social learning formulation of the aetiology of obsessive-compulsive disorder', in P. Emmelkamp, W. Everard, F. Kraaimaat and M. van Son (eds), *Annual Series of European Research in Behaviour Therapy*, vol. IV: *Fresh Perspectives on Anxiety Disorders*. Amsterdam: Swets and Zeitlinger.

Hogarty, G., Schooler, N., Ulrich, R., Hussare, F., Ferro, P. and Herron, E. (1979) 'Fluphenazine and social therapy in the aftercare of schizophrenic patients', *Archives of General Psychiatry*, 36: 1283–94.

Holden, N. and Robinson, P. (1988) 'Anorexia nervosa and bulimia nervosa in British blacks', *British Journal of Psychiatry*, 152: 544–9.

Horvarth, A. and Symonds, B. (1991) 'Relation between working alliance and outcome in psychotherapy: a meta-analysis', *Journal of Consulting Clinical Psychology*, 38: 139–49.

van Horn, J. and McManus, I. (1992) 'Ventricular enlargement in schizophrenia: a meta-analysis of studies of the ventricle brain ratio', *British Journal of Psychiatry*, 160: 687–97.

Hwu, H., Tan, H., Chen, C. and Yeh, L. (1995) 'Negative symptoms at discharge and outcome in schizophrenia', *British Journal of Psychiatry*, 166: 61–7.

Humphrey, L. (1986) 'Stuctural analysis of parent–child relationships in eating disorders', *Journal of Abnormal Psychology*, 95: 395–402.

Humphrey, L. (1988) 'Relationships within subtypes of anorexics, bulimics and normal families', *Journal of the American Academy of Child and Adolescent Psychiatry*, 27: 544–55.

Ineischen, B. (1984) 'Psychiatric hospital admissions in Bristol: geographic and ethnic factors', *British Journal of Psychiatry*, 145: 660–9.

Ingleby, D. (ed.) (1980) *Critical Psychiatry: the Politics of Mental Health*. New York: Pantheon Books.

Jablensky, A., Sartorius, N. Emberg, G. et al. (1992) 'Schizophrenia: manifestations, incidence and course in different cultures: a WHO ten-country study', *Psychological Medicine*, monograph supplement: 20.

Jack, R. (1992) *Women and Attempted Suicide*. Hillsdale, NJ: Erlbaum.

Jackson, H. (1990) 'Are there biological markers of schizophrenia?', in R. Bentall (ed.), *Reconstructing Schizophrenia*. London: Routledge.

Jackson, M. (1995) 'Learning to think about schizoid thinking' in J. Ellwood (ed.), *Psychosis: Understanding and Treatment*. London: Jessica Kingsley Publications.

Jackson, M. and Williams, P. (1994) *Unimaginable Storms*. London: Karnac Books.

Jaspers, K. (1963) *General Psychopathology*. Manchester: Manchester University Press.

Jenkins, J. (1991) 'Anthropology, expressed emotion and schizophrenia', *Ethos*, 10: 387–432.

Joffe, R. (1991) 'Work with suicidal adolescents at a walk-in centre in Brent', in R. Szur and S. Miller (eds), *Extending Horizons*. London: Karnac Books.

Johnson, M. (1988) 'Discriminating the origin of information', in J. Ottmanns and B. Maher (eds), *Delusional Beliefs*. New York: Wiley.

Kakar, S. (1982) *Shamans, Mystics and Doctors: a Psychological Inquiry into India and its Healing Traditions*. London: Unwin.

Kaplan, A. and Woodside, D. (1987) 'Biological aspects of anorexia nervosa and bulimia nervosa', *Journal of Consulting and Clinical Psychology*, 5: 645–53.

Karno, M., Golding, J., Sorensen, S. and Burman, M. (1988) 'The epidemiology of obsessive-compulsive disorder in five US communities', *Archives of General Psychiatry*, 45: 1094–9.

Keller, M. (1985) 'Chronic and recurrent affective disorders: incidence, course and influencing factors', in D. Kemali and G. Recagni (eds), *Chronic Treatments in Neuropsychiatry*. New York: Raven Press.

Keller, M. (1988) 'Diagnostic issues and clinical course of unipolar illness', in A. Francis and R. Hales (eds), *Review of Psychiatry*. Washington: American Psychiatric Press.

Kety, S., Rosenthal, D., Wender, P. and Schulsinger, F. (1976) 'Studies based on a total sample of adopted individuals and their relatives', *Schizophrenia Bulletin*, 2: 413–28.

Kernberg, O. (1975) *Borderline Conditions and Pathological Narcissism*. New York: Jason Aronson.

Kernberg, O. (1984) *Severe Personality Disorders*. New Haven: Yale University Press.

Keys, A. et al. (1950) *The Biology of Human Starvation*. Minneapolis: University of Minnesota Press.

Khan, A. (1983) 'The mental health of the Asian community in an East London District', in *Care in the Community – Keeping it Local*. London: Report of MIND Annual Conference.

Kinderman, P. (1994) 'Attentional bias, persecutory delusions and the self-concept', *British Journal of Medical Psychology*, 67: 33–9.

Kingdon, D. and Turkington, D. (1994) *Cognitive Behaviour Therapy of Schizophrenia*. Sussex: Guildford Press

Kingdon, D. and Turkington, D. (1991) 'The use of cognitive behaviour therapy with a normalising rationale in schizophrenia', *Journal of Nervous and Mental Disease*, 179(4): 207–11.

Kingdon, D., Turkington, D. and John, C. (1994) 'Cognitive behaviour therapy of schizophrenia', *British Journal of Psychiatry*, 164: 581–7.

Klerman, G. (1987) 'Clinical epidemiology of suicide', *Journal of Clinical Psychiatry*, 48 (suppl.): 33–8.

Klerman, G. and Weissman, M. (1989) 'Increasing rates of depression', *Journal of the American Medical Association*, 281: 2229–35.

Klerman, G. and Weissman, M. (1992) 'The course, morbidity and costs of depression', *Archives of General Psychiatry*, 41: 229–37.

Kohut, H. (1971) *The Analysis of the Self*. New York: International Universities Press.

Kozac, M., Foe, E. and McCarthy, P. (1988) 'Obsessive-compulsive disorder', in C. Last and M. Herson (eds), *Handbook of Anxiety Disorders*. New York: Pergamon Press.

Kraeplin, E. (1905) *Lectures on Clinical Psychiatry*. London: Ballière Tindall.

Kral, M. and Sakinofsky, I. (1994) 'A clinical model for suicide risk assessment', in A. Leenaars, J. Maltsberger and R. Neimeyer (eds), *Treatment of Suicidal People*. Washington: Taylor and Francis.

Laing, R. (1959) *The Divided Self*. London: Tavistock.

Laing, R. and Esterson, A. (1970) *Sanity, Madness and the Family: Families of Schizophrenics*. Baltimore: Penguin.

Lane, T. and Borkovec, T. (1984) 'The influence of therapeutic expectancy/demand on self-efficacy ratings', *Cognitive Therapy and Research*, 8: 85–106.

Langs, R. (1975) 'Therapeutic misalliances', *International Journal of Psychoanalytic Psychotherapy*, 4: 77–105.

Lansky, M. (1977) 'Schizophrenic delusional phenomena', *Comprehensive Psychiatry*, 18(2): 157–68.

Lask, B. and Bryant-Waugh, R. (1992) 'Early onset anorexia nervosa and related eating disorders', *Journal of Child Psychology and Psychiatry*, 33: 281–300.

Lawrence, M. (1984) *The Anorexic Experience*. London: The Women's Press.

Leenaars, A. (1994) 'Crisis intervention with highly lethal suicidal people', in A. Leenaars, J. Maltsberger and R. Neimeyer (eds), *Treatment of Suicidal People*. Washington: Taylor and Francis.

Leenstra, A., Ormel, J. and Griel, R. (1995) 'Positive life change and recovery from depression and anxiety', *British Journal of Psychiatry*, 166: 335–43.

Leff, J., Berkowitz, R., Shavit, E. et al. (1990) 'A trial of family therapy v. a relatives group for schizophrenia: two-year follow-up', *British Journal of Psychiatry*, 157: 571–7.

Leff, J., Wig, N., Ghosh, A. and Bed, H. (1987) 'Influence of relatives' expressed emotion on the course of schizophrenia in Chandigarh', *British Journal of Psychiatry*, 151: 166–73.

Lester, D. (1990) 'If women are more often depressed, why don't more of them kill themselves', *Psychological Reports*, 66: 258.

Levi-Strauss, C. (1955) *Triste Tropiques*. Paris: Librarie Plou.

Lewinshon, P. (1974) 'A behavioural approach to depression', in R. Friedman and M. Katz (eds), *The Psychology of Depression: Contemporary Theory and Research*. New York: John Wiley.

Lewis, M. (1990) 'Challenges to the study of developmental psychopathology', in M. Lewis (ed.), *Handbook of Developmental Psychopathology*. New York: Plenum Press.

Linehan, M., Heard, H. and Armstrong, E. (1993) 'Naturalistic follow-up of behavioural treatment of chronically parasuicidal borderline patients', *Archives of General Psychiatry*, 50: 971–4.

Lishman, W. (1987) *Organic Psychiatry*. London: Blackwell.

Littlewood, R. and Lipsedge, M. (1989) *Aliens and Alienists: Ethnic Minorities and Psychiatry*. London: Penguin.

Lyons-Ruth, K., Connell, D., Zoll, D. and Stahl, J. (1987) 'Infants at social risk: relations among infant maltreatment, maternal behaviour and infant attachment behaviour', *Developmental Psychology*, 23(2): 223–32.

McDougall, J. (1989) *Theatres of the Body*. London: Free Association Books.

McDougall, J. (1990) *Plea for a Measure of Abnormality*. London: Free Association Books.

McFarland, C., Ross, M. and de Courville, N. (1987) 'Women's theories of menstruation and biases in recall of menstrual symptoms', *Journal of Personality and Social Psychology*, 57(3): 522–31.

McFarlane, A. (1989) 'The aetiology of post-traumatic morbidity: predisposing, precipitating and perpetuating factors', *British Journal of Psychiatry*, 154: 221–8.

McGhie, A. and Chapman, J. (1961) 'Disorders of attention and perception in early schizophrenia', *British Journal of Medical Psychology*, 34: 103–16.

McGhinley, E. and Rimmer, J. (1993) 'The trauma of attempted suicide', *Psychoanalytic Psychotherapy*, 7(1): 53–68.

McGuffin, P. and Katz, R. (1986) 'Nature, nurture and affective disorders', in J. Deakin (ed.), *The Biology of Depression*. London: Gaskell Press.

McGuffin, P. and Thapar, A. (1992) 'The genetics of personality disorder', *British Journal of Psychiatry*, 160: 12–23.

McIntosh, J. and Jewell, B. (1986) 'Sex difference trends in completed suicide', *Suicide and Life Threatening Behaviour*, 16: 16–27.

McLelland, L., Mynors-Wallis, L. and Treasure, J. (1991) 'Sexual abuse, disordered personality and eating problems', *British Journal of Psychiatry*, 158(10): 63–8.

Maher, B. (1988) 'Anomalous experiences and delusional thinking: the logic of explanations', in I. Oltmans and B. Maher (eds), *Delusional Beliefs*. New York: John Wiley.

Main, T. (1957) 'The ailment', *British Journal of Medical Psychology*, 30(3): 129–45.

Malan, D. (1979) *Individual Psychotherapy and the Science of Psychodynamics*. London: Butterworth–Heinemann.

Maltsberger, J. (1994) 'Calculated risk taking in the treatment of suicidal patients: ethical and legal problems', in A. Leenaars, J. Maltsberger and R. Neimeyer (eds), *Treatment of Suicidal People*. Washington: Taylor and Francis.

Maltsberger, J. and Buie, D. (1974) 'Countertransference hate in the treatment of suicidal patients', *Archives of General Psychiatry*, 30: 625–33.

Margraf, J. and Ehlers, A. (1988) 'Panic attacks in non-clinical subjects', in I. Hand and H. Wittchen (eds), *Panic and Phobias*. Berlin: Springer-Verlag.

Maslow, A. (1968) *Toward a Psychology of Being*. New York: Van Nostrand Reinhold.

Masson, J. (1990) *Against Therapy*. London: Picador.

Masten, A. and Coatsworth, D. (1995) 'Competence, resilience and psychopathology', in D. Cicchetti and D. Cohen (eds), *Developmental Psychopathology*, vol. 2. New York: Wiley.

Matthews, A. and MacLeod, C. (1985) 'Selective processing of threat cues in anxiety states', *Behaviour Research and Therapy*, 23: 563–9.

Matthews, A. and MacLeod, C. (1988) 'Current perspectives on anxiety', in E. Hiller and P. Cooper (eds), *Adult Abnormal Psychology*. London: Churchill Livingstone.

Meltzer, H. and Stahl, S. (1976) 'The dopamine hypothesis of schizophrenia: a review', *Schizophrenia Bulletin*, 2: 18–76.

Mendlewicz, J. and Rainer, J. (1977) 'Adoption study supporting genetic transmission in manic-depressive illness', *Nature*, 268: 327–9.

Merleau-Ponty, M. (1962) *The Phenomenology of Perception*. London: Routledge and Kegan Paul.

Michelson, L. and Marchione, K. (1991) 'Behavioural, cognitive and pharmacological treatments of panic disorder with agoraphobia: critique and synthesis', *Journal of Consulting and Clinical Psychology*, 59: 100–14.

Millon, T. (1995) 'Foreword', in J. Derksen, *Personality Disorder: Clinical and Social Perspectives*. London: Wiley.

Millon, T. and Davis, R. (1995) 'The development of personality disorders', in D. Cicchetti and D. Cohen (eds), *Developmental Psychopathology*, New York: Wiley.

Minuchin, S., Rosman, B. and Baker, L. (1978) *Psychosomatic Families: Anorexia Nervosa in Context*. Cambridge, Mass.: Harvard University Press.

Mischel, W. (1973) 'Towards a cognitive social learning reconceptualisation of personality', *Psychological Review*, 80: 252–83

Monahan, J. (1992) 'Mental disorder and violent behaviour: perceptions and evidence', *American Psychologist*, 47(4): 511–21.

Moorey, H. and Soni, S. (1994) 'Anxiety symptoms in stable chronic schizophrenics', *Journal of Mental Health*, 3: 257–62.

Mueser, K. and Berenbaum, H. (1990) 'Psychodynamic treatment of schizophrenia: is there a future?' *Psychological Medicine*, 20: 253–62.

Mullen, P. (1979) 'Phenomenology of disordered mental function', in P. Hill, R. Murray and A. Thorley (eds), *Essentials of Postgraduate Psychiatry*. London: Academic Press.

Mumford, D., Whitehouse, A. and Plattes, M. (1991) 'Sociocultural correlates of eating disorders among Asian schoolgirls in Bradford', *British Journal of Psychiatry*, 158: 222–8.

Murray, L. and Stein, A. (1989) 'The effects of postnatal depression on the infant', *Ballière's Clinical Obstetrics and Gynaecology*, 3(4): 921–33.

Murray, R. and Castle, D. et al. (1992) 'A neurodevelopmental approach to the classifications of schizophrenia', *Schizophrenia Bulletin*, 18: 319–32.

Neuringer, C. (1988) 'The thinking process in suicidal women', in D. Lester (ed.), *Why Women Kill Themselves*. Springfield, Ill.: Charles C. Thomas.

Nezu, A., Nezu, C. and Perri, M. (1989) *Problem Solving Therapy for Depression: Theory, Research and Clinical Guidelines*. New York: Wiley.

Nitsun, M., Wood, H. and Bolton, W. (1989) 'The organisation of psychotherapy services: a clinical psychology perspective', *Clinical Psychology Forum*, 23: 32–6.

Nolen-Hoeksema, S. (1990) *Sex Differences in Depression*. Stanford: Stanford University Press.

Norman, R. and Malla, A. (1993) 'Stressful life events and schizophrenia: a review of the research', *British Journal of Psychiatry*, 162: 161–6.

Nwaefuna, A. (1981) 'Anorexia nervosa in a developing country', *British Journal of Psychiatry*, 138: 270–4.

Nylander, I. (1971) 'The feeling of being fat and dieting in a school population', *Acta Sociomedico Scandinavica*, 3: 17–26.

O'Callaghan, E., Cotter, D., Colgan, K., Larkin, C., Walsh, D. and Washington, J. (1995) 'Confinement of winter birth excess in schizophrenia to the urban born and its gender specificity', *British Journal of Psychiatry*, 166: 51–4.

O'Donnell, I. and Farmer, R. (1995) 'The limitations of official suicide statistics', *British Journal of Psychiatry*, 166: 458–61.

O'Hara, H., Zekoski, M., Philipps, L. and Wright, E. (1990) 'Controlled prospective study of postpartum mood disorders', *Journal of Abnormal Psychology*, 99(1): 3–15.

Ollendick, T., Matson, J. and Helsel, W. (1985) 'Fears in children and adolescents: normative data', *Behaviour Research and Therapy*, 23: 465–7.

Orbach, S. (1986) *Hunger Strike*. London: Faber and Faber.

Patel, V. and Winston, M. (1994) 'Universality of mental illness: assumptions, artefacts and new directions', *British Journal of Psychiatry*, 165: 437–40.

Paykel, E. and Dieuelt, N. (1971) 'Suicidal attempts following acute depression', *Journal of Nervous and Mental Disease*, 153: 234–43.

Paykel, E. and Priest, R. (1992) 'Recognition and management of depression in clinical practice: consensus statement', *British Medical Journal*, 305: 1198–202.

Penfold, S. and Walker, G. (1984) *Women and the Psychiatric Paradox*. Milton Keynes: Open University Press.

Pianta, R. and Egeland, B. (1990) 'Life stress and parenting outcomes in a disadvantaged sample: results of the mother and child interaction project', *Journal of Clinical Child Psychology*, 19(4): 329–36.

Pilgrim, D. and Rogers, A. (1993) *A Sociology of Mental Health and Illness*. Milton Keynes: Open University Press.

Pinto, R. and Hollandsworth, J. (1989) 'Using videotape modelling to prepare children psychologically for surgery', *Health Psychology*, 8: 79–95.

Piontelli, A. (1992) *From Foetus to Child: an Observational and Psychoanalytic Study*. London: Routledge.

Platt, S., Bille-Brache, U., Kerkof, A., Schnuoltke, A., Bjerke, T., Crepet, P. et al. (1992) 'Parasuicide in Europe: the WHO/EURO multicentre study on parasuicide I', *Acta Psychiatrica Scandinavica*, 85: 97–104.

Plomin, R. and Daniels, D. (1987) 'Why are children in the same family so different from one another?', *Behavioural and Brain Sciences*, 10: 1–60.

Podvoll, E. (1990) *The Seduction of Madness*. London: Century.

Pollard, C. and Henderson, J. (1988) 'Four types of social phobia in a community sample', *Journal of Nervous and Mental Disease*, 776: 440–5.

Popper, K. (1968) *Conjectures and Refutations: the Growth of Scientific Knowledge*. New York: Harper and Row.

Pouillon, J. (1972) 'Doctor and patient: same and/or the other?', *The Psychoanalytic Study of Society*, 5: 9–32.

Quinton, D., Gulliver, L. and Rutter, M. (1995) 'A 15–20 year follow up of adult psychiatric patients', *British Journal of Psychiatry*, 167: 315–23.

Quinton, D., Pickles, A., Maugham, B. and Rutter, M. (1993) 'Partners, peers and pathways: assortative pairing and continuities in conduct disorder', *Developmental Psychopathology*, 5: 763–83.

Quinton, D. and Rutter, M. (1985) 'Parenting behaviour of mothers raised in care', in A. Nicol (ed.), *Longitudinal Studies in Child Psychology and Psychiatry*. Chichester: Wiley.

Rachman, S. (1977) 'The conditioning theory of fear acquisition: a critical examination', *Behaviour Research and Therapy*, 15: 375–87.

Rachman, S. (1985) 'An overview of clinical and research issues in obsessional-compulsive disorders' in M. Marissakalian, S. Turner and L. Michelson (eds), *Obsessive Compulsive Disorder*. New York: Plenum Press.

Rachman, S. (1990) *Fear and Courage*. New York: W.H. Freeman.

Raimbault, G. and Eliacheff, C. (1989) *Les Indomptables: Figures de l'Anorexie*. Paris: Odile Jacob.

Rende, R. and Plomin, R. (1993) 'Families at risk of psychopathology: who becomes affected and why', *Development and Psychopathology*, 5: 529–40.

Riegel, K.F. (1978) *Psychology, Mon Amour: a Countertext*. Boston, Houghton Mifflin.

Rippere, V. (1994) 'Depression', in S. Lindsay and G. Powell (eds), *The Handbook of Clinical Adult Psychology*. London: Routledge.

Roberts, G. (1991) 'Delusional belief systems and meaning in life: a preferred reality?', *British Journal of Psychiatry*, 159 (suppl. 14): 19–28.

Rogler, L. and Hollingshead, A. (1965) *Trapped: Families and Schizophrenia*. New York: Wiley.

Rosenfeld, H. (1965) *Psychotic States*. London: Karnac.

Rosenfeld, H. (1987) *Impasse and Interpretation*. London: Routledge.

Rosenhan, D. (1973) 'On being sane in insane places', *Science*, 179: 250–8.

Rosenthal, D., Wender, P., Kety, S., Welner, J. and Schielsinger, F. (1971) 'The adopted-away offspring of schizophrenics', *American Journal of Psychiatry*, 123: 307–11.

Ross, L. (1977) 'The intuitive psychologist and his shortcomings: distortions in the attribution process', in L. Berkowitz (ed.), *Advances in Experimental Social Psychology*, vol. 10. New York: Academic Press.

Roth, A. and Fonagy, P. (in press) *The Search for Effective Psychotherapy: Limitations and Implications of the Psychotherapy Research Literature*. New York: Guildford Press.

Russell, G. (1979) 'Bulimia nervosa: an ominous variant of anorexia nervosa', *Psychological Medicine*, 9: 429–48.

Russell, G., Szmuckler, G., Dorf, C. and Eisler, I. (1987) 'An evaluation of family therapy in anorexia nervosa and bulimia nervosa', *Archives of General Psychiatry*, 444: 1047–56.

Rutter, M. (1990) 'Psychosocial resilience and protective mechanisms' in J. Rolf, A. Masten, D. Cicchetti, K. Neuch-Kerlein and S. Weintraub (eds), *Risk and Protective Factors in the Development of Psychopathology*. New York: Cambridge University Press.

Rutter, M. (1992) 'Transitions and turning points in development'. Paper presented at the British Psychological Society Conference, December 1992.

Sacks, O. (1995) *An Anthropologist on Mars*, London: Picador.

Sadler, J. and Hulgus, Y. (1994) 'Enriching the psychosocial content of a multiaxial nosology', in J. Sadler, U. Wiggins and M. Schwarz (eds), *Philsophical Perspectives on Psychiatric Diagnostic Classification*, London: Johns Hopkins University Press.

Salkovskis, P., Atha, C. and Storer, D. (1990) 'Cognitive behavioural problem solving in the treatment of patients who repeatedly attempt suicide', *British Journal of Psychiatry*, 157: 871–6.

Salokangas, R. (1983) 'Prognostic implications of the sex of schizophrenic patients', *British Journal of Psychiatry*, 142: 145–51.

Salzman, L. (1995) *Treatment of Obsessive and Compulsive Behaviours*. Northvale, NJ: Jason Aronsen.

Sameroff, A.J. (1993) 'Models of development and developmental risk', in C. Zeanah Jr (ed.), *Handbook of Infant Mental Health*. London: Guildford Press.

Sameroff, A.J. and Chandler, M.J. (1975) 'Reproductive risk and the continuum of caretaking casualty', in F. Horowitz, E. Hetherington, S. Scarr-Salapatek and G. Siegal (eds), *Review of Child Developmental Research*, vol. 4. Chicago: University of Chicago Press.

Sarbin, T. and Juhasz, J. (1967) 'The historical background of the concept of hallucination', *Journal of the History of the Behavioural Sciences*, 3: 339–58.

Sarbin, T. and Juhasz, J. (1978) 'The social psychology of hallucinations', *Journal of Mental Imagery*, 2: 117–14.

Sartorius, N., Jablensky, A., Gulbiuat, W. and Eruberg, G. (1980) 'WHO collaborative study: assessment of depressive disorders', *Psychological Medicine*, 10: 743–9.

Scheff, T. (1966) *Being Mentally Ill: a Sociological Theory*. Chicago: Aldine.

Schneider, K. (1959) *Clinical Psychopathology*. London: Grune and Stratton.

Scott, D. (1986) 'Anorexia nervosa in the male', *International Journal of Eating Disorders*, 5: 799–819.

Scott, M. and Stradling, S. (1992) *Counselling for Post-Traumatic Stress Disorder*. London: Sage.

Searles, H. (1965) *Collected Papers on Schizophrenia and Related Subjects*. London: Hogarth Press.

Searles, H. (1979) *Countertransference and Related Subjects*. Connecticut: International Universities Press.

Sedgwick, P. (1973) 'Illness – mental or otherwise', in *The Hastings Center Studies*, vol. 1(3). New York: Institute of Society, Ethics and Life Sciences.

Seifer, R. and Dickstein, S. (1993) 'Parental mental illness and infant development', in C. Zeander Jr (ed.), *Handbook of Infant Mental Health*. London: Guildford Press.

Seifer, R., Sameroff, A., Baldwin, C. and Baldwin, A. (1992) 'Child and family factors that ameliorate risk between 4 and 13 years of age', *Journal of the American Academy of Child and Adolescent Psychiatry*, 31: 893–903.

Seligman, M. (1971) 'Phobias and preparedness', *Behaviour Therapy*, 2: 307–20.

Shaikh, A. (1985) 'Cross-cultural comparison: psychiatric admission of Asian and indigenous patients in Leicestershire', *International Journal of Social Psychiatry*, 31: 3–11.

Sham, P., O'Callaghan, E. and Takei, N. (1992) 'Schizophrenia following pre-natal exposure to influenza epidemics between 1939 and 1960', *British Journal of Psychiatry*, 160: 390–7.

Shapiro, D., Barnham, P., Rees, A., Reynolds, S. and Startup, M. (1994) 'Effects of treatment duration and severity of depression on the effectiveness of cognitive behavioural and psychodynamic/ interpersonal psychotherapy', *Journal of Consulting Clinical Psychology*, 62: 522–34.

Shea, M., Wishiger, T. and Klein, M. (1992) 'Co-morbidity of personality disorders: implications for treatment', *Journal of Consulting Clinical Psychology*, 660: 857–62.

Shields, G. (1973) 'Heredity and psychosocial abnormality', in H. Eysenck (ed.), *Handbook of Abnormal Psychology*. London: Pitman.

Siegler, M. and Osmond, H. (1974) *Models of Madness, Models of Medicine*. New York: Macmillan.

Sinason, V. (1992) *Mental Handicap and the Human Condition*. London: Free Association Books.

Siris, S. (1991) 'Diagnosis of secondary depression in schizophrenia', *Schizophrenia Bulletin*, 17: 75–98.

Slaby, A. (1994) 'Psychopharmacotherapy of suicide', in A Leenaars, J. Maltsberger and R. Neimeyer (eds), *Treatment of Suicidal People*. Washington: Taylor and Francis.

Solyom, L., Ledwidge, B. and Solyom, C. (1986) 'Delineating social phobia', *British Journal of Psychiatry*, 149: 464–70.

Soomro, G., Crisp, A., Lynch, D. et al. (1995) 'Anorexia nervosa in "non-white" populations', *British Journal of Psychiatry*, 167: 385–9.

Spielberger, C., Gorush, R. and Lushene, R. (1970) *Manual for the State-Trait Anxiety Inventory*. Palo Alto: Consulting Psychologist Press.

Spitzer, R., Endicott, J. and Robins, E. (1978) *Research Diagnostic Criteria for a Selected Group of Functional Disorders*. New York: Biometrics Research.

Starr, P. (1982) *The Social Transformation of American Medicine*. New York: Basic Books.

Steiner, J. (1994) 'Foreword', in M. Jackson and P. Williams, *Unimaginable Storms: a search for meaning in psychosis*. London: Karnac Books.

Stephen, G. and Graham, G. (1994) 'Voices and selves', in J. Sadler, O. Wiggins and M. Schwartz (eds), *Philosophical Perspectives on Psychiatric Diagnostic Classification*. London: Johns Hopkins University Press.

Strean, H. (1989) *The Severed Soul*. New York: St Martin's Press.

Szasz, T. (1960) 'The myth of mental illness', *American Psychologist*, 15: 113–18.

Szasz, T. (1961) *The Myth of Mental Illness*. New York: Harper and Row.

Szmukler, G. and Tantum, D. (1984) 'Anorexia nervosa: starvation dependence', *British Journal of Medical Psychology*, 57: 303–10.

Takei, N., Sham, P. and O'Callaghan, E. (1994) 'Prenatal influenza and schizophrenia: is the effect confined to females?', *American Journal of Psychiatry*, 151: 117–19.

Tantam, D. and Whittaker, J. (1993) 'Self-wounding and personality disorder', in P. Tyrer and G. Stein (eds), *Personality Disorder Reviewed*. London: Gaskell.

Tarrier, N. (1994) 'Management and modification of residual positive psychotic symptoms', in M. Birchwood and N. Tarrier (eds), *Psychological Management of Schizophrenia*. London: Wiley.

Tarrier, N., Barrowclough, C., Vaughn, C. et al. (1989) 'The community management of schizophrenia: a two-year follow-up of a behavioural intervention with families', *British Journal of Psychiatry*, 154: 625–8.

Taylor, S. (1984) *Durkheim and the Study of Suicide*. London: Macmillan.

Teasdale, J. (1990) 'Cognitive vulnerability to persistent depression'. Paper presented at the Howard Morton Trust Symposium on Depression, University of Sheffield.

Thomas, C., Stone, K., Osborn, M. et al. (1993) 'Psychiatric morbidity and compulsory admission among UK born Europeans, Afro-Caribbeans and Asians in Central Manchester', *British Journal of Psychiatry*, 163: 91–9.

Tollinton, G. and Grinsted, J. (1992) 'The Children Act requirement for close co-operation between agencies: some implications for clinical psychologists', *ACCP Newsletter*, 14(4): 168–72.

Toth, S., Manly, J. and Cicchetti, D. (1992) 'Child maltreatment and vulnerability to depression', *Development and Psychopathology*, 4: 323–39.

Tsuang, M. and Faraone S. (1990) *The Genetics of Mood Disorders*. Baltimore: The Johns Hopkins University Press.

Turner, R. and Wagenfeld, M. (1967) 'Occupational mobility and schizophrenia: an assessment of the social causation and social selection hypotheses', *American Sociological Review*, 32: 104–13.

Turner, S., Beidel, D., Dancer, C. and Keys, D. (1986) 'Psychopathology of social phobia and comparison to avoidant personality disorder', *Journal of Abnormal Psychology*, 95: 389–94.

Turner, T. (1988) 'Community care', *British Journal of Psychiatry*, 152: 1–3.

Tyrer, P., Casey, P. and Ferguson, B. (1993) 'Personality disorders in perspective', in P. Tyrer and G. Stein (eds), *Personality Disorder Reviewed*. London: Gaskell.

Ussher, J. (1989) *The Psychology of the Female Body*. London: Routledge.

Ussher, J. (1991) *Women's Madness*. London: Harvester Wheatsheaf.

Ussher, J. and Wilding, J. (1991) 'Performance and state changes during the menstrual cycle, conceptualised within a broad band testing framework', *Social Science and Medicine*, 32(5): 525–34.

Vaillant, G. (1987) 'A developmental view of old and new perspectives of personality disorders', *Journal of Personality Disorders*, 1: 146–56.

Wallace, E. (1994) 'Psychiatry and its nosology: a historic-philosophical overview', in J. Sadler, O. Wiggins and M. Schwartz (eds), *Philosophical Perspectives on Psychiatric Diagnostic Classification*. Baltimore: The Johns Hopkins University Press.

Waller, G. (1992a) 'Sexual abuse as a factor in eating disorders', *British Journal of Psychiatry*, 159: 664–71.

Waller, G. (1992b) 'Sexual abuse and the severity of bulimic symptoms', *British Journal of Psychiatry*, 161: 90–3.

Waller, J., Kaufman, M. and Deutsch, F. (1940) 'Anorexia nervosa: psychosomatic entity', *Psychosomatic Medicine*, 2: 3–16.

Warner, R. (1994) *Recovery from Schizophrenia*. London: Routledge.

Warr, P. (1982) 'Psychological aspects of employment and unemployment', *Psychological Medicine*, 12: 7–11.

Watson, J. and Rayner, R. (1920) 'Conditioned emotional reactions', *Journal of Experimental Psychology*, 3: 1–14.

Watt, N., Anthony, E., Wynne, L. and Rolf, J. (eds) (1984) *Children at Risk for Schizophrenia: a Longitudinal Perspective*. Cambridge: Cambridge University Press.

Watts, D. and Morgan, G. (1994) 'Malignant alienation: dangers for patients who are hard to like', *British Journal of Psychiatry*, 164: 11–15.

Weiss, D.B. (1982) 'Confidentiality expectations of patients, physicians and medical students', *Journal of the American Medical Association*, 247(19): 2685–7.

Weissman, M. (1993) 'The epidemiology of personality disorders: a 1990 update', *Journal of Personality Disorders*, suppl.: 44–62.

Weissman, M., Gammon, G., John, K. et al. (1987) 'Children of depressed parents', *Archives of General Psychiatry*, 44: 847–53.

Welbourne, J. and Purgold, J. (1984) *The Eating Sickness*. Sussex: Harvester Press.

Werner, E. (1993) 'Risk, resilience and recovery: perspectives from the Kanai longitudinal study', *Development and Psychopathology*, 5: 503–15.

Werner, E. and Smith, R. (1992) *Overcoming the Odds: High Risk Children from Birth to Adulthood*. New York: Cornell University Press.

Wessely, S., Buchanan, A., Reed, A., Cutting, J. et al. (1993) 'Acting on delusions', *British Journal of Psychiatry*, 163: 69–76.

Wiggins, O. and Schwartz, M. (1994) 'The limits of psychiatric knowledge and the problem of classification', in J. Sandler, O. Wiggins and M. Schwartz (eds), *Philosophical Perspectives on Psychiatric Diagnostic Classification*. Baltimore: The Johns Hopkins University Press.

Williams, M. and Wells, J. (1989) 'Suicidal patients', in J. Scott, M. Williams and A. Beck (eds), *Cognitive Therapy in Clinical Practice*. London: Routledge.

Williams, R. and Morgan, H. (1994) *Suicide Prevention*. London: HMSO.

Wing, K (1978) 'The social context of schizophrenia', *American Journal of Psychiatry*, 135: 1333–9.

Winnicott, D. (1945) 'Primitive emotional development', in *Through Paediatrics to Psychoanalysis – collected papers*. London: Karnac Books.

Winnicott, D. (1960) 'Ego distortion in terms of true and false self', in *The Maturational Process and the Facilitating Environment*. London: Karnac Books.

World Health Organization (1991) *The International Pilot Study of Schizophrenia*, Vol. 1. Geneva: WHO.

World Health Organization (1973) *Causes of Death*. Geneva: WHO.

Yalom, I. (1980) *Existential Psychotherapy*. New York: Basic Books.

Yager, J., Kurtzman, F., Landswerk, J. and Weismeier, E. (1988) 'Behaviour and attitudes related to eating disorders in homosexual male college students', *American Journal of Psychiatry*, 145: 495–7.

Zanarini, M., Frankenburg, F., Chauncey, D. and Gunderson, J. (1987) 'The diagnostic interview for personality disorders: interrater and test–retest reliability', *Comprehensive Psychiatry*, 28: 467–80.

Zetzel, E. (1968) 'The so-called good hysteric', in *The Capacity for Emotional Growth*. London: Hogarth Press.

Index